D1599987

The Threads
of *The Scarlet Letter*

The Threads
of *The Scarlet Letter*

A Study of
Hawthorne's Transformative Art

Richard Kopley

DELAWARE

Newark: University of Delaware Press
London: Associated University Presses

Associated University Presses
2010 Eastpark Boulevard
Cranbury, NJ 08512

Associated University Presses
Unit 304 The Chandlery
50 Westminster Bridge Road
London SE1 7QY, England

Associated University Presses
P.O. Box 338, Port Credit
Mississauga, Ontario
Canada L5G 4L8

The paper used in this publication meets the requirements of the American National Standard for Permanence of Paper for Printed Library Materials Z39.48-1984.

Library of Congress Cataloging-in-Publication Data

Kopley, Richard.
 The threads of The scarlet letter : a study of Hawthorne's
transformative art / Richard Kopley.
        p. cm.
Includes bibliographical references and index.
 ISBN 0-87413-769-1 (alk. paper)
1. Hawthorne, Nathaniel, 1804–1864. Scarlet letter—Sources. 2.
Historical fiction, American—History and criticism. 3. Lowell, James
Russell, 1819–1891. Legend of Brittany. 4. Wheelwright, Ebenezer,
1800–1877. Salem belle. 5. Poe, Edgar Allan, 1809–1849. Tell-tale
heart. 6. Intertextuality. 7. Literary form. I. Title.
PS1868 .K67 2003
813'.3—dc21

                                                2002151282

For My Mother,
Irene Kopley,
With Much Love

Contents

Acknowledgments

G ATHERING *T HE T HREADS OF "T HE S CARLET L ETTER"* HAS BEEN A LABOR OF love. Many institutions and individuals have contributed to that labor, and I am pleased to acknowledge them.

I am deeply grateful to those institutions where I did extensive archival research: the Microtexts Division of the Boston Public Library; the Rare Book and Manuscript Library of Butler Library, Columbia University; the Houghton Library of Harvard University; the Massachusetts Historical Society; the New England Historic Genealogical Society; the Berg Collection of the New York Public Library; and the Phillips Library of the Peabody Essex Museum. I am indebted, too, to the American Antiquarian Society; the Congregational Library of the American Congregational Association; the Rare Books and Manuscripts Division of the Boston Public Library; the Howard B. Lee Library of Brigham Young University; the Concord Free Public Library; the Reference and Bibliography Section of the Copyright Office (Washington, D.C.); the Cumberland Public Library (Cumberland, Virginia); the Burton Historical Collection of the Detroit Public Library; the Library of the First Presbyterian Church of Newburyport, Massachusetts; Historical Collections of the Baker Business Library, Harvard Business School; the Andover–Harvard Theological Library of Harvard Divinity School; the Harvard University Archives of the Pusey Library, Harvard University; the Schlesinger Library of the Radcliffe Institute, Harvard University; the Widener Library of Harvard University; the Historical Society of Old Newbury; Rare Books/Long Island Studies of Hofstra University; the Huntington Library; the Lilly Library of Indiana University; Special Collections and Archives at Kent State University; the Holder Museum of the Clinton Historical Society, Lancaster Historical Commission; the Lancaster Public Library; the Library of Congress; the Fogler Library of the University of Maine; the Pierpont Morgan Library;

the National Archives and Records Administration, Northeast Region (Boston); the New-York Historical Society; the Newburyport Public Library (Newburyport, Massachusetts); the Palmyra Public Library (Palmyra, New York); the Portsmouth Athenaeum; the Salem Custom House; the Archives of American Art of the Smithsonian Institution; Special Collections of the Tampa Campus Library, University of South Florida; the Department of Archives at the Supreme Judicial Court (Boston, Massachusetts); the Harry Ransom Humanities Research Center at the University of Texas at Austin; the Albert and Shirley Small Special Collections Library of the University Library, University of Virginia; and the Beinecke Rare Book and Manuscript Library of Yale University.

Of special note is my home library, the Pattee/Paterno Library of Penn State, including its Rare Books and Manuscripts Room, its Interlibrary Loan Department, and its Microforms Department, where I first read *The Salem Belle*.

For permission to quote from archival materials, I wish to thank the Rare Book and Manuscript Library of Butler Library, Columbia University; Special Collections of the Concord Free Public Library; the Burton Historical Collection of the Detroit Public Library; Dun and Bradstreet; the First Presbyterian Church of Newburyport, Massachusetts; Historical Collections of the Baker Library, Harvard Business School; Houghton Library of Harvard University; the Harvard University Archives of Pusey Library, Harvard University; the Schlesinger Library of the Radcliffe Institute, Harvard University; the Widener Library of Harvard University; Rare Books/Long Island Studies of Hofstra University; the Huntington Library; the Lilly Library of Indiana University; Special Collections and Archives of Kent State University; the Massachusetts Historical Society; the Pierpont Morgan Library; the National Archives and Records Administration, Northeast Region (Boston); the New England Historic Genealogical Society; the Berg Collection of the New York Public Library; the Phillips Library of the Peabody Essex Museum; the Archives of American Art of the Smithsonian Institution; Special Collections of the Tampa Campus Library of the University of South Florida; the Albert and Shirley Small Special Collections Library of the University Library of the University of Virginia; and the Beinecke Rare Book Room and Manuscript Library, Yale University. I am glad to acknowledge Mary Loeffelholz, editor of *Studies in American Fiction,* for permission to publish as chapter 1 of this volume a revised version of an article that appeared in that journal.

For their generous support over the years, I wish to thank Penn State DuBois and the DuBois Educational Foundation; the Commonwealth College of Penn State; the Research and Graduate Studies Office of the College of the Liberal Arts of Penn State; and the Institute for the Arts and Humanistic Study (now the Institute for the Arts and Humanities), also of the College of the Liberal Arts. And for a Summer Stipend in 1992, I am grateful to the National Endowment for the Humanities.

I wish to note the generous assistance of numerous librarians, archivists, and curators: Jean Ashcroft (Rare Book and Manuscript Library, Columbia University), Scott Andrew Bartley (New England Historic Genealogical Society), Elizabeth C. Bouvier (Supreme Judicial Court, Boston, Massachusetts), Fred Burchstead (Widener Library, Harvard University), Paul Eugen Camp (University of South Florida), MaryAnn Campbell (Phillips Library, Peabody Essex Museum), Rebecca C. Cape (Lilly Library), Maggie Castellani (Kent State University), Joanne Chaison (American Antiquarian Society), Eva M. Chandler (University Library, University of Virginia), Donna Chin (Library, Church of the Latter-Day Saints, State College, Pennsylvania), Chris Cordon (Phillips Library, Peabody Essex Museum), Bobbi DeVore (Pattee/Paterno Library, Penn State), Tim Driscoll (Baker Business Library, Harvard Business School), Jean-Robert Durbin (Huntington Library), the late Kim Fisher (Pattee/Paterno Library, Penn State), Kathy M. Flynn (Phillips Library, Peabody Essex Museum), John Frayler (Salem Custom House), Karen Fuller (Penn State DuBois), Wayne Furman (Special Collections, New York Public Library), Michelle Gauthier (Andover–Harvard Theological Library, Harvard Divinity School), Marla Gearhart (Phillips Library, Peabody Essex Museum), Cara Gilgenbach (Kent State University), Jessica Gill (Newburyport Public Library), Nicholas Graham (Massachusetts Historical Society), George H. Hardy (First Presbyterian Church, Newburyport, Massachusetts), Nicole M. Hayes (Baker Library, Harvard Business School), Walter Hickey (National Archives and Records Administration, Northeast Region [Boston]), Sue Hoadley (Lancaster Public Library), Harley P. Holden (Harvard University Archives, Harvard University), John Hooper (Boston Public Library), Ann Hummer (Penn State DuBois), Stephen C. Jones (Beinecke Rare Book and Manuscript Library, Yale University), William Joyce (Pattee/Paterno Library, Penn State), Britta Karlberg (Phillips Library, Peabody Essex Museum), Sue Kellerman (Pattee/Paterno Library, Penn State), Barbara Kelly (Hofstra University), David Keyser (Salem Custom House), Ann Kinsey (Cumberland Public Library [Cumberland, Virginia]), Tom Knowles (American Antiquarian Society), Lynda Leahy (Widener Library, Harvard College Library), Jennifer B. Lee (Rare Book and Manuscript Library, Columbia University), William LeMoy (Phillips Library, Peabody Essex Museum), Deborah Lloyd (Copyright Office), Linda Martin (Copyright Office), Russell Martin (American Antiquarian Society), Sylvia McDowell (Schlesinger Library, Radcliffe Institute, Harvard University), Philip Melito (Special Collections, New York Public Library), George Miles (Beinecke Rare Book and Manuscript Library, Yale University), Leslie A. Morris (Houghton Library, Harvard University), Marla Y. Muse (Copyright Office), Christie Nelson (Pierpont Morgan Library), Betty Ogborn (Lancaster Public Library), Virginia Olexy (Pattee/Paterno Library, Penn State), Jim Owens (National Archives and Records Administration, Northeast Region [Boston]), Betsy Paradis (Fogler Library, University of Maine), Charles E. Pierce Jr. (Pierpont Morgan Library), Cecille Pimental (Newburyport Public Library), George Rodney Phillips (Special Collections, New York Public Library), Michael Plunkett (University Library, University of Virginia), Paula Bradstreet Richter (Peabody Essex Museum), Nicole Rioles (Phillips Library, Peabody Essex Museum), Mary Robertson (Huntington Library), Timothy Salls (New England Historic Genealogical Society), Joel Silver (Lilly Library), Virginia Smith (Massachusetts Historical Society), Geri E. Solomon (Long Island Studies Institute, Hofstra University), Shannon Stark (Pierpont Morgan Library), Sandra K. Stelts (Pattee/Paterno Library, Penn State), Brian A. Sullivan (Harvard University Archives, Harvard College Library), Jennifer Tolpa (Massachusetts Historical Society), Miriam Touba (New-York Historical Society), Jane Ward (Phillips Library, Peabody Essex Museum), Richard J. Wattenmaker (Archives of American Art, Smithsonian Institution), Jay Williamson (Historical Society of Old Newbury), Leslie P. Wilson (Special Collections, Concord Free Public Library), Harold F. Worthley (Congregational Library, American Congregational Association), David S. Zeidberg (Huntington Library), and R. Eugene Zepp (Rare Books and Manuscripts, Boston Public Library).

I wish to thank profoundly Nina Baym, who read an intermediate draft of the whole manuscript and provided welcome encouragement and comment. I thank, too, Buford Jones, who read an intermediate draft of the first chapter prior to its journal publication; Victor A. Doyno, who read several chapters; and Richard Wilbur and Frederick Crews, who read the proofs of the book. And I am grateful to Joel Myerson and David S. Reynolds for their belief in my work.

I would also like to express my thanks to David Grant, J. Gerald Kennedy, and Alan Price, and to two former Penn State students, Jill Landis and Beth Roszkowski.

I have enjoyed critical support from Penn State administrators. I wish to thank, in particular, Diane M. Disney, Dean of Penn State's Commonwealth College; Joseph Strasser, former Dean of Penn State's Commonwealth College; Sandra E. Gleason, Associate Dean of Faculty and Research at the Commonwealth College; Nancy L. Herron, Associate Dean for Academic Programs at the Commonwealth College; Claudia Limbert, former Chief Executive Officer at Penn State DuBois; Robert Loeb, Director of Academic Affairs at Penn State DuBois; Don Bialostosky, former Head, Department of English, Penn State, University Park; Marie Secor, former Interim Head, Department of English, Penn State, University Park; Robert L. Caserio Jr., Head, Department of English, Penn State, University Park; Raymond E. Lombra, Associate Dean, Research and Graduate Studies, College of the Liberal Arts, Penn State; Ronald Filippelli, Associate Dean, Administration and Undergraduate Studies, College of the Liberal Arts, Penn State; Susan Welch, Dean, College of the Liberal Arts, Penn State; and Robert Secor, Vice Provost for Academic Affairs, Penn State.

And I wish to acknowledge with much appreciation the good fellowship of my colleagues in the English Division of Penn State's Commonwealth College.

I am indebted to Donald C. Mell, Chair, Board of Editors, University of Delaware Press; Karen Druliner, Managing Editor, University of Delaware Press; J. A. Leo Lemay, H. F. Du Pont Winterthur Professor of English, University of Delaware; Christine Retz, Managing Editor, Associated University Presses; and Julien Yoseloff, Director, Associated University Presses. It has been my very good fortune to work with these fine people on this project.

I will close by acknowledging what is really beyond words—the love and support of my best friend, my wife, Amy Golahny; our two children Emily and Gabe; my mother-in-law and father-in-law, Berta and Yuda Golahny; and my mother, Irene Kopley.

The Threads
of *The Scarlet Letter*

Introduction

A CRITICAL SUBTEXT IN *The Scarlet Letter* IS THE ISSUE OF ORIGINS. WITH regard to historical origins—those of the Puritan community (1:64) and the Election Day ceremony (1:230), for instance—Hawthorne is fairly straightforward.[1] But with regard to matters of his own creation, he is more ambiguous. Most famously, with his account of the "half a dozen sheets of foolscap" of Surveyor Pue (1:33), Hawthorne offers an engaging but imaginary origin for his story of Hester Prynne (1:32–33). Only seeming to resolve the nature of the novel's beginnings, he provides a nonexistent manuscript that serves to foster greater interest in the subject. Hawthorne comically revisits imaginary origin when the Reverend John Wilson asks Hester's daughter Pearl, "Canst thou tell me, my child, who made thee?": she mischievously replies that her mother had picked her off a rosebush (1:111–12).

Hawthorne conveys a notable ambivalence with regard to the method of determining origins. Roger Chillingworth asks about Pearl—"the scarlet letter endowed with life!" (1:102)—"Would it be beyond a philosopher's research . . . to analyze that child's nature, and, from its make and mould, to give a shrewd guess at the father?" (1:116). Hawthorne later implies the evident effectiveness of this method when Hester says to Dimmesdale of Pearl, "I know whose brow she has!" and Dimmesdale responds, in part, "Methought . . . that my own features were partly repeated in her face, and so strikingly that the world might see them!" (1:206). Nonetheless, Mr. Wilson answers Chillingworth's inquiry about an effort to deduce Pearl's paternity by declaring, "Nay; it would be sinful, in such a question, to follow the clew of profane philosophy" (1:116). With this response, Hawthorne is clearly building character consistent with Puritan theology, but he may also be revealing his own reservations about tracing certain origins—

17

his own wish for deference with regard to the origins of his work. With a similar implicit ambivalence, Hawthorne mentions a method for determining the origins of the cloth scarlet letter—but only by asserting that method's futility: "It [the scarlet letter] had been wrought, as was easy to perceive, with wonderful skill of needlework; and the stitch (as I am assured by ladies conversant with such mysteries) gives evidence of a now forgotten art, not to be recovered even by the process of picking out the threads" (1:31). The scholar seeking Hawthorne's literary art might take these passages about the sinfulness or futility of tracing origins as a warning. Yet inasmuch as a method is mentioned, Hawthorne offers an invitation, too. If Hawthorne felt an anxiety of influence, he also knew the allure of revelation. Attention to the "make and mould" of *The Scarlet Letter* does indeed help to reveal the novel's origins. "Picking out the threads" of *The Scarlet Letter* does indeed enable us to recover the novel's "now forgotten art."

Clearly, many threads have already been suggested—the bibliographical appendix furnished at the end of this text surveys the history of the study of the origins of Hawthorne's masterpiece. However, despite the considerable and illuminating work that has been done, there are yet more threads to find. This is not surprising in light of Hawthorne's wide reading and his responsiveness to it. Robert Stanton's comment in 1956 on this issue remains relevant: "Hawthorne's romances still contain many undetected—because so well integrated—echoes of his literary favorites." Also relevant is Arlin Turner's assertion in 1973 that one of the areas holding "most promise of yielding new facts helpful to our understanding of Hawthorne the man and the novelist" is "his reading and his response to what he read."[2] Certainly, with *The Scarlet Letter*, a reader may discover new pretexts. The present study will identify and examine new pretexts for *The Scarlet Letter*—new threads for Hawthorne's narrative fabric and new patterns for that fabric—thereby permitting further recovery of Hawthorne's "wonderful skill of needlework."

Edward Wagenknecht once wrote of *The Scarlet Letter*, "Unquestionably . . . the most important sources are American."[3] The first three chapters of this book tend to bear him out. Furthermore, these chapters reveal the particular power of contemporary American works on Hawthorne's writing.

Chapter 1, "A Tale by Poe," contends that chapter ten of *The Scarlet Letter*, "The Leech and His Patient," involves, in part, Hawthorne's reshaping elements of Edgar Allan Poe's famous short story "The Tell-Tale Heart." Noting that Hawthorne would have encountered the tale in *The Pioneer* and probably recognized several of the sources for the tale, this chapter presents correspondences between "The Tell-Tale Heart" and *The Scarlet Letter* in plot, setting, theme, and language. Hawthorne transformed the murderous narrator and the sleeping old man of Poe's story into the vengeful Roger Chillingworth and the sleeping Arthur Dimmesdale. Hawthorne subtilized his source, eliminating the physical murder, offering a spiritual one. But still, the hues of Poe's work modulate and inform his own. Hawthorne artfully employed a thread from Poe to include with related literary threads as he stitched his extraordinary cloth. And he would do this again when he borrowed for *The House of the Seven Gables* from another Poe tale concerning crime and guilt—another vital literary thread—"MS. Found in a Bottle."

Chapter 2, "A Poem by Lowell," argues that Hester's relationship with Dimmesdale involves, in part, Hawthorne's selective adaptation of the relationship of Margaret with Mordred in his friend James Russell Lowell's narrative poem, "A Legend of Brittany"—a much-reviewed work that Hawthorne would clearly have known. Of greatest importance is the notable parallel between the celebrated church organ passage in Lowell's poem and the remarkable passage about Dimmesdale's voice in the church in *The Scarlet Letter*. Poem and novel share common elements of plot, character, setting, theme, and language. And even as Hawthorne diminished the violence of the Poe tale in his novel, he diminished the sexual suggestiveness of Lowell's church organ passage in *The Scarlet Letter*. Yet that suggestiveness is still present and implies a balancing of the scarlet letter's censure with the acknowledgment of the "consecration" of passionate love. Furthermore, Hawthorne borrowed for the Election Sermon from a passage on poesy in Lowell's essay "The Old English Dramatists" (refashioned in *Conversations on Some of the Old Poets*). In light of that passage, the erotic in both "A Legend of Brittany" and *The Scarlet Letter* may shadow forth the poetic enterprise itself. Accordingly, Hawthorne borrowed threads from Lowell not only to enrich his own fabric, but also to comment on the making of that fabric.

Hawthorne's debt to an engaging 1842 narrative, *The Salem Belle: A Tale of 1692*, is the focus of chapter 3, "A Novel by Ebenezer Wheelwright." Hawthorne would have known the work through James Russell Lowell or Elizabeth Palmer Peabody or his own publisher (also the publisher of *The Salem Belle*), and through the many book reviews and notices. We may see his reliance on this novel for plot and setting, and secondarily for language, by comparing selected passages in Ebenezer Wheelwright's *The Salem Belle* with the passages in *The Scarlet Letter* concerning the conversation of Hester Prynne and Arthur Dimmesdale in the forest, the presence of the escape ship in Boston Harbor, and the confession of the minister at the scaffold. Again Hawthorne subtilized—he attenuated the emphasis on witchcraft in *The Salem Belle*. Yet he preserved the novel's concern with persecution, guilt, and atonement. No doubt aware of the identity of the anonymous author of *The Salem Belle* (through his publisher), Hawthorne would have found the 1842 novel an especially resonant work to subtilize—Ebenezer Wheelwright's most famous ancestor was a leader in the Antinomian Controversy, an event that serves as a critical leitmotif in *The Scarlet Letter*. And, as chapter 3 will contend, the Antinomian Controversy suggests a biblical subtext.

Hawthorne's modulation of the sources to be presented here is consonant with the Hawthornean modulation recognized elsewhere. Regarding the supernatural in Hawthorne, George Ripley wrote that it is "relieved, softened, made tolerable, and almost attractive, by a strong admixture of the human." Leslie Stephen stated, "Hawthorne never introduces the supernatural without toning it down by a supposed legendary transmission." Regarding the historical in Hawthorne, Alfred S. Reid commented, "source elements entering Hawthorne's mind from the legal or physical plane emerged on a higher moral or spiritual plane. . . . This process of spiritualization of materials . . . appears to be so fundamental to Hawthorne's creative processes that it may well be one of the distinctive characteristics of his artistic imagination." And regarding sensationalism in Hawthorne, David S. Reynolds writes, "Both the 'Custom-House' section and the novel itself operate simultaneously as modern sensational texts and as critiques of modern sensational texts." Indeed, he adds, "The careful apportionment of Subversive imagery in a unified artistic structure is the author's highest achievement."[4] Hawthorne's artistic method—whether termed a softening, a toning down, a spiritualizing, or an apportioning—is evident in his treatment in *The Scarlet Letter* of "The Tell-Tale Heart," "A Legend of Brittany," and *The Salem Belle*. It is precisely Hawthorne's skillful attenuation of these texts that warrants attention. To return to our figure, Hawthorne subdued his literary threads: in the interest of the aesthetic wholeness of his fabric, he allowed individual threads to fade. Yet their relatedness may still be discerned.

Finally, chapter 4, "The Matter of Form," shifts from a concern with individual threads to the overall pattern of threads, from contemporary American sources to traditional literary conventions. This chapter contends that the well-framed meteor that turns midnight to noon and creates a moment suggestive of the Last Judgment is the Sun of Righteousness, Christ come in judgment, the critical image at the center of works written in the providential form. Hawthorne's greatest work is a multilayered narrative of the Fall—a work of providentially-overseen sin and expiation.

This chapter goes on to note that Hawthorne's expression of the meteoric judgment—"an immense letter,—the letter A" (1:155)—is the central chiasmus that links importantly to the plot, the characterization, and the theme of the novel, as well as to similar phrasing at the center of other literary works. Hawthorne clearly elaborated a highly unified pattern of threads, one adapted from earlier patterns.

There is much pleasure in helping to clarify the genesis of a great work of literature. And there need be no reductiveness, no dismissiveness, no diminishment. Conducted with high regard and care, the search for origins may invigorate our reading and enhance our understanding. And, too, it may yield a sense of renewal.

1

A Tale by Poe

THE RELATIONSHIP OF ROGER CHILLINGWORTH TO ARTHUR DIMMESDALE is succinctly intimated in one of Hawthorne's 17 November 1847 note-book entries: "A story of the effects of revenge, in diabolizing him who indulges in it" (8:278, see also 8:27). Scholars have linked the diabolized doctor to three clusters of previous writings: those works that involve or relate to the devil (John Milton's *Paradise Lost*, John Bunyan's *Pilgrim's Progress*, and versions of Faust); those works that concern psychological probing (accounts of Francis Cheynell's torment of William Chilling-worth, accounts of William Prynne's torment of Archbishop Laud, William Godwin's *Caleb Williams*, and James Malcolm Rymer's *Varney the Vampire*); and those works that involve murder (accounts of the murder of Sir Thomas Overbury and accounts of the murder of Captain Joseph White).[1] The three clusters reinforce the burden of the critical tenth chapter of *The Scarlet Letter*: a satanic figure, probing the psyche of a guilty man, commits a spiritual murder. However, none of the sources in these clusters seems to be the immediate prompt for Chillingworth's intrusion upon the sleeping Dimmesdale and his discovery of Dimmesdale's secret. That incident may find its model in a work by Hawthorne's one peer in the short story in 1840s America, Edgar Allan Poe.

Nathaniel Hawthorne highly respected the fiction of Poe. In the fall of 1842, he acknowledged as much in his short story "The Hall of Fantasy," including Poe in a select company of poets and writers in the Hall of Fantasy "for the sake of his imagination" (although threatening him with "ejectment" for his criticism) (10:636).[2] And Hawthorne wrote to Poe on 17 June 1846, "I admire you rather as a writer of Tales, than as a critic upon them. I might often—and often do—dissent from your opinions, in

the latter capacity, but could never fail to recognize your force and origi-
nality, in the former" (16:168). Poe's May 1842 *Graham's Magazine*
review of *Twice-Told Tales*—a review acknowledging "force" and "origi-
nality," but incorrectly accusing Hawthorne of plagiarism (*Complete
Works* 11:104–13)—must have particularly antagonized Hawthorne.[3] Yet
Poe's literary artistry clearly impressed him.

George Ripley's already-quoted early review of *The Scarlet Letter* stim-
ulates inquiry into the possibility of a Hawthorne debt to Poe. The 1 April
1850 critique notes several parallels between the work of Hawthorne and
that of Poe: "the same terrible excitement . . . the same minuteness of
finish—the same slow and fatal accumulation of details, the same exquisite coolness of coloring, while everything creeps forward with irresistible
certainty to a soul-harrowing climax." Then Ripley qualifies his observation, noting Hawthorne's softening of the supernatural. Although he quotes
amply from *The Scarlet Letter*, he does not go on to identify a specific related Poe tale.[4] Nevertheless, Ripley's general observation clearly provides
encouragement for a consideration of Hawthorne's possible reliance on
Poe.

Scholars have occasionally engaged in this consideration. Arlin Turner
rightly stated, "similarities in details and in method [in the stories of Hawthorne and Poe] indicate that [Hawthorne] possibly came in some measure
under Poe's influence." However, the relationships that Turner suggests
are not developed. Maurice Beebe nicely elaborated parallels in setting
and characters between Hawthorne's novel *The House of the Seven Gables*
(1851) and Poe's short story "The Fall of the House of Usher" (1839), but
he did not argue for Hawthorne's indebtedness. Millicent Bell intimated
that Hawthorne borrowed for "The Birthmark" (1843) from Poe's "The
Oval Portrait" (1842), and Joel Pfister concurred, but the case is still not
altogether conclusive.[5] The initial considerations are suggestive, though,
and there remains a wide field for further inquiry. Such inquiry is re-
warded: evidence suggests a strong, but hitherto unrecognized, correspondence between *The Scarlet Letter* and Poe's classic short story "The
Tell-Tale Heart."

Hawthorne would have read "The Tell-Tale Heart" when it was first
published, in January 1843. The story appeared in the first number of
James Russell Lowell's literary magazine, *The Pioneer*, a monthly periodical that Hawthorne would have had reason to anticipate—Lowell had solicited a contribution.[6] And on 17 December 1842, Hawthorne sent Lowell
a piece for *The Pioneer*, the aforementioned "The Hall of Fantasy," which
would appear in the second number (15:663). On 4 January 1843, Haw-

thorne's wife Sophia Hawthorne wrote admiringly about "The Hall of Fantasy" to her sister-in-law Louisa Hawthorne, and added, "James [Russell] Lowell . . . has sent us the first [number of *The Pioneer*], but that has nothing of Nathaniel's" (15:667). However, that number had Lowell's highly commendatory review of Hawthorne's *Historical Tales for Youth*. And that first issue of the magazine featured, too, Poe's intense tale of murder and guilt, "The Tell-Tale Heart"—a work praised by Lowell, who referred to the author's "powerful imagination."[7] Hawthorne would surely have read this issue of *The Pioneer* with interest, and with particular interest Poe's remarkable contribution.

Contemporary response to the first publication of "The Tell-Tale Heart" was emphatic, if we judge from the second number of Lowell's magazine, which offered comments on Poe's tale in three reprinted reviews of *The Pioneer*'s first number. It was probably Horace Greeley who wrote in a New York *Tribune* review—with a mixture of admiration and distaste—that "The Tell-Tale Heart" was "a strong and skilful, but to our minds overstrained and repulsive analysis of the feelings and promptings of an insane homicide." A critic asserted in a Boston *Bay State Democrat* review that the tale was "an article of thrilling interest." And N. P. Willis remarked in his *Brother Jonathan* review—with unmixed admiration for Poe's tale—that "Mr. Poe's contribution is very wild and very readable, and that is the only thing in the number that most people would read and remember."[8] Doubtless Hawthorne would have shared the views of the anonymous critic and Willis, especially in light of his own favorable comment on Poe's imagination in "The Hall of Fantasy," the lead-off piece in that second number of *The Pioneer*. Hawthorne would have been much engaged by the tale's dark theme and its guilt-wracked protagonist.

And he would surely have been fascinated by the tale's indebtedness to works familiar to him—Daniel Webster's speech to the jury at the Joseph White murder trial, Shakespeare's *Macbeth*, and his own biographical sketch, "Thomas Green Fessenden." Our perceiving Hawthorne's probable recognition of some of the origins of "The Tell-Tale Heart" permits greater insight regarding his attraction to Poe's story.

As T. O. Mabbott has observed, in writing "The Tell-Tale Heart" Poe relied critically on Daniel Webster's prosecutorial speech regarding John Francis Knapp, who was accused (and found guilty) of participating in a conspiracy responsible for the murder of Captain Joseph White, a crime that took place on 6 April 1830 in Salem, Massachusetts. Webster imagined the very deliberate murderer, Richard Crowninshield Jr., entering the room of the sleeping "old man," striking his helpless victim, and later, unable to contain his guilt, confessing his deed. Webster identified the story as "a new lesson for painters and poets," and Poe, probably reminded of the speech by quotations from it in a Mary Rogers article in the *Brother Jonathan* of 21 August 1841, clearly took the lesson: "The Tell-Tale Heart" concerns just the sequence of events described (*Collected Works* 3:789–91).[9]

Webster's published speech, a synthesis of the summations that the famous lawyer had made at the two trials of John Francis Knapp, appeared in Salem in late 1830 in the *Appendix to the Report of the Trial of John Francis Knapp*.[10] This celebrated speech would have been known to Hawthorne, who was a resident of North Salem at the time of the murder and that of the trials (August to December 1830). Scholars have noted that Hawthorne might even have heard Webster speak at the trials.[11] Certainly Hawthorne would have heard much about the sensational murder and the trials—and he wrote a letter to his cousin John S. Dike in September 1830 concerning, in part, the convicted John Francis Knapp and his accused brother Joseph and their family (15:206–9). He also referred to the White murder in two subsequent letters, one of these to his younger sister Maria Louisa and the other to Dike (15:214, 217). Furthermore, Hawthorne recurred to that murder in later years—in 1837, he wrote in his notebook about a cabinet in the Essex Historical Society containing old portraits, clothes, manuscripts, and "[t]he club that killed old Jo. White" (23:177);[12] in 1847, he imagined a story based on the Committee of Vigilance that had been created to find the murderers of Captain White (8:279); and in 1852, he listed the birth of Joseph White, adding, "Murdered, more than fourscore years afterwards, in Salem" (8:550). Hawthorne's son-in-law George Parsons Lathrop connected the Joseph White murder with the alleged guilt of Clifford Pyncheon for the death of his uncle, in *The House of the Seven Gables*; also, David S. Reynolds linked the Knapp brothers with Roger Chillingworth. F. O. Matthiessen specifically related the Webster speech to the murder of Judge Pyncheon, and Margaret Moore has recently linked Webster's dramatic speech to Reverend Dimmesdale's urge to confess.[13] Certainly Hawthorne would have recognized what Mabbott termed "the chief inspiration" for "The Tell-Tale Heart" (*Collected Works* 3:789).[14]

And Hawthorne would also very probably have recognized an important indebtedness in "The Tell-Tale Heart" to an even more famous work concerning the murder of an old man in his bed—Shakespeare's *Macbeth*. At the very center of Poe's story, his narrator directs a ray of light upon the old man's veiled eye—what he terms "the damned spot" (*Collected Works* 3:795). As Richard Wilbur has noted, Poe thus alludes to the guilt-ridden

Lady Macbeth, who, in the renowned sleepwalking scene, apostrophizes the blood she perceives on her hand, "Out, damn'd spot! Out, I say!" (5.1.35). Hawthorne had alluded to *Macbeth* in an 1839 letter to Sophia ("Hurley-Burley," 15:316 [see *Macbeth* 1.1.3]) and in the 1842 story "The Lily's Quest" (the stream stained with a murderer's blood, 9:446 [see *Macbeth* 2.2.57–60]), and he had alluded specifically to Lady Macbeth's words in her sleepwalking scene in his 1835 travel piece, "Sketches from Memory" ("all the perfumes of Arabia," 11:299 [see *Macbeth* 5.1.50–51].[15] It is interesting to add that Hawthorne would read Shakespeare to his wife in 1844 (16:13), and she would allude to *Macbeth* in a letter in 1845 (regarding Una's "murthered" sleep, 16:109 [see *Macbeth* 2.2.33]). And he would later teach his children passages from Shakespeare, and his son Julian would readily draw on *Macbeth* (regarding an older woman's "golly locks" [see *Macbeth* 3.4.49–50]).[16] As he read "The Tell-Tale Heart" in January 1843, Hawthorne would surely have been struck not only by its reliance on Daniel Webster's speech, but also by its allusion to Shakespeare's *Macbeth*.

Finally, Hawthorne would very likely have recognized another important source for Poe's "The Tell-Tale Heart"—his own essay, "Thomas Green Fessenden." Scholars have noted Poe's occasional reliance on Hawthorne: Seymour Gross has suggested that Poe revised "Life in Death" (soon to be "The Oval Portrait") because of his reading Hawthorne's "The Birthmark" (appearing in the third number of *The Pioneer*, in March 1843); Robert Regan has maintained that in writing "The Masque of the Red Death" Poe drew on "The Legends of the Province House" in *Twice Told Tales* (second edition, 1842)—"Howe's Masquerade," "Lady Eleanore's Mantle," "Edward Randolph's Portrait," and "Old Esther Dudley"; and D. M. McKeithan has confirmed Regan with regard to "Howe's Masquerade" and "Lady Eleanore's Mantle" and has linked Poe's "The Oval Portrait" with Hawthorne's "The Prophetic Pictures."[17] Consistent with these views is the view that Poe's writing of "The Tell-Tale Heart" was influenced by his reading of Hawthorne's 1838 sketch of Fessenden. This point requires brief elaboration.

Poe lived in New York City from January 1837 through mid-1838. Having worked as the editor of Richmond's distinguished monthly magazine, the *Southern Literary Messenger*, from August 1835 through January 1837—and probably seeking similar employment in New York—he announced his presence at the celebrated 30 March 1837 Booksellers' Dinner by toasting "The Monthlies of Gotham—Their Distinguished Editors, and their vigorous Collaborateurs." Notably, he had, at that time, a library including "magazines bound and unbound."[18] Of all the American magazines then published, the *American Monthly Magazine* would have particularly commanded his attention—he had termed it in January 1837 a periodical "for whose opinions we still have the highest respect" (*Complete Works* 9:273), and he would write in October 1846 that that magazine "[is] one of the best journals we have ever had" (*Complete Works* 15:121). Edited by Park Benjamin, the *American Monthly Magazine* featured in the May 1837 issue an account of the Booksellers' Dinner; in the June 1837 issue Poe's tale, "Von Jung, the Mystific"; and in the July 1837 issue the unsigned Hawthorne tale, "Incidents from the Journal of a Solitary Man."[19] Moreover, the periodical offered in the November 1837 issue Benjamin's review of *The Token* for 1838, where the editor referred to his "admiration of the genius of NATHANIEL HAWTHORNE," alluding to his remark in a review of *The Token* for 1837 that Hawthorne was a "man of genius." The December 1837 issue included Benjamin's announcement that "A valued friend" would soon write a "biographical sketch" of the recently deceased editor and poet Thomas Green Fessenden, and the January 1838 issue provided that sketch of Fessenden, signed by that "valued friend," that "man of genius," Nathaniel Hawthorne.[20] Poe would probably have been very curious about Hawthorne at this time and perhaps somewhat competitive with him; he surely would have seen Hawthorne's sketch of Fessenden in the *American Monthly Magazine* and read the piece with interest.[21]

And Poe might well have already heard significantly of Fessenden—especially during his 1827 stay in Boston. Then looking for "employment on any of the large journals," Poe would very likely have known of "the most widely circulated agricultural journal in New England," Fessenden's *New England Farmer*, the office of which was located at 52 North Market Street, opposite Faneuil Hall.[22] Pertinently, Fessenden listed his *New England Farmer's Almanack, for 1828* for sale at one bookstore in Boston—Bowles and Dearborn, located at 72 Washington Street, only a few blocks from Faneuil Hall. Poe would have come upon this bookstore since it was between the offices of the *North American Review* and *United States Literary Gazette* at 74 Washington Street and the office of Calvin F. S. Thomas, the printer of his 1827 *Tamerlane and Other Poems*, at 70 Washington Street.[23] Probably Bowles and Dearborn would have sold, too, the *New England Farmer* itself. Especially noteworthy in that periodical, in light of the "*scarabæus*" of Poe's prize-winning 1843 tale "The Gold-Bug," is the 31 August and 7 September 1827 front-page article titled "Remarks on the Scarabæus Roseus, or Rose-Bug." (It should be added that Poe joined the army while he was living in Boston, and in late October 1827 his battery was sent to Sullivan's Island, in the harbor of Charleston, South Carolina, an island that he would later use as the setting for "The

Gold-Bug.")[24] The evidence is primarily circumstantial but quite suggestive—it does seem reasonably likely that Poe would have heard significantly of Fessenden in 1827. If he had, then Hawthorne's 1838 Fessenden piece would have held even greater meaning. And perhaps, too, it would have been an even more probable work from which Poe might borrow.

Hawthorne had lived with Fessenden in 1836 and had clearly been devoted to him; he declared towards the close of his Fessenden sketch his affection for the senior editor.[25] In this regard, we should recall, in Poe's "The Tell-Tale Heart," the murderous narrator's notoriously asserting, "I loved the old man" (*Collected Works* 3:792) and his identifying the old man's disturbing features as his filmy eye and his beating heart. We may well be struck, then, by Hawthorne's feelingly stating of Fessenden, "On my part, *I loved the old man*, because his *heart* was as *transparent* as a fountain" (23:106–7; emphasis added). The great probability that Poe read this statement in the *American Monthly Magazine* and the identity of the assertion of love in Hawthorne and in Poe suggest Poe's debt to Hawthorne. Furthermore, Poe's ironic treatment of that assertion in "The Tell-Tale Heart" is strengthened by an inversion of Hawthorne's explanation. I would propose that even as Poe, in *The Narrative of Arthur Gordon Pym*, inverted the Isaiahan prophecy of the peace of Jerusalem—"not one of the stakes thereof shall ever be removed, neither shall any of the cords thereof be broken" (Isaiah 33:20)—to convey the destruction of Jerusalem—natives pull "cords" attached to a line of "stakes," causing a landslide (*Collected Writings* 1:184–85)[26]—so, too, did Poe, in "The Tell-Tale Heart," invert the cause for Hawthorne's love for the old man—Fessenden's *transparent* heart—to serve as the provocation of the narrator's hostility to the old man—his victim's *filmy* eye, his *veiled* eye. I would propose, too, that Poe further inverted that transparent heart by creating a secret-bearing heart, a tell-tale heart. According to this view, Hawthorne's statement of love in the Fessenden sketch was both acknowledged and subverted by Poe. Arguably, in "The Tell-Tale Heart," the beloved editor Thomas Green Fessenden became Poe's stern foster father John Allan.

In his November 1847 review of Hawthorne, Poe specifically remembered the March 1838 *American Monthly Magazine* review of Hawthorne (probably by Park Benjamin) (*Complete Works* 13:142)—it seems wholly plausible, therefore, that when he wrote "The Tell-Tale Heart" in 1842, Poe would have remembered the January 1838 *American Monthly Magazine* sketch of Fessenden by Hawthorne. Perhaps Poe had a copy of the January 1838 issue of the magazine—whether "bound or unbound"—in his possession or at least accessible; very likely he had Hawthorne's unabashedly expressive language in mind.

Reading "The Tell-Tale Heart," Hawthorne would surely have recognized its debt to the Webster speech, Shakespeare's *Macbeth*, and his own Fessenden sketch. As engaged by the work as he would have been given its authorship, its characterization, and its thematics, he would have been even more beguiled by the work because of its genesis.

It is relevant to add that after Hawthorne's story "The Birth-Mark" was published in the third and final number of *The Pioneer* (March 1843), Henry Wadsworth Longfellow (also mentioned in the "Hall of Fantasy" [10:635]) praised the work to Hawthorne in a letter of 19 March 1843, and then admonished, "But you should have made a Romance of it, and not a short story only. But more of that on Tuesday." On Tuesday, 21 March 1843, Hawthorne dined with Longfellow in Cambridge (8:368) and undoubtedly learned more of Longfellow's assessment. Perhaps the two writers also discussed *The Pioneer*'s inclusion of "The Tell-Tale Heart"— especially since that tale opened with a stanza from Longfellow's "A Psalm of Life" (*Collected Works* 3:792). In any case, as Hawthorne considered the suggestion that he write a romance, he would still have had Poe's recently-published work, "The Tell-Tale Heart," fresh in his mind.[27]

And Hawthorne may have had occasion to encounter "The Tell-Tale Heart" again. Although it was not reprinted in Poe's 1845 *Tales* (a copy of which Hawthorne owned [16:158]), it did appear in the 23 August 1845 issue of the *Broadway Journal*—the same issue in which Poe offered a paragraph of comment on Hawthorne as a "prose poet" deserving greater financial success (*Collected Writings* 3:225). But regardless of whether Hawthorne saw the *Broadway Journal* publication of "The Tell-Tale Heart," he would not likely have forgotten the work's intensity or its familiar origins. Clearly he could well have had Poe's memorable tale of guilt in mind in late September 1849 as he "began work in earnest" on *The Scarlet Letter*. And he would soon have had an unexpected but compelling reason to call to mind the Poe tales he admired: on 7 October 1849, Poe died. And then followed the broad press consideration of Poe's life and work.[28] There is ample reason to infer that Hawthorne would have had reason to think of "The Tell-Tale Heart" as he wrote his first novel.

Evidence for Hawthorne's use of Poe in that novel is a clear pattern of parallels between "The Tell-Tale Heart" and *The Scarlet Letter*. In Poe's story, for seven nights at "about midnight" a young man "thrust[s]" his head inside the "chamber" of a sleeping "old man" with an "Evil Eye," and opens a lantern "cautiously (for the hinges creaked)" and shines it upon this "Evil Eye" (*Collected Works* 3:792–93). On the eighth night, the young man is "more than usually cautious in opening the door" of the room of the "old man," but the sound of the young man's chuckling startles his sleeping victim, who is therefore "lying awake" (*Collected Works* 3: 793–94). The young man opens his lantern "stealthily" and shines it upon the "Evil Eye," then jumps into the room and kills the "old man" because of his "Evil Eye" and his loudly beating heart (*Collected Works* 3:794–95). In Hawthorne's novel, an "old man" (1:129, 131, 137, 139, 141, 167, 169, 172, 174, 175, 179, 194, 195, 224, 229, 252, 253, 256, 260) with an "evil eye"—the physician Roger Chillingworth—seeks something "far worse than death" (1:196): the violation of the guilty heart of the adulterous young minister, Arthur Dimmesdale. In the critical tenth chapter of *The Scarlet Letter*, "The Leech and His Patient," Poe's story is approximated by Hawthorne's presentation of a related figurative event and a similarly related literal one. Initially, Hawthorne writes that Chillingworth, as he probes for Dimmesdale's secret, "groped along as stealthily, with as cautious a tread, and as wary an outlook, as a thief entering a chamber where a man lies only half asleep,—or, it may be, broad awake" (1:130). Hawthorne adds, "In spite of his premeditated carefulness, the floor would now and then creak." And just as Poe's "old man" sensed "the unperceived shadow" of "Death" (*Collected Works* 3:794), so, too, does Dimmesdale "become vaguely aware" of "the shadow of [Chillingworth's] presence" (1:130).[29] The figurative becomes literal when Chillingworth, this "old man" with an "evil eye," actually enters "at noonday" the room of the sleeping young man, lays "his hand upon [the minister's] bosom," "thrust[s] aside the vestment," and discovers the scarlet letter on Dimmesdale's breast—the sign of the minister's secret guilt (1:138). Chillingworth has trespassed, causing a spiritual exposure "far worse then death." Poe's intruder had taken a life; Hawthorne's intruder thinks he has taken a soul.

In "The Tell-Tale Heart," after the murder of the old man, Poe's intruder "smile[s] gaily" (*Collected Works* 3:795), but soon thereafter, in great agony, confesses his deed (*Collected Works* 3:797). In *The Scarlet Letter*, after the violation of the minister, Hawthorne's intruder is in "ecstasy" (1:138), and although Chillingworth does not acknowledge his guilt, Dimmesdale earlier asked the diabolical doctor a question that recalls the confession of the narrator in "The Tell-Tale Heart": "Why should a wretched man, guilty, we will say, of murder, prefer to keep the dead corpse buried in his own heart, rather than fling it forth at once, and let the universe take care of it?" (1:132). And Dimmesdale does eventually, after great agony, confess his deed (1: 254–55).

In both Poe's story and Hawthorne's novel, the heart is "tell-tale." The imagined, perhaps projected beating of the buried heart of the murdered old man provokes Poe's narrator's confession of murder (*Collected Works* 3:797); and the evident stigma, the *A* upon Dimmesdale's chest, emerging from the minister's "inmost heart" (1:258–59), indicates his sin of adultery. In both works, a heart reveals the heart's secret.[30]

Appropriately, Hawthorne relied in chapter 10 of his novel on the Shakespearean play to which Poe alluded in "The Tell-Tale Heart," *Macbeth*. The "air-drawn lines and figures of a geometrical problem" (1:129)—to which Chillingworth's view of the elements of his investigation is compared—recall Lady Macbeth's speaking to Macbeth of "the air-drawn dagger which you said / Led you to Duncan" (3.4.61–62). Clearly Shakespeare's "charm" was "firm and good," and Poe and Hawthorne honored it in their allusive creations.

George Ripley's general comment may be applied specifically: Poe's "The Tell-Tale Heart" and Hawthorne's *The Scarlet Letter* do both possess a "terrible excitement," a "minuteness of finish," a "slow and fatal accumulation of details," a "coolness of coloring," and a "soul-harrowing climax." But they share more than that. Poe's tale and chapter 10 of Hawthorne's novel share language—"old man," "awake," "chamber," "creak," "shadow," "cautious," "stealthily," and "thrust"—and the "old man" in both tale and novel possesses the "evil eye." Furthermore, "The Tell-Tale Heart" and the tenth chapter of *The Scarlet Letter* share a dramatic situation (anticipated figuratively, then rendered literally in that tenth chapter): at twelve o'clock, one man enters the room of another man, asleep or awakened, and assaults him, causing death or a violation thought worse than death. Also, tale and novel share the crucial theme of man's sinfulness, guilt, and need for confession. Significantly, chapter 10 of *The Scarlet Letter* specifically mentions a tormented murderer's need to confess his crime. Furthermore, in both the short story and the novel, a seemingly supernatural heart lays open man's sin. And both works feature a covert reference to the murder of the sleeping Duncan in *Macbeth*.[31]

As Hawthorne borrowed, he also transformed. Ripley notes that Hawthorne softened the supernatural of Poe; we may note other modifications here. Even as Poe had inverted elements of "Thomas Green Fessenden" for "The Tell-Tale Heart" and Hawthorne inverted elements of *Macbeth* and the Webster speech (notably, the relative ages of murderer and victim) for *The Scarlet Letter*, so, too, did Hawthorne invert elements of "The Tell-Tale Heart" for his novel. Hawthorne switched the young man and the old man—the former became the sleeper and the latter the intruder. And he switched the time, as well—midnight became noon. Furthermore, he modified the motive of the intruder—the narrator's desire to alleviate his nameless terror became Chillingworth's desire to determine definitively his

wife's lover. And he modified the nature of the helpless victim—the terri-
fied old man in "The Tell-Tale Heart" became the remorseful minister in
The Scarlet Letter. Hawthorne also refashioned the heart in Poe's story—
the provocative heart of the old man in "The Tell-Tale Heart" became the
object of the scrutiny of the old man in *The Scarlet Letter*. And Hawthorne
adapted the murder in Poe's work to his own purpose, spiritualizing that
murder, turning it into the violation of "the sanctity of a human heart"
(1:195)—a violation that he considered, in his short story "Ethan Brand,"
the "Unpardonable Sin" (11:90, 94, 98–99; see also 8:251). Unlike the sin
of murder in Poe's story, this sin in Hawthorne's novel is never confessed—though Dimmesdale does confess his adultery and duplicity.

Finally, and, crucially, Hawthorne transformed the damnation of Poe's
work to the salvation of his own. Poe's narrator in "The Tell-Tale Heart"
had "heard many things in hell" (*Collected Works* 3:792) and had presumably developed his horror of the old man's "Evil Eye" because of its
knowledge of his damnation—he later states of his burial of the old man,
"no human eye—not even *his*—could have detected anything wrong"
(*Collected Works* 3:796). Trying to destroy the condemning eye—that
"damned spot"—through murder, the narrator only increased his own
damnation. His painful confession suggests momentary escape, but there
is no evidence of redemption or salvation. The narrator is as damned at the
tale's close as he had been at its beginning—indeed, if possible, even
more so. In contrast, the investigation of Dimmesdale in chapter 10 of *The
Scarlet Letter* has a salvific purpose, which Hawthorne acknowledges immediately before and after that chapter. Before chapter 10, Hawthorne
writes that "[t]his diabolical agent [Chillingworth] had the Divine permission, for a season, to burrow into the clergyman's intimacy, and plot
against his soul" (1:128); after that chapter, Hawthorne writes that "Providence" was "using the avenger and his victim for its own purposes, and,
perchance, pardoning, where it seemed most to punish" (1:139–40). And
Dimmesdale does eventually confess, thankful to his "afflictions," his
"agonies" (1:256–57)—including Chillingworth's burrowing into his own
suffering—for permitting his "victory" (1:255). Dimmesdale defeats
Chillingworth's "evil eye," acknowledging instead "God's eye" (1:255).

When Poe alluded in his December 1844 "Marginalia" to his (erroneous) May 1842 claim in his review of *Twice-Told Tales* that Hawthorne
had used "William Wilson" for "Howe's Masquerade," he stated that he
was "honored in the loan" and added that "[Hawthorne's] handling is
always thoroughly original" (*Complete Works* 16:43). One imagines that
in light of his response to an imagined borrowing, an actual borrowing
(suggested by parallels between "The Tell-Tale Heart" and *The Scarlet*

Letter in language, plot, setting, theme, and literary touchstone) would have led Poe again to be "honored in the loan." And the noted transformations of the former work in the latter would have confirmed him in his opinion that Hawthorne's "handling" was "always thoroughly original."

In view of the telling parallels identified, including parallels in language, we may consider "The Tell-Tale Heart" to be an important source for Hawthorne's writing of Chillingworth's discovery of Dimmesdale's secret—a significant addition to the cluster of works about murder (*Macbeth*, the Overbury accounts, the Webster speech) on which Hawthorne relied for chapter 10 of his novel. We may infer that by recalling these works, as well as those in the clusters concerning the devil and psychological probing, Hawthorne was well prepared to write of Chillingworth's assault upon Dimmesdale. We may extrapolate from this instance and, returning to the figure of our title, infer that as Hawthorne fashioned *The Scarlet Letter*, he bore in mind threads from other literary and historical narratives—threads relevant to his planned character development, theme, and plot—so as to strengthen his imaginative effort. Still, to preserve the desired hue of his fabric, he toned down individual threads. As Hawthorne stitched these threads, more or less evidently, into his narrative, he deepened the work and challenged his readers.

Arlin Turner wrote that Hawthorne "had one prevailing method of expanding each idea—a method involving what we may call the catalogue or procession." In the case of *The Scarlet Letter*, Turner added, that catalog consists of scenes involving Hester Prynne and Arthur Dimmesdale. Turner noted, too, that Hawthorne relied on his life experiences and his reading.[32] We may advance this point by returning to the term "catalog." Ironically, even as Hawthorne dramatized the idea of secret guilt in *The Scarlet Letter* in a catalog of scenes, he elaborated each scene with the help of a catalog of secret sources—or clusters of secret sources. Yet Hawthorne was—as he advised his readers to be—"true" (1:260)—he offered detail (primarily language) through which the sources "may be inferred." And not adultery, but artistry, is revealed. Although one scholar has asserted that "[Hawthorne's] sources are not readily traceable, because they appear in his ideas and effects but hardly ever in his phrasing," this statement is not accurate.[33] In fact, some of Hawthorne's sources may be traceable especially because of his phrasing—or at least his wording—as his allusions to "The Tell-Tale Heart" in *The Scarlet Letter* make apparent.

We may return to our primary figure—as Hawthorne stitched, he borrowed others' threads that would inspire him and enhance his handiwork. He allowed these threads to fade, but not so much as to preclude identification. Hawthorne could sew with subtlety and dexterity; he could reveal faintly. Indeed, Hester's "delicate and imaginative skill" (1:81) was also his own.

It seems fitting to close this chapter by noting that even after he wrote *The Scarlet Letter*, Hawthorne continued to rely on Poe. Hawthorne's phrasing in *The House of the Seven Gables* reveals his debt. And it wasn't only "The Fall of the House of Usher" that he employed in that novel.

In chapter 20, "The Flower of Eden," Holgrave shows to Phoebe, in the reception room of the Pyncheon house, a miniature of the dead Judge Pyncheon—the corpse itself is seated in the next room. Holgrave does not say how Judge Pyncheon died, although the repeated descriptions of the suspicious "Grimalkin" (2:247, 281, 298; emphasis added) near the death scene suggest that *kin* of *Maule* may have been responsible. (Perhaps the name's earlier use for the witch's familiar—"Graymalkin"—in *Macbeth* [1.1.9] encourages conjecture regarding murder.)[34] In any case, Holgrave tells Phoebe (truthfully or not) that he had heard that Judge Pyncheon was missed, and "*A feeling which I cannot describe—an indefinite sense of some catastrophe*, or consummation—impelled me to make my way into this part of the house, where I discovered what you see [the dead Judge]" (2:303; emphasis added). Hawthorne's language with regard to this House of the Dead corresponds closely with Poe's language in his tale of a Ship of the Dead, the Death Ship, the Flying Dutchman, a vessel whose men had been punished for some terrible crime: the award-winning tale, "MS. Found in a Bottle." Although Hawthorne may have read the story in the 1850 Griswold edition of Poe, it is also possible that he read the work in *The Gift for 1836*—after all, both Hawthorne's "Howe's Masquerade" and Poe's "William Wilson" may well have been drawn from Washington Irving's "An Unwritten Drama of Lord Byron," which appeared in *The Gift for 1836*. And it was in that giftbook that "MS. Found in a Bottle" was first reprinted.[35]

Holgrave's "*A feeling which I cannot describe—an indefinite sense of some catastrophe*" may be linked backward to the language of Poe's narrator as he sees the dead crew and captain on the Death Ship: "*An indefinite sense of awe*, which at first sight of the navigators of the ship has taken hold of my mind, was perhaps the principle of my concealment"; "*A feeling for which I have no name*, has taken possession of my soul" (*Collected Works* 2:140–41; emphasis added). The correspondences in phrasing are unobtrusive yet unmistakable. By alluding to Poe's tale about the Death Ship, Hawthorne underscored the presence of the dead in the Pyncheon house, increased the sense of mystery and possible discovery, and again paid tribute to Edgar Allan Poe. As he relied on "The Tell-Tale

Heart" in *The Scarlet Letter*, so, too, did he rely on "MS. Found in a Bottle" for *The House of the Seven Gables*. "For the sake of [Poe's] imagination"—especially with regard to crime and guilt—Hawthorne employed Poe's fictions in his own, sewed Poe's threads into his own fabric.

2

A Poem by Lowell

ARTHUR DIMMESDALE MAY BE LINKED WITH THE OBJECTS OF THE VARIOUS possible Chillingworth figures, including Robert Carr's Thomas Overbury, Caleb Williams's Mr. Falkland, Dr. Chillingworth's Sir Francis Varney, Richard Crowninshield and the Knapp brothers' Joseph White, and the narrator's sleeping foe in Poe's famous tale, but, of course, other historical and literary connections may be mentioned, as well. One of these is the biblical David, the adulterous king depicted in the tapestry of Dimmesdale's apartment (1:126). Others, suggested by scholars, include Nathaniel Manning, a maternal ancester of Hawthorne, who had committed incest with his two sisters Anstiss and Margaret; Michael Wigglesworth, the Puritan poet; Jean-Jacques Rousseau's Saint-Preux, the former lover of a now-married woman; J. G. Lockhart's Adam Blair, a remorseful adulterous widowed minister; and James K. Paulding's Walter Avery, the seducer of beautiful young Phoebe Angevine. John Cotton, the minister of the heroic woman with whom Hawthorne links Hester Prynne, Anne Hutchinson, has also been proposed. Once again, we may infer that Hawthorne was working from a catalog of sources—once again, we may see that he relied on an array of matching threads.[1]

Dimmesdale's Election Sermon, concerning the "high and glorious destiny for the newly gathered people of the Lord" (1:249), has naturally attracted much attention. Some scholars have sought links to prior writing: Reiner Smolinski notes that Hawthorne withdrew from the Salem Athenaeum the *Election Sermons* (and other books of sermons) in 1828, Thomas F. Walsh shows that Dimmesdale's Election Sermon features a vocabulary typical of election sermons, and Frederick Newberry relates the characterization of Dimmesdale's delivery of that sermon to the "rushing mighty wind" of Acts 2:2.[2] It is precisely Hawthorne's characterization

of Dimmesdale's delivery of the Election Sermon—as well as the response
to that sermon—that warrants further attention here, attention that will
lead to a new and important source.

Dimmesdale's voice is sensitively elaborated throughout *The Scarlet
Letter*. Hawthorne first describes Dimmesdale's plaintive speech to the
condemned Hester:

> The young pastor's voice was tremulously sweet, rich, deep, and broken.
> The feeling that it so evidently manifested, rather than the direct purport of
> the words, caused it to vibrate within all hearts, and brought the listeners
> into one accord of sympathy. (1:67)

The implicit sorrow in Dimmesdale's voice is owing to his love for Hester,
his guilt for his adultery, and his failure to acknowledge his part. As the
narrative proceeds, Hawthorne writes that Dimmesdale's voice was
"sweet, tremulous, but powerful" (1:114), that "though still rich and sweet,
[it] had a certain melancholy prophecy of decay in it" (1:120), that it
became "more tremulous than before" (1:122), and that, if not for
Dimmesdale's sin, his voice might have been "listened to and answered"
by "the angels" (1:142). Then, for the Election Sermon passage, Hawthorne describes Dimmesdale's "very peculiar voice" (1:243) with exceptional fullness. Hawthorne's allusion to the extraordinary preaching on the
day of Pentecost in Acts is altogether fitting, as Newberry shows, but an
allusion to another work may be identified, as well. We may best understand Hawthorne's rendering of Dimmesdale's voice here by considering a
critically informing text, a narrative poem by Hawthorne's friend James
Russell Lowell, a work once acclaimed, but long since neglected: "A
Legend of Brittany."

Lowell's first book of poetry, *A Year's Life*, was published in January
1841. Although Lowell later wrote to Poe that it was "a volume of rather
crude productions (in which there is more of everybody else than of
myself)" (Poe, *Complete Works* 17:144) and to Longfellow that it was
"crude and immature," it did elicit numerous positive reviews, often for its
perceived elevated sensibility.[3] Poet Elizabeth B. Barrett wrote to Lowell,
encouragingly, on 31 March 1842, "I hope that you will write on, and not
suffer your 'Year's Life' to be only *one* year's life."[4] Lowell continued to
write poetry (including "Rosaline," concerning a man's murder of his
beloved), contributed essays to the *Boston Miscellany*, and prepared for
his new journal, *The Pioneer*. Only a few months after the *The Pioneer*
ceased publication—due, in large part, to an unworkable agreement with
its distributors—Lowell found himself particularly excited about a poem

that he was writing, one with a thematic affinity with "Rosaline."[5] He stated in a letter of 15 June 1843 to his friend George B. Loring,

> I am now at work on a still longer poem in the *ottava rima*, to be the first in my forthcoming volume. I feel more and more assured every day that I shall yet do something that will keep my name (and perhaps my body) alive. My wings were never so light and strong as now. So hurrah for a niche and a laurel![6]

Indebted for the form of "A Legend of Brittany" primarily to previous works written in *ottava rima*—such as Lord Byron's *Don Juan* (1819–24), John Keats's "Isabella; or the Pot of Basil" (1820), and Percy Shelley's "The Witch of Atlas" (1824)—Lowell was vitally indebted for the poem's story to a fourteenth-century French ballad, "Les Trois Moines Rouges" ("The Three Red Monks").

Charles Oran Stewart, who discovered this source, notes that young Lowell was taught French by his mother Harriet and his older sister Mary. Indeed, when he was not yet eight years old, Lowell wrote to his brother Robert, "I read french stories." Lowell continued to develop his skills in French, reading Old French volumes when he was at Harvard. He would have found the seminal French ballad, "Les Trois Moines Rouges," most probably in the 1839 or 1840 volume *Chants Populaires de la Bretagne*, translated by Theodor Hersart de la Villemarqué.[7] The background for the ballad involved the belief that Knights Templar would anoint an idol with the fat of a child produced by the union of a Templar and a virgin. According to the ballad, three Knights Templar kidnap a young woman, get her pregnant, and, months later, bury her and her baby alive beneath the altar of the church. Before her burial, she seeks only baptism for her baby and extreme unction for herself. A knight who witnesses the digging of her tomb tells the bishop, and the woman and her baby are disinterred. The mother is dead or dying, having done violence to herself in her despair. But, amazingly, the baby, in three days' time, identifies the murderers, who are then burned alive.[8] Lowell adapted this horrific tale for his purposes, crafting a long narrative poem about a love affair, a terrible crime, and the attainment of an otherworldly peace. His elaborate reshaping and expansion of the French ballad might well be compared to Washington Irving's reshaping and expansion of the German folktale, "Peter Klaus the Goatherd," for "Rip Van Winkle." But while Irving's debt was known by his contemporaries, Lowell's debt does not seem to have been known by the readers of his time.[9] Lowell's friend Charles F. Briggs asked in a 22 January 1845 letter, "Pray do you never write a story? It strikes me that you might, if you invented the Legend of Brittany."[10]

Lowell did not invent the story of "A Legend of Brittany," but he did fully transform "The Three Red Monks" for his poem. "A Legend of Brittany" was published by Christmas 1843 in Lowell's second volume of poetry, titled simply *Poems*.[11] Hawthorne would have read his friend's book and would have been aware of some of the considerable critical response that its featured poem prompted.

Hawthorne had a growing relationship with Lowell in the period before the publication of *Poems*. Edward Everett Hale wrote that "Lowell probably met [Hawthorne] for the first time at Elizabeth Peabody's" (at 13 West Street) and that "Hawthorne soon after married her charming sister [Sophia Peabody]." Accordingly, Lowell and Hawthorne would have first met shortly before 8 July 1842, the date of the wedding of Sophia and Nathaniel, an event that also took place at the West Street house. Lowell's fiancée since November 1840, Maria White, had been a "childhood friend" of Sophia's—indeed, according to Rose Hawthorne Lathrop, "had long been an intimate friend" of hers. On 6 November 1839, the two women had attended the first class of Margaret Fuller's "Conversations," also at West Street.[12]

On first meeting Hawthorne, Lowell would have been well aware of the distinguished reputation of the author of *Twice-Told Tales*; in fact, in April 1851, Lowell wrote to Hawthorne, "I became a disciple [of yours] in my eighteenth year" (in 1837, when *Twice-Told Tales* first appeared).[13] Of Hawthorne's most recent work, Lowell certainly knew the short story "A Virtuoso's Collection," which had appeared in the May 1842 issue of the *Boston Miscellany*, preceding the second number of Lowell's series, "The Old English Dramatists." Lowell mentioned that short story in his own (unsigned) short story, "The First Client," appearing later in the same issue.[14] Similarly, Hawthorne would have known of Lowell's rising reputation, especially with regard to the poet's first book of poems, *A Year's Life*, published only eighteen months before the first Hawthorne-Lowell meeting and reviewed by Hawthorne's friend George S. Hillard, as well as by Orestes Brownson, William Wetmore Story, Margaret Fuller, and by Charles J. Peterson in the same issue of *Graham's Magazine*—that of April 1842—in which Poe first reviewed Hawthorne.[15] And, of course, of Lowell's most recent work, Hawthorne would have known the aforementioned series in the *Boston Miscellany*, "The Old English Dramatists." When Lowell undertook *The Pioneer* in the fall of 1842, he naturally turned to Hawthorne for a contribution, and Hawthorne readily obliged.

Lowell's fiancée Maria White wrote to her friend "Kiddy"—Caroline King, of Salem—on Tuesday, 4 October 1842, "James has gone to Portland today to engage John Neill [Neal] as a contributor [to *The Pioneer*] and will go this week to Concord to see Hawthorne and obtain his services." Possibly, Lowell, by himself, did then visit Hawthorne in Concord—perhaps this is when, according to Sophia Hawthorne, "[Lowell] offered Mr. Hawthorne *any* price for his articles."[16] Her husband later suggested the rate that was provided by editor Epes Sargent, five dollars per page (15:663). Perhaps, too, it was during this visit that Lowell and Hawthorne talked at a Revolutionary War gravesite near Hawthorne's home, as mentioned in "The Old Manse" (10:9). Possibly, too, at this time, Lowell spoke of his planned work, which might have included the long poem that he would soon be writing, "A Legend of Brittany"—the piece that would commence his next volume, *Poems*. However, the conversations may also have taken place during Lowell's visits with Maria to the Hawthornes.

Shortly after Sunday, 2 October 1842, Mary Peabody reported to her sister Sophia Hawthorne what Maria White's brother William White had said: "James Lowell & Maria are going up to see you in about a fortnight." On Sunday, 9 October 1842, Sophia Hawthorne requested that her mother, Mrs. Elizabeth Palmer Peabody, invite James Russell Lowell and Maria White to visit the Hawthornes in Concord "*next week,*—not this week."[17] It was to be several weeks, in fact, before the visit took place—the Hawthornes were in Boston and Salem from 23 October through 31 October (8:363)—but Lowell and his fiancée did call on the Hawthornes in Concord on Wednesday, 2 November. On Friday, 4 November, Maria wrote to family friend Sarah Shaw, "I went on Wednesday with James to spend the day with Mr. & Mrs. Hawthorne. They seemed very blissful and our time passed delightfully."[18]

Some time after that visit, Hawthorne completed his sketch "The Hall of Fantasy," which he sent to Lowell on 17 December (15:663). Hawthorne described Lowell in that work as "the poet of the generation that now enters upon the stage" (10:636). (The story appeared in the second issue of *The Pioneer*; Hawthorne's story "The Birth-mark" [sent on 1 February 1843 (15:669)] appeared in the third issue.) Lowell, in turn, would write by mid-December his admiring review of Hawthorne's *Historical Tales for Youth* (for the first issue of *The Pioneer*), identifying Hawthorne as "a man of acknowledged genius."[19]

The two writers became more friendly as time passed: Hawthorne closed his 17 December 1842 letter "Yours truly, Nath. Hawthorne." (15:663), and he closed his (circa) May 1843 letter—one about his inability to fulfill Poe's request for a story for the *Stylus*—"I shall not forget your promised visit," and signed it (despite problems in receiving payment for his *Pioneer* work), "Truly your friend, Nath. Hawthorne." (15:684).[20]

Apparently the Lowells again visited the Hawthornes some time during 1844 after 3 March since they saw the baby girl, Una. In December 1844, the soon-to-be-married (or lately married) Lowell—who wed Maria White on 26 December—arranged to have Hawthorne sent a copy of his new volume, *Conversations on Some of the Old Poets*, "with author's love." (And that book offered two references to Hawthorne, who, Lowell wrote, "has a right in any gathering of poets.") Then, on 16 January 1845, Lowell's wife Maria wrote to Sophia Hawthorne from Philadelphia, "James desires his love to Mr. Hawthorne and yourself and sends a kiss to Una, for whom he conceived quite a passion when he saw her in Concord."[21]

In light of the increasing friendship between Hawthorne and Lowell in 1842, 1843, and 1844, Hawthorne was sure to have read "A Legend of Brittany" soon after it appeared as the first and longest work in Lowell's *Poems*. Perhaps Lowell even gave Hawthorne one of the twenty copies of the book that he had received from his publisher.[22] And certainly Hawthorne would have been much engaged by the story of "A Legend of Brittany." Mordred, a Knight Templar, loves the beautiful young Margaret, whom he makes pregnant, but he loves power more. He controls her, and then, concerned about his vow of celibacy and his ambition to become grand master, he kills her and hides her body beneath the altar of the church. After the townspeople have gathered at the church for a festival, and after extraordinary organ music is heard in the church, and then the chant of the responding choir, Margaret's spirit, come from heaven, speaks. Although she is still in love with Mordred and hopes to be reunited with him in the hereafter, Margaret's spirit reveals the crime that has been committed so that she may ask that her dead infant be baptized. Finding Margaret's body, the priests baptize the unborn infant, whose spirit, with his mother's, ascends to heaven. Mordred, hearing Margaret's spirit and witnessing the baptism, is relieved; he then dies, with an amaranth flower upon his chest, a token of eternal life—perhaps, by implication (after penance is done and faith has grown), with the murdered Margaret. (As a reader of *The Faerie Queen* and *Paradise Lost*, Hawthorne might well have recalled Spenser's treatment of the amaranth as the flower to which the grieving lover Amintas was transformed [bk. 3, canto 6, st. 45] and Milton's description of the amaranth as a flower of Eden, "but soon for man's offense / To heav'n removed" [bk. 3, lines 353–56]. Lowell had earlier treated the amaranth in "The Ballad of the Stranger," and he later employed it in *Conversations on Some of the Old Poets*.)[23]

Hawthorne would have encountered in Lowell's poem a reminder of the beginning of one of his own early notebook entries: "A man, to escape detection for some offence, immures a woman whom he has loved in some cavern or other secret place" (23:153). Furthermore, Hawthorne would have encountered in that poem some of his own great themes: human passion, one individual's violation of another, secret guilt, penance, and ultimate redemption. He would have recognized a tale of the Fall and its consequences. And he would have encountered familiar language—in light of his March 1843 story, "Egotism, or the Bosom Serpent" (written, according to John J. McDonald, between 2 February and 15 February 1842), Hawthorne would probably have been intrigued to read that a desire for power, prompting a man's murder of his lover, was characterized by Lowell as "a serpent in his breast," "the black serpent . . . round his heart." And even as the poem would have interested him for its story, themes, and language, it would also have interested him simply because it was by his friend Lowell. We should recall here the comment of Hawthorne's son Julian about his father's attitude toward the writing of his friends:

> we may concede, too, in general, that Hawthorne was human enough to love best the literature which, other things being equal, or nearly so, had for him the warmest personal associations. If he loved a writer, he was apt to read some of his liking into that writer's productions.[24]

Hawthorne's attention to Lowell's "A Legend of Brittany" would very likely have been heightened because of the critical response it elicited. Most notable was the unsigned laudatory review in the March 1844 issue of *Graham's Magazine*, a piece that Hawthorne would not have missed. He would have been following *Graham's* because he awaited publication there of the story that he had completed by 9 January 1844, "Earth's Holocaust," and had sent on to the magazine.[25] Unfortunately, the work remained unpublished (and presumably unpaid for) for several months. On 24 March 1844, Hawthorne wrote to his friend George S. Hillard, "Unless he [George R. Graham] publishes it ["Earth's Holocaust"] next month, I shall reclaim it—having occasion for it elsewhere" (16:23). (The tale was published, probably in late April 1844, in the May 1844 issue of *Graham's* [10:579].) Looking for "Earth's Holocaust" in the March 1844 issue of *Graham's*, Hawthorne would have come upon the very favorable review of Lowell's *Poems*.

This unsigned review was by Poe. Writing to Lowell on 19 October 1843, Poe had promised a review: "I am seeking an opportunity to do you justice in a review, and may find it, in 'Graham,' when your book [*Poems*] appears." Three years later, in response to an astute query from George W.

Eveleth, Poe acknowledged having found that opportunity in *Graham's*: "The notice of Lowell's 'Brittany' *is* mine."[26] Poe began his review of *Poems* with a strong encomium:

> This new volume of poems by Mr. Lowell will place him, in the estimation of all whose opinion he will be likely to value, *at the very head* of the poets of America. For our part, we have not the slightest hesitation in saying, that we regard the "Legend of Brittany" as by far the finest poetical work, of equal length, which the country has produced. (*Complete Works* 11:243)

Poe's high opinion of "A Legend of Brittany" here seems all the more striking in light of the fact that, in responding to Lowell's uncertainty about his as-yet-unpublished narrative poem, Poe had warned against writing narrative poetry.[27] (But, of course, Poe's greatest success, coming in early 1845, would be one of his own narrative poems, "The Raven.") Poe followed two paragraphs of introduction in his review of *Poems* with a paragraph of plot summary for "A Legend of Brittany" and a paragraph on the "*sublimity* of human love" as illustrated by extracts from the second part of Lowell's poem, six stanzas of Margaret's otherworldly plea. And then Poe offered an exceptional paragraph of intense and focused tribute to ten stanzas appearing before these extracts, the first four stanzas of which concern an extraordinary church organ:

> The description of the swelling of the organ—immediately preceding these extracts—surpasses, in all the loftier merits, any similar passage we have seen. It is truly magnificent. For those who have the book, we instance the forty-first stanza of the second book, and the nine stanzas succeeding. We know not where to look, in all American poetry, for anything more richly ideal, or more forcibly conveyed. (*Complete Works* 11:246)

Here is the peak of Poe's commendation. With the phrase "richly ideal," Poe appears to imply what he had termed in his 1836 Drake-Halleck review "the beautiful . . . the sublime . . . the mystical" and "the beautiful . . . the mystical . . . the august" (*Complete Works* 8:282–83, 301; see also 10:64)—a suggestive undercurrent intimating to the reader "the Hope of a higher Intellectual Happiness hereafter" (*Complete Works* 8:283), "a far more ethereal beauty *beyond*" (*Complete Works* 10:65–66). And this undercurrent is produced by "the sentiment of Poesy," "the Poetic Sentiment" (*Complete Works* 8:282, 284). The remaining paragraphs of Poe's review of *Poems* offer some additional praise of "A Legend of Brittany," a caution with regard to its didacticism and smaller faults, very brief comment on other poems in the book, and brief summary (*Complete Works*

11:249). This review would have compellingly focused Hawthorne's attention on "A Legend of Brittany," and, particularly, on its remarkable church organ passage.[28]

And some of the other reviews might have also called his attention to the poem and its church organ passage. The anonymous and mixed review in the 30 January 1844 issue of the New York *Tribune* noted the "great sweetness, beauty and ease of style" of "A Legend of Brittany," objected to the poem's familiar account of seduction and its unfamiliar language, and identified the organ music passage as "original" and "full of truth," quoting from "Part Second" stanzas 41 and 42 (the first two of the four stanzas in the passage).[29] A positive, anonymous review in the February 1844 issue of the *Knickerbocker* described the poem as "a romantic story, fringed with rhyme," and quoted the second part's stanzas 39 and 41, terming them and the treatment of the choir "equally beautiful." Charles J. Peterson's highly praising review in the March 1844 issue of the *Ladies' National Magazine*—a review resembling the *Graham's* review of *Poems* by Peterson's former colleague on that magazine, Poe—stated that "A Legend of Brittany" "displays a genius of the very highest order" and that "[w]e know no sustained poem by an American author equal to it." The Peterson review quoted "Part Second"'s stanzas 41 through 49, asserting that the nine stanzas constitute "the finest passage in the poem," and that "[h]ere is the highest imagination combined with a graphic power rarely equalled."[30] An anonymous review in the March issue of the *New Jerusalem Magazine* (a review not cited by Alvan R. McFadyen) quoted five early stanzas of "A Legend of Brittany" and then stanzas 41, 43, and 44 in the poem's second part; the writer for this Swedenborgian periodical praised Lowell's "pure and elevated affections." Another anonymous review in the 15 April 1844 issue of *The Critic* of London quoted the same stanza 41 and observed its "power." And an additional anonymous review, appearing in the London *Inquirer* and reprinted in the November 1844 issue of *Littell's Living Age*, described "A Legend of Brittany" as "full of beauty, lavished on a repulsive subject," an old story "clothed . . . with fresh interest and beauty," and this piece quoted the second part's stanzas 41 through 44, a passage considered "almost perfect in its way."[31] Hawthorne would assuredly have seen Poe's appreciative comments regarding "A Legend of Brittany" and its church organ passage, and he may well have seen one or more of these other instances of such comments, with reprintings of that passage.

One review that praised "A Legend of Brittany" but did not focus on the church organ passage was especially likely to have come to Hawthorne's attention: the extended analysis in the April 1844 issue of the prestigious

North American Review, an assessment written by C. C. Felton, the distinguished Harvard professor and member of the "Five of Clubs" (with Hawthorne friends and acquaintances George Hillard, Henry Wadsworth
Longfellow, Charles Sumner, and Henry Russell Cleveland [15:82]). Suggesting various possible improvements for Lowell's poems—including
"compression"—and not quoting from "A Legend of Brittany" because
"we prefer to leave it to be read as a whole," Felton did comment, "The
first poem, 'A Legend of Brittany,' is written with great beauty and
pathos."[32]

Lowell's *Poems* sold well—indeed, Lowell wrote to Poe on 6 March
1844, "It will please you to hear that my volume will soon reach a third
edition. The editions are of five hundred each, but 'run over,' as printers
say, a little so that I suppose about eleven hundred [copies] have been
sold" (Poe, *Complete Works* 17:159–60). Poe responded on 30 March
1844, "I sincerely rejoice to hear of the success of your volume. To sell
eleven hundred copies of a bound book of American poetry, is to do wonders."[33] And Poe continued to acknowledge the virtues of "A Legend of
Brittany": he offered additional praise of the poem in the 11 January 1845
issue of the New York *Evening Mirror*, in his first identifiable book review
in that newspaper, a review of Lowell's *Conversations on Some of the Old
Poets*:

> We have few men among us of any kind, who think or write at once so
> earnestly, so purely, and so originally as Lowell; and certainly we have no
> man among us who can do all this, in prose, as well as he, and at the same
> time compose a "Legend of Brittany."

Probably in large part because of the considerable critical regard expressed
for "A Legend of Brittany"—and especially its church organ passage—
Rufus Wilmot Griswold excerpted the second section's stanzas 41 through
48 for the eighth edition of his popular anthology, *The Poets and Poetry of
America*, a book that appeared between 24 April and 22 May 1847.[34] And
these stanzas would be included in subsequent editions, as well.

Poe returned to his acclaim of "A Legend of Brittany" in his March
1849 *Southern Literary Messenger* review of Lowell's *A Fable for Critics*,
the volume that features the oft-quoted couplet, "There comes Poe, with
his raven, like Barnaby Rudge, / Three fifths of him genius and two fifths
sheer fudge." Lowell had not remained Poe's friend: genial relations had
ended because of Poe's drinking, Poe's alienating Lowell's friend Charles
F. Briggs (of the *Broadway Journal*), and Poe's accusing Lowell of pla-

giarism (*Collected Writings* 3:211). Poe wrote, nonetheless, in the context of a highly negative review, that "A Legend of Brittany" is "decidedly the noblest poem, of the same length, written by an American" (*Complete Works* 13:168).[35] Finally, Griswold added a fuller biographical introduction to the Lowell section of the tenth edition of *The Poets and Poetry of America*—a volume that was available on 15 December 1849—and that introduction discussed "A Legend of Brittany." Griswold wrote, "'A Legend of Brittany,' is without any of the striking faults of [Lowell's] previous compositions, and in imagination and artistic finish is the best poem [Lowell] has yet printed." After recounting the narrative, Griswold commented, "The illustration of this story gives occasion for the finest of Mr. Lowell's exhibitions of love, and the poem is in all respects beautiful and complete."[36]

Although it is unclear whether Hawthorne knew of Poe's continuing praise for "A Legend of Brittany," it certainly seems probable that he would have known of the inclusion of a passage from that poem in Griswold's *The Poets and Poetry of America* in 1847. Hawthorne had sent Griswold a copy of *Mosses from an Old Manse* in 1846 (16:158, 167), and his work was reprinted and excerpted in Griswold's prose anthology, *The Prose Writers of America*, in 1847.[37] If Hawthorne did not own or borrow a copy of the eighth, ninth, or tenth edition of *The Poets and Poetry of America*—all of which included the church organ passage from "A Legend of Brittany"—then perhaps he saw a copy at Elizabeth Peabody's West Street bookshop or the Old Corner Bookstore or the Boston Athenaeum's Reading Room or the Salem Athenaeum or the Salem bookstores. And perhaps, too, Lowell might have mentioned to Hawthorne the growing reputation of "A Legend of Brittany."

Hawthorne and Lowell continued their friendship in the period from the publication of Lowell's *Poems* through Hawthorne's writing *The Scarlet Letter*. The two writers' mutual regard is evident in their occasional writings about one another. Hawthorne, in his April 1845 tale "P's Correspondence," referred to Lowell as one of the "most fervent and worthiest worshippers" of Keats (10:375). And Hawthorne wrote in his introduction to the 1846 *Mosses from an Old Manse*, "The Old Manse," that Lowell had told him a "deeply impressive" story at the Concord grave of two British soldiers (10:9). Indeed, Hawthorne wrote that Lowell's story of a Concord youth's axing to death a wounded British soldier (a story prompting Hawthorne's inference that the youth's "soul was tortured by the blood-stain") "has borne more fruit for me, than all that history tells of the fight" (10:10).

Lowell wrote in his 1848 satirical poem *A Fable for Critics* an unsatiri-
cal appreciation of Hawthorne:

> There is Hawthorne, with genius so shrinking and rare
> That you hardly at first see the strength that is there;
> A frame so robust, with a nature so sweet,
> So earnest, so graceful, so lithe and so fleet,
> Is worth a descent from Olympus to meet![38]

Also, Lowell gave to Hawthorne a copy of his two-volume *Poems* of 1849,
the first volume of which began with the revised "A Legend of Brittany."
The poet inscribed that volume, "Nathaniel Hawthorne from the author."
Presumably Lowell presented this set at the time of its publication, December 1849—when Hawthorne was writing *The Scarlet Letter*.[39] Lowell,
responding to Poe's criticism of the didacticism of "A Legend of Brittany,"
had eliminated some of the preachiness for this new edition, and, responding to C. C. Felton's criticism in the *North American Review*, had com-
pressed the work. He must also have considered the response of Elizabeth
B. Barrett—"a woman whose genius I admire," Lowell had written. She
offered her criticism of the poem in an 1844 letter (the mutilations in
which necessitate occasional ellipses):

> Your "Legend of Brittany" is full of beautiful touches, . . . to go no far-
> ther,—and the whole of the cathedral scene presents signs of no ordinary
> power. . . . that your object is (a noble one!) to teach not merely the holiness
> but hallowingness of love, I still shrink a little at the sudden escape from
> guilt & its results, which you confer on Mordred.

One imagines that Barrett's reservation may have led Lowell to delete the
promised redemption of Mordred in the revised version of "A Legend of
Brittany" for the 1849 *Poems*.[40] However, he let the church organ passage
stand—not surprisingly, in light of the critical recognition it had received.

Finally, on 13 January 1850, as Hawthorne approached his writing the
final three chapters of *The Scarlet Letter*, Lowell wrote letters to friends
soliciting financial support for Hawthorne.[41] Lowell addressed one of the
editors of the New York *Literary World*, Evert A. Duyckinck, noting that
money for Hawthorne had already been raised "in this neighborhood" and
asking, "Could not something be also done in New York? I know that you
appreciate him, and that you will be glad to do anything in your power. I
take it for granted that you know personally all those who would be most
likely to give." The letter to Duyckinck indicates that Lowell was writing,
as well, to the former editor of the *Democratic Review*, John O'Sullivan.

And Lowell penned a letter to the president of the Eastern Pennsylvania Anti-Slavery Society, Edward M. Davis, of Philadelphia, asking if he could provide money for Hawthorne (through writer and theologian William Henry Furness)—after all, Lowell wrote, "Hawthorne is a man of rare genius and we all owe him a debt."[42] The irony is that Hawthorne was then incurring a debt to Lowell—specifically for "A Legend of Brittany," another "deeply impressive" story that had "borne . . . fruit" for Hawthorne.

The edition of "A Legend of Brittany" that we may most profitably rely on here is that of the 1844 *Poems*—it is longer and more suggestively detailed than the later version in the 1849 *Poems*. Clearly Hawthorne would have known both versions, but he would have had six years to muse about the first of these, and only days and weeks to consider the second. Furthermore, neither the first version's didacticism (which irked Poe), nor its length (which seems to have troubled Felton), nor its redemption of Mordred (which disturbed Barrett) would have been very likely to bother Hawthorne.[43]

Before examining the church organ passage in Lowell's poem and the rendering of Dimmesdale's voice in the Election Sermon passage, we should note correspondences between the story of Mordred and Margaret in "A Legend of Brittany" and that of Arthur Dimmesdale and Hester Prynne in *The Scarlet Letter*. In Lowell's poem and in Hawthorne's novel, an innocent young woman has a love affair with a man of religious station, a love affair that results in pregnancy or the birth of a child. The unborn infant or child imbibes the sorrow of its mother. In both narratives, the man, anxious about others' disapproval and about his possible loss of professional standing (for breaking a vow of celibacy or committing adultery), tries to hide the love affair (through murder or silence) and consequently feels great guilt. In both narratives, the woman continues to love the man and seeks reunion with him in heaven. During a festival at which the townspeople have gathered at the church, the man's crime (of murder or adultery) is revealed to the awestruck crowd, and the unborn infant is released to heaven or the child is released to the world.[44] Relieved that all is now known, the guilty man dies, with a supernatural amaranth or *A* on his chest. The man will do penance or has done penance and will probably be reunited with his beloved in the next world.

Although significant differences exist between the two stories—clearly the manipulative and murderous Mordred possesses some of the diabolical qualities of Chillingworth—the parallels in plot are sufficient to warrant consideration. Hawthorne had been gripped by Lowell's Revolutionary

War tale of violence and implicit guilt; he would again have been gripped by Lowell's medieval tale of violence and explicit guilt. The correspondences observed suggest the influence of the poem on the novel and invite attention to correspondences between the poem's celebrated passage about the music of the church organ and the response to that music, and the novel's treatment of Dimmesdale's voice in his final sermon and the response to that voice.

Leading to the climactic church organ passage in "A Legend of Brittany" are Margaret's meeting Mordred in "a little dell" that was "[d]eep in the forest" (16) and her returning home with him, where "Her summer nature felt a need to bless, / And a like longing to be blest again" (22). Leading to the climactic Election Sermon in *The Scarlet Letter* is Hester's meeting her former lover Arthur in "a little dell" that is "deep into the wood," where the minister witnesses Hester's provocative casting off of the scarlet letter, her release of her confined hair, and her "smile, that seemed gushing from the very heart of womanhood," her "crimson flush," and the return of "[h]er sex, her youth, and the whole richness of her beauty" (1:202–3). Furthermore, like Margaret in the forest, who "would have gone, / Yet almost wished it might not be alone" (19), Hester says to her beloved, "Thou shalt not go alone!"(1:198).[45]

The church organ passage in "A Legend of Brittany" is introduced by two stanzas concerning the gathering of the people to the church on the occasion of a festival (50–51); the passage about Dimmesdale's "vocal organ" in *The Scarlet Letter* is introduced with the procession of gentlemen soldiers (linked by Hawthorne to "Knights Templars") and civic and religious leaders to the church on the occasion of a holiday, Election Day (when the new governor will be installed) (1:236–40). The concluding action of each work is imminent. In "A Legend of Brittany," the music of the church organ will lead to the music of the choir and the speech of the murdered Margaret, followed by the performance of the baptism, the release of the unborn infant, and the death of Mordred; in *The Scarlet Letter*, Dimmesdale will give the Election Sermon in the church, and the people will respond with much talk and a great shout; then, on the scaffold, supported by Hester, he will confess his guilt for adultery, acknowledge Pearl, and die.

Verbal parallels begin to be evident on comparison of the much-hailed stanza 41 of the second part of "A Legend of Brittany" with a portion of the passage about Dimmesdale's voice in the church in *The Scarlet Letter*. These parallels concern the rising and sinking of a majestic sound in (or from) a church:

"A Legend of Brittany"
Part Second, Stanza 41
Then swelled *the organ*: up through choir and nave
     The *music* trembled *with an* inward thrill
Of bliss at its own *grandeur*: wave on wave
     Its flood of mellow thunder *rose, until*
The hushed air shivered with the throb *it* gave,
     Then, poising for a moment, *it* stood still,
And *sank* and *rose* again, to burst in spray
That wandered into silence far away.

(51; emphasis added)

The Scarlet Letter
Chapter 22

This vocal *organ* was in itself a rich endowment. . . . Like all other *music*, it breathed passion and pathos, and emotions high or tender, in a tongue native to the human heart. . . . Now she [Hester Prynne] caught the low undertone, as of the wind *sinking* down to repose itself; *then* ascended with it, as *it rose* through progressive gradations of sweetness and power, *until its* volume seemed to envelop her *with an* atmosphere *of* awe and solemn *grandeur*.

(1:243; emphasis added)

The verbal parallels about the noble ascent of the "music" become more marked in stanza 42 (and lines in stanza 43) and the subsequent portion of the Election Sermon passage. Comparison reveals in both texts the music's filling the church and "bursting" the walls:

"A Legend of Brittany"
Part Second, Stanza 42
(and lines from Stanza 43)
Like to a *mighty heart* the music seemed,
     That yearns with melodies it cannot speak,
Until, in grand despair of what it dreamed,
     In the *agony* of effort it doth break,
Yet triumphs breaking; on it rushed and streamed
     And wantoned in its might, *as when* a lake,
Long pent among the mountains, *bursts its walls*
And in one crowding *gush* leaps forth and falls.

Deeper and deeper shudders shook *the air*,
     As the huge bass kept gathering heavily,
. . . .
It *grew up* like a darkness everywhere,
     Filling the vast *cathedral*. . . .

(52; emphasis added)

The Scarlet Letter
Chapter 22

And yet, majestic as the voice sometimes became, there was for ever in it an essential character of plaintiveness. A loud or low expression of *anguish*,— the whisper or the shriek . . . that touched a sensibility in every bosom! . . . But even *when* the minister's voice *grew high* and commanding,—*when* it *gushed* irrepressibly *upward*—*when* it assumed its utmost breadth and power, so *overfilling the church as* to *burst its* way through the solid *walls, and* diffuse itself in *the* open *air*,—still, if the auditor listened intently, and for the purpose, he could detect the same cry of pain. What was it? The complaint of a human *heart*, sorrow-laden, perchance guilty, telling its secret, whether of guilt or sorrow, to the *great heart* of mankind.

(1:243; emphasis added)

The correspondences between the passage regarding the church organ and that concerning the "vocal organ" conclude with the similar rendering of the music's effect. In the poem, the church organ prompts the "rich chant" of the "full-toned choir," and "*fifty voices in one strand* did twist / Their varicolored tones" (52–53; emphasis added). In the novel, Dimmesdale's voice prompts in his listeners both rapturous speech (1:248) and "that more impressive sound than the organ-tones of the blast, or the thunder, or the roar of the sea; even that mighty swell of *many voices, blended into one great voice*" (1:250; emphasis added).

The verbal correspondences are evident. The "music" of the church "organ," music of some "grandeur," music that "rose" and "sank," that "grew up," "filling the vast cathedral," music like a lake that "leaps forth" "in one crowding gush," having "bursts its walls," causing "fifty voices" to form "one strand," in "A Legend of Brittany," resonates with the "music" of Dimmesdale's "vocal organ," a sound of some "grandeur," that "rose" and sank, that "grew high," "gushed irrepressibly upward," "over-filling the church as to burst its way through the solid walls," causing "many voices" to form "one great voice," in *The Scarlet Letter*. Having read his friend Lowell's "A Legend of Brittany"—the lead poem in both the 1844 and 1849 editions of Lowell's *Poems* and a work frequently acclaimed—Hawthorne drew upon its plot and its setting, and, with regard to its most admired passage, some of its language as well. Even as Hawthorne had fashioned a passage concerning a spiritual murder by relying, in part, on Poe's account of a literal murder, he shaped a passage concerning a climactic speech in a church by relying, in part, on Lowell's treatment of similarly climactic organ music in a church. Perhaps in turning to Lowell's treatment, Hawthorne sought for his Election Sermon passage the "richly ideal" quality that Poe had mentioned in his review of "A

Legend of Brittany" in *Graham's Magazine*—or the "almost perfect" rendering that a British critic had noted in a reprinted appraisal in *Littell's Living Age*—or the "great beauty and pathos" that Felton had observed in his critique in the *North American Review*. Clearly, by alluding to Lowell's church organ passage, Hawthorne provided an added dimension to Dimmesdale's presentation of his Election Sermon, subtly imbuing one impassioned triumph with another.

The notable pattern of correspondences plainly argues against mere coincidence, but a reader might propose that Hawthorne need not have been aware of his debt to Lowell—he could have relied on what Henry James termed "the deep well of unconscious cerebration," so honored by John Livingston Lowes in *The Road to Xanadu*.[46] This view cannot be definitively disproved—unquestionably Hawthorne's imaginative process involved unconscious, as well as conscious workings. Yet the considerable critical attention to "A Legend of Brittany" in the 1840s, Hawthorne's growing friendship with Lowell in that period, and the degree of correspondence between "A Legend of Brittany" and *The Scarlet Letter*—including verbal parallels—tend to indicate that more probably Hawthorne was aware of his borrowing. While his unconscious no doubt did exert some influence over the reworking of the church organ passage, in all likelihood Hawthorne knowingly relied on "A Legend of Brittany" for his novel.

Not surprisingly, even as Hawthorne modified his source passage in Poe for *The Scarlet Letter*—and, as scholars have shown, other source passages for the novel, as well—so, too, did he modify his source passage in Lowell. Through Hawthorne's imaginative reformulation, the despair of the organ music over its ever attaining full expression, in "A Legend of Brittany," became the despair in Dimmesdale's voice over his ever attaining relief from his guilt, in *The Scarlet Letter*. Serving the theme and characterization in his novel, Hawthorne replaced a sense of frustration with a more abiding sense of sin. Furthermore, the erotic energy that seems suggested by Lowell's passage—evident in such language as "swelled," "trembled," "inward thrill," "bliss," "shivered," "throb," and "burst in spray"—is diminished in Hawthorne's passage. Still, that energy remains present in the gushing, bursting organ. As with the violent in Poe, with the erotic in Lowell, Hawthorne refined and preserved at the same time. We shall return to this point later in this chapter.

The correspondences between the denouement of Lowell's poem and that of Hawthorne's novel may be briefly stated. In "A Legend of Brittany," the music of the church organ and the choir ceases suddenly as "a nameless fear . . . leapt along from heart to heart"—a fear that causes all, with "a dark, freezing awe," to look to the altar—where Margaret is buried (53–54). In *The Scarlet Letter*, "The shout died into a murmur, as one portion of the crowd after another obtained a glimpse" of the "feeble and pale" Dimmesdale. As the minister pauses at the foot of the scaffold, "The crowd . . . looked on with awe and wonder" (1:252). The great quiet in both works leads to the revelation: Margaret's spirit, come from heaven, reveals Mordred's responsibility for her unborn infant and intimates his guilt for her murder, and Dimmesdale reveals his own guilt for adultery.

And then comes the release. After Margaret's spirit asks for baptism for her infant to allow him to enter heaven, the priests perform the rite, the crowd hears "A sigh, as of some heart from travail sore / Released," and the spirits of mother and son, singing *"Misereatur Deus"* ("God have mercy"), rise to heaven (62). Dimmesdale asks for his daughter Pearl's kiss, so long denied; she kisses him on the lips, and "A spell was broken": her tears on her father's cheek are "the pledge that she would grow up amid human joy and sorrow, nor for ever do battle with the world, but be a woman in it" (1:256). In both poem and novel, the revelation of a secret passion yields redemption for the consequence of that passion—for Margaret's unborn infant and for Pearl. Furthermore, Margaret's spirit says to Mordred, "Yes, ages hence, in joy we yet may meet, / By sorrow thou, and I by patience, tried" (61); Hester, less certain, asks the dying Dimmesdale, "Shall we not meet again? Shall we not spend our immortal life together?" (1:256).

After Margaret's speech and the baptism, Mordred dies, and "Upon his breast a little blossom lay / Of amaranth, such as grows not in earth's mould" (63); Dimmesdale, having acknowledged God's mercy, dies with the scarlet letter *A* upon his breast (1:258). And while Margaret's spirit said to Mordred, "If thou wast false, more need there is for me / Still to be true" (57), Hawthorne comments on the story of Dimmesdale by advising his reader to allow his or her worst to be inferred: "Be true! Be true! Be true!" (1:260).

"A Legend of Brittany" was a particularly important thread for Hawthorne in his composition of *The Scarlet Letter*. It offered suggestive plot detail, characterization, setting, and language. There are, of course, major differences: for example, Lowell offers a medieval tenor, Hawthorne a Puritan one; Lowell offers a manipulative lover, Hawthorne a manipulative cuckold; Lowell treats murder, Hawthorne adultery; and Lowell tells of an unborn boy, Hawthorne a little girl. Still, as has been noted, the two tales share much. The issues in both works that require further consideration here are sex, love, and religion.

Sex is clearly a critical element in both "A Legend of Brittany" and *The Scarlet Letter*. In both works, sexual passion, although never explicitly described, is the catalyst for subsequent events. Lowell's language is sometimes romantic and sentimental—Margaret's "long dreamed-of ecstasy" (26), the "[b]right passion of young hearts" (27), and the "dewy dawn of love" (28), for example. Yet the church organ passage in "A Legend of Brittany"—one that elaborates lines that appeared in Lowell's "The Church"—invites at least consideration of suggestiveness.[47] The swollen, rising, throbbing, trembling organ that bursts in spray does seem to warrant attention in this regard. We should recall Lowell's words in *Conversations on Some of the Old Poets*:

> To be a sensualist in a certain kind and to a certain degree is the mark of a pure and youthful nature. To be able to keep a just balance between sense and spirit, and to have the soul welcome frankly all the delicious impulses which flow to it from without, is a good and holy thing. But it must welcome them as the endearments of a wife, not of a harlot.

And we should note that an older Lowell, arguing in an 1874 letter against licentiousness in literature, did allow that the erotic might find a place in poetry: "Shelley almost alone (take his 'Stanzas to an Indian air,' for example) has trodden with unfaltering foot the scimetar-edged bridge which leads from physical sensation to the heaven of song."[48] The strong evidence of Lowell's church organ passage—evidence reinforced by his critical comments—argues that this passage of spiritual ascent possesses, too, a quality of physical joy.

Certainly Hawthorne does write suggestively (as Frederick Crews has shown): the minister, returning from his forest meeting with the beautiful and vibrant Hester, "leaped across the plashy places, thrust himself through the clinging underbrush, climbed the ascent, plunged into the hollow" (1:216).[49] Emboldened by his encounter with Hester, Dimmesdale imagines violating the faith and innocence of parishioners he meets—including a "maiden" whose "field of innocence" he feels "potent to blight" (1:219–20). Moreover, the minister returns home no longer fearful of Roger Chillingworth, and, with "an impulsive flow of thought and emotion" (1:225), he writes the Election Sermon. The source of Dimmesdale's "impulsive flow" is his newly aroused libidinal energy, as Crews first noted; the minister's sexual excitement will prompt his writing a prophetic sermon that will provoke excitement in his community.[50] But Dimmesdale does not fully recognize the origins of his seeming inspiration, his sublimation: "he . . . only wondered that Heaven should see fit to transmit the grand and solemn music of its oracles through so foul an organ-pipe as he" (1:225).[51]

For his passage on Dimmesdale's voice in the church, surely Hawthorne would have recognized the physical joy in Lowell's church organ passage. Hawthorne did noticeably reduce that passage's suggestiveness in his re-working. However, appropriately (for a sermon prompted by the speaker's libidinal awakening), he did not wholly remove it.[52] Regarding its erotic tones, the thread that Hawthorne borrowed from Lowell was only moder-ately faded. Perhaps with regard to the bursting organ in the Election Sermon passage in *The Scarlet Letter*, we may conclude that, in terms of the balance of subtlety and accessibility, the figure of consummation is consummately figured.

It is true that the regard of Lowell's fiancée Maria White for "A Legend of Brittany" prompted Charles F. Briggs to term the poem "proper reading for pure-minded loving creatures." But we may remember that Sophia Hawthorne was moved by and admiring of Hawthorne's *The Scarlet Letter*, though it also has evident sexual resonance.[53] (Whether she denied or missed the resonance is not clear.) Both Lowell's poem and Haw-thorne's novel have a subtle but strong physical passion.

And that physical passion is an expression of love. Of Margaret, Lowell writes:

> All beauty and all life he was to her;
>   She questioned not his love, she only knew
> That she loved him, and not a pulse could stir
>   In her whole frame but quivered through and through
> With this glad thought . . . (28)

And of her beloved, the murderous Mordred, Lowell acknowledges, "At first he loved her truly" (34).

Hawthorne writes that, after seven years, Arthur was the man whom Hester had "once,—nay, why should we not speak it?—still so passion-ately loved" (1:193). And the writer reinforces this view with a touching biblical allusion—a small portion of what Michael J. Colacurcio calls Hawthorne's "vast store of twice-told words."[54] Chapter 3 of The Song of Solomon begins with a description of a woman bereft of her lover:

> By night on my bed I sought him whom my soul loveth: I sought
> him, but I found him not.
>   I will rise now, and go about the city in the streets, and in the
> broad ways I will seek him whom my soul loveth: I sought him, but I
> found him not. (3:1–2)

When Hester sees the minister in the marketplace as he passes her and ig-
nores her altogether, she sorrowfully concludes that "there could be no real
bond between the clergyman and herself"—and, Hawthorne adds, "she
groped darkly, and stretched forth her cold hands, and found him not"
(1:239–40). Thus, Hawthorne delicately and aptly intimates the passionate
love that animates the action of *The Scarlet Letter*. The bereft woman in
the broad ways—Hester in the marketplace—the two are one—each sought
her lover and "found him not." Hawthorne ably employs some of his
"twice-told words"—artfully sews into his cloth a biblical thread—to hint
at the passion that he must so often subdue.[55]

And Hester is herself loved. Although, as Ernest Sandeen has admitted,
the minister, still so dependent on the rigid structure of Puritan orthodoxy,
is "not a disciple of true love," he is nonetheless susceptible—as the occasion for Hester's punishment suggests. Torn between conscience and passion, Dimmesdale later admits to Hester that he has not been penitent
(1:192)—arguably, as Sandeen has written, because "he is still in love and
can no more regret this passion than Hester can regret hers." Indeed,
Hester says to Arthur, "What we did had a consecration of its own. We felt
it so! We said so to each other! Hast thou forgotten it?" And the minister
responds, "Hush, Hester!" and then, "No; I have not forgotten!" (1:195).
In further support of his view, Sandeen adduces the tremulous voice of
Dimmesdale as he addresses Hester in the first scaffold scene, the joy he
feels as he senses the warmth of Pearl and Hester in the second scaffold
scene, the passion of his writing the new Election Sermon, the emotional
delivery of that sermon, and his public confession in the third and final
scaffold scene—a confession that reveals both conscience and pride and
that redeems the minister's passion. Sandeen writes of Dimmesdale, "we
like him most when he is most the lover." And Sandeen fittingly quotes
Hawthorne on the appearance of sunshine in the forest when Hester's "ra-
diant and tender smile" and "crimson flush" return: "Love, whether newly
born, or aroused from a deathlike slumber, must always create a sunshine,
filling the heart so full of radiance, that it overflows upon the outward
world" (1:203). Sandeen argues that here Hawthorne comes as close as he
will to revealing love to be "the deep force which moves through the
story."[56]

It is relevant to recall here the concluding motto of Hawthorne's novel
and that motto's source. As Robert L. Brant first noted, "ON A FIELD,
SABLE, THE LETTER A GULES" was drawn from the final line of
Andrew Marvell's poem, "The Unfortunate Lover," "In a field sable a
lover gules."[57] Hawthorne's black field with a red letter was originally a

black field with a red lover. The complete final stanza from Marvell's poem reads:

> This is the only banneret
> That ever Love created yet:
> Who though, by the malignant stars,
> Forced to live in storms and wars;
> Yet dying leaves a perfume here,
> And music within every ear:
> And he in story only rules,
> In a field sable a lover gules.[58]

Perhaps Hawthorne is suggesting with his allusion that the two who are marked by the letter A (and who rule only in his novel), the lovers Hester Prynne and Arthur Dimmesdale, though undoubtedly unfortunate, leave behind them, after their deaths, a gladness in those who know their story. Through allusion, Hawthorne subtilized and enriched the romantic passion in his novel, thereby providing a guide, an insight into his own perception of his characters.

Finally, there is assuredly also a strong religious element in both "A Legend of Brittany" and *The Scarlet Letter*. Lowell writes in "A Legend of Brittany" that Art's "fittest triumph is to show that good / Lurks in the heart of evil evermore" (32), and he later asserts that "God doth not work as man works, but makes all / The crooked paths of ill to goodness tend" (37). (The poet thus recalls Milton's Adam in *Paradise Lost* [bk. 12, lines 469–78].) And he suggests in his poem both Satan and an innocent Eve. Lowell writes of Mordred—he with "a serpent in his breast" (35)—"He fell as doth the tempter ever fall, / Even in the gaining of his loathesome end" (37), but he writes of the still-innocent Margaret after the love affair, "Though tempted much, her woman's nature clings / To its first pure belief, and with sad eyes / Looks backward o'er the gate of Paradise" (38). (Mordred's eventual redemption seems later implied by the immortal amaranth flower, which departed Eden for heaven at the time of the Fall.) A Catholic element emerges as the poem proceeds. After Margaret has been killed by Mordred and gone to heaven, she comes to believe that with the help of the Virgin Mary, Mordred may eventually join her: "And thou, dear Mordred, after penance done, / By blessed Mary's grace may'st meet me here" (60). And she asserts that she has been able to plead for her infant's baptism "in Christ's dear name" (59) only through Mary's intercession: "For she it was that pitied my sad moan, / Herself not free from mother's pangs whilere, / And gave me leave to wander forth alone / To ask due rites for him I hold so dear" (60). Although the original fourteenth-century ballad, "The Three Red Monks," offered Catholic detail, it did not feature the marian emphasis of "A Legend of Brittany"; that element was Lowell's addition.

With *The Scarlet Letter*, Hawthorne also offers a providential tale with Catholic elements. The act of adultery constitutes the Original Sin, as Roy R. Male first noted, and Hester and Dimmesdale, repeatedly termed "fallen" (1:73, 110, 117, 118, 159, 195–96, 259), have a child who was "worthy to have been brought forth in Eden"—indeed, "worthy to have been left there, to be the plaything of the angels, after the world's first parents were driven out" (1:90).[59] Pearl comes "by the inscrutable decree of providence" (1:89) to bring her mother's soul to heaven—"to remind [Hester]," as Dimmesdale argues, "at every moment, of her fall,—but yet to teach her, as it were by the Creator's sacred pledge, that, if she bring the child to heaven, the child will also bring its parent thither!" (1:115). Hester comes to see her daughter as evidence of Providence's "design of justice and retribution" and "purpose of mercy and beneficence" (1:180). And, as mentioned in chapter 1, Roger Chillingworth is the providential afflicter of Dimmesdale—the satanic figure who has "the Divine permission . . . to burrow into the clergyman's intimacy" to help the minister achieve salvation (1:128).[60] The minister, confessing all on the scaffold, recognizes Chillingworth's providential role and sees it as evidence of divine mercy (1:256–57). God's providence is intimated, too, in the message of the Election Sermon—the "high and glorious destiny for the newly gathered people of the Lord" (1:249). Like "A Legend of Brittany," *The Scarlet Letter* affirms what Hawthorne termed "celestial guardianship" (1:155). That guardianship is developed further, through the form of the novel, as will be seen in chapter 4.

The Catholic elements in Hawthorne's novel are well known. In the first of the three scaffold scenes that are so crucial to the structure of the novel, Hester holding her baby Pearl is said to resemble, for "a Papist," "the image of Divine Maternity" (1:56). As scholars have noted, the subsequent scaffold scenes also have a Catholic resonance: the second scaffold scene, involving Hester, Pearl, and Dimmesdale, may suggest Mary, Mary Magdalene, and Jesus; the final scaffold scene, involving Hester holding the dying Dimmesdale, suggests Mary and the dying Jesus—the Pietà.[61] Hawthorne later writes about the generous Hester, "She was self-ordained a Sister of Mercy" (1:161), and he asserts that her scarlet letter came to have "the effect of the cross on a nun's bosom" (1:163). In contrast, the minister, still hiding his guilt, beat himself with "a bloody scourge" in his "secret closet"—a practice "more in accordance with the old, corrupted faith of Rome, than with the better light of the church in which he had been born and bred" (1:144). The faith of Rome, both respected and faulted, holds a prominent place in *The Scarlet Letter*.[62]

It is not surprising that Hawthorne considered an additional Catholic element for *The Scarlet Letter*—and confided that fact to Lowell. The poet wrote, in a 12 June 1860 letter to Charles Eliot Norton's sister Jane Norton, about his conversation with Hawthorne in Liverpool: "He said . . . that it had been part of his plan in 'The Scarlet Letter' to make Dimmesdale confess himself to a Catholic priest." And Lowell added, "I, for one, am sorry he didn't. It would have been psychologically admirable."[63]

It is noteworthy that the Catholic motif in Lowell's "A Legend of Brittany" is markedly different from that in *The Scarlet Letter*. Never directly depicted, Mary nonetheless takes a part in the events of Lowell's poem— she permits Margaret to leave heaven and make her plea on earth. Lowell uses the Madonna in a straightforward and dramatic way—she is a part of the providence that the story reveals. On the other hand, Mary takes no part in Hawthorne's novel, providential or otherwise—rather, she is the standard of nurturing motherhood with which Hester is compared—and of innocence, with which Hester is contrasted. Hawthorne employs the Madonna image to intensify his characterization of Hester—even as he writes of the "bloody scourge" in the "secret closet" to intensify his characterization of the guilt-wracked Arthur. The final image of the Pietà intensifies the characterization further, highlighting Hester's maternal strength and Arthur's long suffering and his ultimate triumph.

We may here consider the significance of the presence of the erotic in the church passage in "A Legend of Brittany" and its modulated presence in the church passage in *The Scarlet Letter*. There could well be an aesthetic purpose—the hinted sexual passion in each of these passages effectively balances the original undescribed sexual passion, providing a satisfying symmetry. Perhaps, too, there is a dramatic purpose. Both the poem and the novel are accounts of family lost and recovered, and the erotic tension returns us to the beginning of the family and thus fittingly anticipates the coming recovery of the family: the reunion of Margaret, her baby, and eventually Mordred, in heaven; and the reunion of Hester, Pearl, and Dimmesdale on the scaffold, and, presumably, again in heaven. But beyond the aesthetic and dramatic purposes, there seems to be a religious purpose. We may infer that the presence of a hint of sexual love in each church passage suggests—to adapt a phrase of Elizabeth Barrett's—a hallowing of sexual love. In "A Legend of Brittany," such treatment is not surprising since it was not the sexual love but the will to power that led to the tragedy. But in *The Scarlet Letter*, the hallowing of sexual love may seem remarkable since that love, in the context of an adulterous affair, did lead to the tragedy and was considered, by the minister and the townspeople, sinful. However, with the erotic energy in the church, helping to shape prophecy, Hawthorne provides a counter-balance to the scarlet letter, the badge of the sin of adultery. That the erotic energy occurs within this religious setting and situation may well covertly confirm that the love of Hester and Arthur did indeed have "a consecration of its own" (1:195); that "the whole relation of man and woman" in the case of these two did involve "sacred love" (1:263); that while their union was "unrecognized on earth," it would be recognized at "the bar of final judgment," which would be, as Hester had hoped, "their marriage altar" (1:80). It is surely true that, as Sophia Hawthorne wrote to her sister Mary Mann, *The Scarlet Letter* "shows that the Law cannot be broken" (16:313 n), but, like the claims of law in the novel, the claims of love in this work are also compelling. And certainly the presence of a hint of physical passion in the church passage tends to strengthen these claims. The tension between law and love in *The Scarlet Letter* is unresolvable, but the artistry that created that tension seems clear and beyond challenge.

Providence in both "A Legend of Brittany" and *The Scarlet Letter* is merciful. Lowell's murderous Mordred may well be reunited with Margaret in heaven after he has done his penance. And Hawthorne's adulterous Dimmesdale—granted the opportunity to do penance for his sin (enduring Chillingworth and the scarlet letter) and to confess—achieves salvation. And, despite his doubts, he may be reunited in the afterlife with Hester, who has been brought there through her love of Pearl and, presumably, through her good works for the community. In the poem and in the novel, the sinner is punished, but not damned. Even the satanic Chillingworth is given a qualified reprieve (1:260–61). Both Lowell and Hawthorne reprise the story of the Fall of Man, honoring the human and the divine—and perhaps thereby managing to approach Milton's goal in *Paradise Lost*—to "assert Eternal providence, / And justify the ways of God to men" (bk. 1, lines 25–26).

The parallels observed here argue for the likelihood of additional parallels between Lowell's writing and *The Scarlet Letter*. And one additional correspondence may indeed by noted, involving again Dimmesdale's Election Sermon.

We know that Hawthorne would have encountered Lowell's "The Old English Dramatists," which appeared in the April 1842, May 1842, and August 1842 issues of the *Boston Miscellany*. Nathan Hale Jr., the editor of the *Boston Miscellany* (and former coeditor, with Lowell, of *Harvardiana*), had sent Hawthorne a copy of the January 1842 issue, and Hawthorne had responded on 6 December 1841, "I have read it with great pleasure, and like it very much indeed, both as to its external and material aspect, and its intellectual and spiritual being" (15:598). Hawthorne would surely have seen a review of the new edition of his *Twice-Told Tales* in the February 1842 issue of the *Boston Miscellany*, and, on 28 March 1842, Hawthorne submitted to Hale "A Virtuoso's Collection" (15:619), a work that was published in the May 1842 issue.[64] Furthermore, Lowell reworked the material in "The Old English Dramatists," giving it a conversational form, and this material was a significant portion of his 1845 book, *Conversations on Some of the Old Poets*—a copy of which, as already noted, Lowell gave to Hawthorne, "with author's love."

The first installment of "The Old English Dramatists" was placed prominently as the lead article in the April 1842 *Boston Miscellany*. If we recall Hawthorne's writing that Dimmesdale's Election Sermon culminated with a prophecy of the "high and glorious destiny for the newly gathered people of the Lord," we may well find the opening of the second paragraph of that first installment to be familiar and significant: "It is the high and glorious vocation of poesy to make our daily life and toil more beautiful and holy by the divine ministerings of love." Modified to address the fitness for poetry of a concern with slavery (perhaps because of Maria Lowell's influence), the line appears in *Conversations* thus: "It is the high and glorious vocation of Poesy as well to make our own daily life and toil more beautiful and holy to us by the divine ministerings of love, as to render us swift to convey the same blessing to our brethren."[65] In either version, the key adjective phrase "high and glorious" is present. Hawthorne's use of that phrase—a phrase appearing in two different Lowell works, both of which Hawthorne would have read—suggests another borrowing from Lowell for *The Scarlet Letter*. Although one could assert that the borrowing was only a coincidence, it seems likelier, in light of the Hawthorne-Lowell pattern already demonstrated, that the borrowing is a significant one—whether consciously or unconsciously made—and that it may clarify the Election Sermon itself.

The "high and glorious vocation of Poesy" takes us back to Poe's comment that the church organ passage in "A Legend of Brittany" was "richly ideal," for the ideal is the consequence of "the sentiment of Poesy" (*Complete Works* 8:282). If we read the first paragraph in the first installment of "The Old English Dramatists," we note, in particular, Lowell's assertion that "under the thin crust of fashion and frivolity throb the undying fires of the great soul of man, which is the fountain and center of all poesy, and which will one day burst forth, and wither like grassblades all the temples and palaces which form and convention have heaped over it." And so I offer a tentative inference: the throbbing bursting organ in "A Legend of Brittany," which refers literally to the church organ and its music, suggests figuratively not only a sexual dimension, but also a larger dimension, which the sexual shadows forth: that of the poetic enterprise itself. According to this view, that throbbing bursting organ, like the throbbing bursting "fires of the great soul of man," is the genius of the poet. (In this regard, we should recall Lowell's assertion, in *Conversations*, regarding Wordsworth's Intimations Ode, "The grand symphony of Wordsworth's Ode rolls through me, and I tremble, as the air does with the gathering thunders of the organ." Again, for Lowell, the organ is a figure for poetic genius.) We encounter in the third paragraph of the first installment of "The Old English Dramatists" an analogy between the poet, whose work is the expression of love, and the "angel of love," who leaves Eden, behind Adam and Eve, holding the eternal amaranth—the very flower that Lowell associates with Mordred in "A Legend of Brittany." According to Lowell, the seed of the amaranth "gives a higher hope to the soul or makes life nobler or more godlike" (recalling Poe on the suggestive undercurrent), and this seed is nourished by "the overarching sky of poesy."[66] Lowell's phrase "high and glorious" is both applied to the "vocation of poesy" and embedded in an encomium for the power of poesy. Accordingly, in light of the use of that phrase with reference to the Election Sermon in *The Scarlet Letter*, the minister seems to suggest the poet; Dimmesdale seems to suggest Hawthorne.

It would seem likelier than not that Hawthorne deliberately borrowed Lowell's phrase "high and glorious" and its association. Poe had written that Hawthorne was "a prose poet" (*Collected Writings* 3:225). And, as already noted, Lowell himself had written in *Conversations* that Hawthorne "has a right in any gathering of poets."[67] And Hawthorne wrote to Longfellow on 5 June 1849, "I do not claim to be a poet; and yet I cannot but feel that some of the sacredness of that character adheres to me, and ought to be respected in me" (16:270). That Hawthorne associated the organ with poetry is evident from his narrator's mentioning, in the 1845 piece "P.'s Correspondence," having heard "scraps of poetry . . . a few as grand as organ-peals" (10:379). Perhaps, even as Dimmesdale's prophecy concerns the "high and glorious destiny" of Puritan New England, it also suggests the "high and glorious vocation" of the writer. And perhaps, with this allusion to the "high and glorious vocation of poesy" in his climactic church sermon, Hawthorne was subtly asserting "the sacredness" of the writer's effort—indeed, "the sacredness" of his own vocation.

James Russell Lowell's "A Legend of Brittany"—like *The Scarlet Letter*, a story of secret sin—is yet another source in Hawthorne's catalog of secret sources. Or, to shift to the thread that is worked throughout this study—that is, the figure of threads—"A Legend of Brittany" is one of the preeminent matching threads that Hawthorne employed for exciting his imagination and enhancing his art. And even as the angry hue in the Poe thread (the physical murder) was modulated in *The Scarlet Letter*, so, too, was the brilliant hue in the Lowell thread (the sexual suggestiveness) diminished in Hawthorne's novel. That is, the borrowed threads were, in certain ways, allowed to fade. Although Hawthorne's "wonderful skill of needlework" may be "a now forgotten art" (1:31), if it is studied, that skill may well be partly recovered.

We should recall that, on 9 December 1853, Hawthorne repaid the financial debt that he had earlier incurred by accepting funds raised for him so that he could write *The Scarlet Letter*. He sent to George Hillard "a draft on [George] Ticknor for the sum (with interest included) which was so kindly given me by unknown friends, through you, about four years ago" (17:154). And even as he repaid his financial debt to these "unknown friends," he had earlier repaid his literary debt to Lowell by masterfully transforming—and thereby paying tribute to—"A Legend of Brittany" in *The Scarlet Letter* (even as he had repaid Poe with his transformation of "The Tell-Tale Heart"). It seems very likely that Lowell would have recognized Hawthorne's literary debt to him and Hawthorne's repayment. And in view of Lowell's own borrowing from "The Three Red Monks" for "A Legend of Brittany," the poet would surely have understood well Hawthorne's borrowing. Lowell's thinking about that borrowing may be clarified by a comment that he made later with regard to Edmund Spenser: "It is not what a poet takes, but what he makes out of what he has taken, that shows what native force is in him." Ultimately, Lowell's judgment of what Hawthorne had made of what he had taken was extremely high. Indeed, on 26 February 1862, Lowell wrote to Hawthorne, "It is a pure delight to me to admire any man's work as heartily as I do yours."[68] Lowell's "pure delight" in admiring Hawthorne's first novel would surely have involved his understanding that Hawthorne's "native force" had rendered in *The Scarlet Letter* a beautiful reworking of elements of Lowell's "A Legend of Brittany." Accordingly, Lowell would have had an enormous pride—both in Hawthorne and in himself.

3

A Novel by Ebenezer Wheelwright

THE CRITICAL EPISODES OF THE FINAL THIRD OF *The Scarlet Letter*—FROM the forest meeting of Arthur Dimmesdale and Hester Prynne to the minister's sermon, confession, and death—may be linked with a number of works that Hawthorne knew. Lowell's "A Legend of Brittany" is a vital one of these—especially regarding chapter 22, "The Procession," as discussed—but other works may be noted, as well. For example, in chapters 16, 17, 18, and 19, the minister and Hester in the forest recall the Red Cross Knight and Una in the forest in Spenser's *The Faerie Queen*, Adam Blair and Charlotte Bell in the forest in J. G. Lockhart's *Adam Blair*, and Arthur Kavanagh and Cecilia Vaughan in the forest in Henry Wadsworth Longfellow's *Kavanagh*. A portion of conversation between Hester and the minister may have been suggested by dialogue in Kotzebue's play *Lover's Vows*; Pearl at the brook may have been indebted to Matilda and Beatrice at the brook in Dante's *Divine Comedy*; and a phrase appearing toward the end of the forest scene may have been prompted by a phrase in Emerson's *Nature*. In chapter 20, Dimmesdale's determining, as he left the forest, that he had not "fallen asleep, and dreamed!" (1:214) and his perceiving the town that he returned to as if he had left "years ago"—as if "a single day" had been a "lapse of years" (1:216–17)—may well owe a debt to Washington Irving's "Rip Van Winkle." And the minister's impassioned nighttime writing of his final sermon probably owes a debt to Mr. Pendexter's impassioned nighttime writing of his final sermon in *Kavanagh*. The entire section involving the forest meeting and Dimmesdale's return to Boston echoes ironically Christian's pilgrimage in John Bunyan's *Pilgrim's Progress*. In chapters 22 and 23, Dimmesdale's sermon has been linked to previous Election Sermons and the Bible, as already noted. And Dimmesdale's confession may be related to that of

Samuel Johnson in Uttoxeter market, as recounted by Boswell, an event that Hawthorne would have known as a boy (5:121–22, 132), had mentioned in his notebook in 1838 (8:180; 23:214), and had described in his 1842 *Biographical Stories for Children* (6:239–49). Other historical confessions that Hawthorne would likely have known include those of criminals depicted in *The Record of Crime in the United States*, Overbury jailer Jervase Helwyse, and Judge Samuel Sewall. Among the fictional confessions Hawthorne would likely have encountered was Adam Blair's confession of adultery at a presbytery meeting. And, of course, Hawthorne knew well the confession of Poe's narrator in "The Tell-Tale Heart." Christian iconography was clearly an influence with regard to Dimmesdale's death. And in chapter 24, *Adam Blair* may figure again with regard to details of the aftermath of the story, while assuredly Andrew Marvell's "The Unfortunate Lover" figures in the reading of the tombstone escutcheon.[1]

To this lengthy, but by no means exhaustive, catalog of sources for the final third of Hawthorne's novel may be added another source; to this list of threads may be added another thread: a neglected 1842 novel by Ebenezer Wheelwright, set during the Salem witchcraft period and titled *The Salem Belle: A Tale of 1692*. Wheelwright's narrative includes three important source passages for *The Scarlet Letter*.

The novel has been considered only briefly in literary scholarship. In 1930, G. Harrison Orians termed it "a fairly accurate picture of the public malady at Salem and the terrible engine of power, which the general belief in supernatural agencies put into the hands of 'designing men to punish private wrongs.'" He acknowledged, though, that neither "the ascribed relationships" nor "the action" was "historical" and that neither the first nor the second edition (1847) gave "any hint of the authorship." In 1932, Orians referred again to *The Salem Belle*, listing it as a work of fiction featuring a regicide—the heroine is the granddaughter of General William Goffe. In 1971, Nolan E. Smith offered a tentative attribution for the novel, based on a "pencil notation" in a copy held by what was then the Essex Institute (now the Peabody Essex Museum). The bracketed notation in this copy is "By Mrs. Wm. Cleveland." (Mrs. William Cleveland was the Salem children's book writer, Lucy Cleveland [1780–1866].) Also in 1971, Michael Davitt Bell commented briefly on the novel, mentioning its regicide; its "pattern of proposal, refusal, and accusation"; and its concern with the reemergence of delusion. In 1989, Gabriele Schwab listed the novel as one of the "most important" "works which are direct literary renditions of the Salem events," but she mistakenly attributed the work to

Mary Lyford, its heroine. And in 1991, Sacvan Bercovitch quoted from the novel with regard to the nobility of the Puritans, asserting that the author was "anonymous."[2]

The anonymity of the author of *The Salem Belle* is the evident immediate problem. The present chapter will summarize the book's publication history, note the difficulty of the Lucy Cleveland attribution, yet assert the relevance of her children's book *The Unveiled Heart* (1835) to *The Scarlet Letter*. It will then elaborate the evidence for an Ebenezer Wheelwright attribution regarding *The Salem Belle*; sketch the life of this obscure, but not insignificant, author; and demonstrate the validity of the Ebenezer Wheelwright attribution, with particular reference to Wheelwright's other novel, *Traditions of Palestine* (1864). This chapter will also explore Hawthorne's awareness of *The Salem Belle* through individuals, the publisher, and reviews, and then furnish parallels in plot, setting, and language that will reveal Hawthorne's reliance on *The Salem Belle* for *The Scarlet Letter*. It will argue that Hawthorne employed Wheelwright's book both to subtilize the Salem witchcraft crisis and to recall, however privately, the Antinomian Controversy. The vital link to the latter is Ebenezer Wheelwright's celebrated ancestor, John Wheelwright—the missing man of *The Scarlet Letter*. Finally, this chapter will assert that the story of Anne Hutchinson and John Wheelwright supports a critical biblical subtext in Hawthorne's novel.

The Salem Belle, a romance set during the period of the Salem witchcraft frenzy, was registered for copyright, without an author's name, by Tappan and Dennet in Boston on 25 November 1842.[3] The year of publication was the sesquicentennial of the witchcraft trials. And the publisher was none other than Hawthorne's own. In 1842, Tappan and Dennet published not only *The Salem Belle*, but also Nathaniel Hawthorne's *Biographical Stories for Children*, as well as the second edition of his *Grandfather's Chair: A History for Youth*, the second edition of his *Famous Old People: Being the Second Epoch of Grandfather's Chair*, the third edition of his *Liberty Tree; with the Last Words of Grandfather's Chair,* and his two-volume *Historical Tales for Youth*, comprising *Grandfather's Chair, Famous Old People, Liberty Tree*, and *Biographical Stories*.[4] Although, unlike these books, *The Salem Belle* boasted no celebrated author—indeed, boasted no author at all—it was widely reviewed (as will be discussed shortly), and it must have sold reasonably well: the novel was republished by John M. Whittemore in Boston in July 1847.

The difficulties with the attribution of *The Salem Belle* to Lucy Cleveland are several. *The Salem Belle* does not have a notable resonance with

Lucy Cleveland's writings. In particular, neither the historical setting nor the language patterns of the anonymous work are found in Cleveland's writings.[5] Additionally, *The Salem Belle* begins with a letter addressed to the author, and that letter opens, "Dear Sir" (iii).[6] Furthermore, the review of *The Salem Belle* in *The Pioneer*—a review probably written by Lowell himself—states, "This little novel is, we are informed, the production of a young merchant of this city, whose first attempt in the art of book-making it appears to be." Lowell would most likely have learned about the author from publishers Tappan and Dennet—that firm was the only one advertising in *The Pioneer*—indeed, it took a full page in the first issue of the magazine for Jared Sparks's *The Life of George Washington*.[7] Clearly, sixty-two-year-old Salem writer Lucy Cleveland—who had published a dozen books by 1842—did not fit Lowell's description of the author of *The Salem Belle*.

Nolan E. Smith's tentative attribution, and the "pencil notation" that prompted it, seem questionable. Yet Lucy Cleveland is nonetheless not without relevance here. One of her earlier novels, *The Unveiled Heart,* may well have been a minor thread for *The Scarlet Letter*. It is certainly likely that Hawthorne knew the book—Lucy Cleveland's reputation in Salem (where he lived from 1825 to 1842 and 1845 to 1850) and the provocative title of her novel would probably have engaged Hawthorne's interest. And Sophia Peabody knew Lucy Cleveland from their earlier involvement in a private school in Lancaster. Notably, in 1838, when Hawthorne was courting Sophia, she had lately visited with Lucy Cleveland and was writing to her.[8]

Some of the details of Cleveland's novel of adolescent romance and manipulation correspond clearly with details in *The Scarlet Letter*. The exemplary Emma Southgate sews clothes for the poor, and visits the poor and the sick; she is twice termed a "sister of charity." Cautioning her vain sister Helen about the latter's foolish selfishness, Emma says, "I warn you! Look to it." The man whom Emma eventually marries, Edward Harrison, comes upon a shack in which she is speaking to a poor ill woman, and "The voice, but not the words, were distinguishable, and that was full of music." We may recall that Hester, who also sews clothes for the poor, and visits the poor and the sick, is also termed a "Sister of Charity" (1:215). Furthermore, implicitly warning Dimmesdale as she argues for her keeping her daughter Pearl, she says, "I will not lose the child! Look to it!" Moreover, from outside the church, she listens to the voice of the man she loves—a voice compared to "music"—and, Hawthorne writes, "the sermon had throughout a meaning for her, entirely apart from its indistinguishable words" (1:243). Importantly, in the short story following *The Unveiled*

Heart, "Retribution," another anticipative passage appears—one concerning a specific "retributive justice": a man's "standing up before the gaze of the scoffing multitude with the brand upon his forehead." We may readily recall in *The Scarlet Letter* a Puritan matron's recommending that "they should have put the brand of a hot iron on Hester Prynne's forehead" (1:51) and Dimmesdale's exposing the *A* on his breast to "the gaze of the horror-stricken multitude" (1:255).[9] The parallels are highly suggestive; Lucy Cleveland's 1835 work seems to have a presence in *The Scarlet Letter*. Accordingly, Hawthorne's occasional derogation of women writers seems further undercut.[10]

It is serendipitous that a problematic attribution leads to a new source. But the mystery of the authorship of the original source, *The Salem Belle*, remains. The solution to that mystery may be learned by examining a copy of the first edition of *The Salem Belle* held by the Lilly Library and once owned by Jane Ann Reed of Waldoboro, Maine. (Waldoboro is a small town about thirty-five miles northeast of Brunswick, Maine.) Ms. Reed wrote on the fly-leaf of the volume "Jane Ann Reed's / Waldoboro / Dec. 1842." And she wrote on the title page, above the title, "Jane Ann Reed's," and below the title, "By Mr. Wheelwright."[11]

Jane Ann Reed (1811–81), a woman highly regarded for her letter-writing, was the daughter of Isaac Gardner Reed (1783–1847) and Jane Reed (1779–1856). Isaac Gardner Reed had graduated from Harvard in 1803, and he became a lawyer and postmaster in Waldoboro. Moreover, he had "a strong literary taste, and his mind was enriched with much and various reading." Remarkably, he wrote to his daugher Mary Gardner Reed on 26 January 1843 about his reading *The Salem Belle*. Having completed more than half the book (and referring to several episodes), he added, "I think [this] book, so far, well written—especially the sermons of Willard & of Mather. I have read without an effort to discover 'incongruities', I therefore have found but few. And I am too littled versed in the niceties of history to detect anachronisms, or other errors."[12]

Perhaps Isaac Gardner Reed read his daughter Jane Ann's copy of *The Salem Belle*. Perhaps he read Jane Ann's attribution in that copy—"By Mr. Wheelwright"—and knew precisely who was meant. Indeed, the absence of a first name suggests that for Jane Ann (and, one imagines, for her family, as well) there was just one "Mr. Wheelwright." However, for today's reader, the incomplete attribution teases and entices. Fortunately, clarification is at hand. A 13 October 1841 letter to Mary Gardner Reed from her friend Sarah R. Derby provides a helpful clue. Having inquired about a Boston academy, the Charles Abbott School, and teachers and others in Boston, Sarah asks, "Have you seen Mr. & Mrs. Wheelwright lately? Have they removed from Dover Street?"[13] Examination of the Boston directory for 1841 reveals that only one of the twelve Wheelwrights listed lived on Dover Street: Ebenezer Wheelwright. And the Boston directory for 1842 shows that he did indeed move from Dover Street—to 3 Temple Place, the same address as that of Charles Tappan of Tappan and Dennet, the publisher of *The Salem Belle*.

In order to corroborate the validity of the attribution of *The Salem Belle* to Ebenezer Wheelwright, we must briefly explore his life and his other writing. Further study will bear out the compelling inference—Ebenezer Wheelwright did write *The Salem Belle*.

Ebenezer Wheelwright Jr. was born to Ebenezer Wheelwright Sr. (a shipowner) and Anna Coombs Wheelwright in Newburyport, Massachusetts, on 12 February 1800. The most well-known of his seven siblings was to be William, who became an industrialist in South America. The Wheelwright children were brought up strictly, and the family belonged to the First Presbyterian Church ("The Old South"). In 1818, young Ebenezer and John Andrews Jr. formed a booksellers and stationers firm in Newburyport. However, in 1821 Ebenezer moved to Portsmouth, New Hampshire, and became a flour merchant. On 21 January 1823, he married Sarah Boddily, and they had five children, three of whom lived to adulthood: Henry Blatchford, Sarah, and Mary Abney. He moved his family to Boston in 1835 and shifted, over the next few years, from flour merchant to West Indies merchant. He did not succeed in his business—perhaps owing to the Panic of 1837, or his great trust in others, or both—and with the passage of the Bankruptcy Act of 1841, he petitioned for bankruptcy on 5 March 1842. He was declared bankrupt on 10 May 1842. On 25 November 1842, *The Salem Belle* was deposited for copyright by Tappan and Dennet. Perhaps Wheelwright's status as a bankrupt argued against his identifying himself in the book or in the copyright documents. In any case, Lowell's characterization of the author of *The Salem Belle* fairly describes Ebenezer Wheelwright—at forty-two, he was "a young merchant of this city," Boston. And *The Salem Belle* was his "first attempt in the art of book-making." That first book was widely reviewed, and more favorably than not.[14]

Wheelwright was an abolitionist early on, and he wrote antislavery pieces. He may well have been one of the Boston merchants who requested that the United States recognize the independence of Haiti in 1852. He moved back to Newburyport in 1853, but continued to do business in Boston, associated with the firm of Nehemiah P. Mann and Company. He also continued to publish—anonymously. His 1853 booklet, *A*

Review of Dr. Dana's Remonstrance, Addressed to the Trustees of Phillips Academy, supported Daniel Dana's attack on the allegedly too-liberal views of Professor Edwards Amasa Park of Phillips Academy. Although Wheelwright remained involved with his business, his finances did not improve—by 1858, he was said to have "failed twice or more" and to be "in v[er]y low cr[edit]." During the Civil War, he contributed modestly to the relief of soldiers' families and hung a mourning emblem from his house after Lincoln was assassinated. He also remained a congregant in the Old South Church.[15]

On 2 October 1863, *Traditions of Palestine; or, Scenes in the Holy Land in the Days of Christ* was deposited for copyright by its publisher, M. H. Sargent. This book, which concerned the coming of Jesus, was published anonymously, but Wheelwright acknowledged on 10 October 1867 that he had written "several works—one of which, *Traditions of Palestine* has seen three editions." (A genealogist asserted that Wheelwright had written "several children's books." Since *The Salem Belle* and *Traditions of Palestine* would have been accessible to adolescent readers—indeed, the former volume refers to "our young readers" [90] and the latter to "our youthful readers" [15]—these may be those "children's books.") Wheelwright was said to be "well known in Massachusetts in the religious world and by the best men"; he inscribed one copy of *Traditions of Palestine* to Dr. Andrew Preston Peabody, Plummer Professor of Christian Morals at Harvard University. And he edited the Boston evangelical Congregationalist magazine *The Panoplist* in 1867 and 1868.[16]

Wheelwright's financial status remained bleak. In an 1867 credit rating, he was described as "good for 0." He wrote on 27 November 1873 that he was "barely solvent" and that "everything I possess has been required to pay my business debts, which I have not yet been able to do." He added, by way of further explanation, to John A. Vinton, who sought funding for the publication of his Wheelwright genealogy, "my business affairs have been and are now so perplexed and entangling that I have had and now have as much as I can do, to discharge the duties I owe to my creditors & others." He noted the assistance of his brother William, but stated, "I have been unfortunate in my business and have lost all he has given me." A credit rating in 1874 observed of Ebenezer Wheelwright, "Has been poor for years & hardly makes a living. Has no real basis for cr[edit]." Ebenezer Wheelwright died of a heart ailment on 10 June 1877.[17]

A lengthy memorial piece spoke of Wheelwright's good character and excellent ancestry. And two obituaries recognized Ebenezer Wheelwright's literary skill. One of them characterized him as "an accomplished writer and essayist." And yet another stated, "he was a caustic and correct writer, and if he had applied himself to literature would doubtless have distinguished himself in that line." Perhaps the writer of the latter obituary did not know of his subject's anonymous novels. Ebenezer Wheelwright did apply himself to literature, and he did achieve some distinction. If his writing is, by some standards today, too pious, it is nonetheless earnest, varied, and interesting. And, indeed, one of his novels became an important source for *The Scarlet Letter*. His authorship of the earlier novel, *The Salem Belle*, may be confirmed by its correspondences with his later novel, *Traditions of Palestine*.[18]

Traditions of Palestine, comprising fifteen chapters, was published serially, in fifteen installments, in the *Newburyport Herald*, every Saturday from 27 June 1863 through 3 October 1863. That newspaper termed the unnamed author "one of the best writers in this city," and the work itself "a very interesting story," "of great interest, and beautifully written." "We hope nobody will fail to read this work," the editor declared, "which we are publishing from the manuscript." Readers who wished "to preserve the connection of the narrative" were encouraged to "take care of their papers." At least one reader took the encouragement to heart: in the library of Old South Church is a book of letters into which clippings of all fifteen installments were pasted. The narrative also appeared in a weekly religious newspaper from Newburyport, *Herald of Gospel Liberty*, beginning 9 July 1863. It was subsequently published in book form, slightly revised, with a preface and an appendix. Publisher M. H. Sargent was superintendent of the Sabbath School of Old South Church and later treasurer of the Congregational Sunday School and Publishing Society. The work embeds the story of the coming of Jesus into the lives of diverse fictional characters of the period. We know that *Traditions of Palestine* was written near the time of *The Salem Belle* because Wheelwright writes in the preface, "this narrative was written more than twenty years ago" (v). Calling to mind Wheelwright's antislavery work, the book is dedicated to Benjamin C. Clark, an advocate for Haiti and an African American poet.[19]

The Salem Belle and *Traditions of Palestine* resemble one another in theme, plot, and language. The former concerns the hoped-for triumph of Christianity over superstition; the latter concerns the triumph of Christianity over ritual. Both works tell the story of a virtuous and beautiful young woman (Mary Lyford in *The Salem Belle*, Flavia Marcella in *Traditions of Palestine*) who escapes a public execution and marries one of the men who aided her (Walter Strale, Lucius). Each of these women is hiding a secret and has two names. Furthermore, *The Salem Belle* relates the hanging of a minister falsely accused of wizardry, George Burroughs, even as *Traditions of Palestine* recounts the crucifixion of Jesus. Both works focus on intense guilt (that of Trellison in *The Salem Belle*, that of Hakem and Pilate in *Traditions of Palestine*) and the possibility of Christian redemption.

The verbal parallels are plentiful; a selection will suffice. The introduction of *The Salem Belle* refers to "this little work" (iii) and "the object of the following pages" (vii); the dedication to *Traditions of Palestine* refers to "This Little Volume" (iii), and the preface mentions "the great purpose of these pages" (vi). Both works consider "true piety towards God" (*SB* 86; *TP* 29) and "True Religion" (*SB* 238; *TP* 216). Both books offer the human response of "amazement and terror" (*SB* 60; *TP* 79); describe characters as "perplexed and overawed" (*SB* 168; *TP* 134); and identify a large group as an "immense congregation" (*SB* 134; *TP* 90, 92), "a vast assembly," and an "awe-struck multitude" (*SB* 230; *TP* 29). In one instance, the books' renderings of nature especially resonate with one another. *The Salem Belle* states, "The wind sighed mournfully along, as if in sympathy with the sadness which had fastened deeply on the minds of brother and sister" (175); *Traditions of Palestine* states, "the winds . . . sighed mournfully along, as if they bore on their wings the dying cadences of the Nazarene's voice" (39). In another instance, the endings of scenes in the two volumes also echo, one with the other. Trellison in *The Salem Belle* "disappeared among the trees" (230) while Jesus in *Traditions of Palestine* "disappeared among the olive-trees of the wood" (20). And in yet a third instance, references to futurity in the two books correspond significantly. Mary Lyford's brother James, in *The Salem Belle*, states, "Time will soon disclose all; meanwhile have courage, my dear sister" (176), while Carmi in *Traditions of Palestine* states, "Time will reveal his [Jesus'] character and mission. Meanwhile, he seems to me a Messenger from God" (124–25).

The evident correspondences between *The Salem Belle* and *Traditions of Palestine* in theme, plot, and language indicate that the two books are by one hand. Ebenezer Wheelwright acknowledged having written *Traditions of Palestine* in his 10 October 1867 letter to John A. Vinton; accordingly, he must also have written *The Salem Belle*. Jane Ann Reed's handwritten attribution, "By Mr. Wheelwright," is indeed correct.

It is satisfying to see that when Ebenezer Wheelwright edited the *Panoplist* in 1868, he included not only an advertisement for the third edition of *Traditions of Palestine,* but also an unattributed short work, "A Sabbath in Boston in 1692"—a reprinting (albeit not identified as such) of most of chapter 9 and all of chapter 10 of *The Salem Belle*.[20]

The Salem Belle would have come to Hawthorne's attention through his friend James Russell Lowell, possibly through his sister-in-law Elizabeth

Palmer Peabody, and through his publisher Tappan and Dennet, and the various book reviews.

It was Lowell, in all likelihood, who wrote the review of *The Salem Belle* for the January 1843 issue of *The Pioneer* (since fellow editor Robert Carter did not claim it as his own). As noted, the review begins, "This little novel is, we are informed, the production of a young merchant of this city, whose first attempt in the art of book-making it appears to be." Lowell would have had several possible sources for this information. His father, Charles Lowell, might have known of Ebenezer Wheelwright (and his ancestors) through family connections—Charles's own father, John Lowell, and grandfather, John Lowell, had roots in Newburyport. James Russell Lowell's great-grandfather, pastor of the Old South Church, had welcomed George Whitefield in 1740. Alternatively, the father of James Russell Lowell's fiancée (and later his wife) Maria White— Abijah White, of Watertown—had been a West Indies merchant; he therefore might have known a younger West Indies merchant, Ebenezer Wheelwright, of Boston. The likeliest source, however, was the publisher of *The Salem Belle*. Tappan and Dennet would clearly have known the identity of the book's author, and, in light of its advertising in the first issue of *The Pioneer*, the firm might well have been in contact with Lowell. As elaborated in chapter 2, Hawthorne's relationship with Lowell became a close one; Lowell might well have mentioned the novel *The Salem Belle* and its author to his friend Hawthorne, who, as a fiction writer, antiquary, and resident of Salem, would have had no small interest in a fictional narrative about historic Salem.[21]

Furthermore, Elizabeth Palmer Peabody, Hawthorne's sister-in-law, might have told Hawthorne about *The Salem Belle*. Publisher of the first editions of *Grandfather's Chair*, *Famous Old People*, and *Liberty Tree*, she may have served as an intermediary between Hawthorne and Tappan and Dennet (and Sophia Peabody may have provided the illustrations in the reissued works) (6:294–95). Clearly the 109 Washington Street address that Peabody occasionally used placed her across the street from Tappan and Dennet at 114 Washington Street. And 13 West Street, the Peabody home and Elizabeth Peabody's bookshop, was just one block from the 3 Temple Street residence of Charles Tappan and Ebenezer Wheelwright. Perhaps Elizabeth Peabody already knew that (as she later reported) Hawthorne as a young man had "made himself thoroughly acquainted with the ancient history of Salem, and especially with the witchcraft era." Certainly, as the publisher of *Famous Old People*, Elizabeth Peabody would have known of Hawthorne's ongoing interest in the "melancholy affair" of the Salem witchcraft mania (see 6:77–79, 94). Accordingly, she might well have conveyed to Hawthorne the intriguing fact that his publisher Tappan and Dennet was publishing or had already published a novel titled *The Salem Belle: A Tale of 1692*. And perhaps she also knew who the unnamed author of that novel was.[22]

And the firm of Tappan and Dennet would have brought *The Salem Belle* to Hawthorne's attention. Communication between the publisher and the author would sometimes have been direct. Disagreeing somewhat with the "Historial Introduction" to volume 6 of the Hawthorne edition, Bruce Ronda states, "He [Hawthorne] engaged Tappan and Dennet to publish succeeding editions [of his children's books]." Hawthorne specifically mentioned Tappan and Dennet in a very formal letter to Elizabeth Palmer Peabody of 19 February 1842 (in which he promised to "seek an explanation with Messrs. Tappan and Dennet" regarding "remnants of the books" published by James Munroe & Company [15:609–10]). He also mentioned the firm in a letter to R. C. Waterston of 1 September 1842 regarding permission from Tappan and Dennet to reprint Hawthorne's story of Samuel Johnson. He believed that permission would be granted, given his "free consent," if Waterston "will be kind enough to call on them [Tappan and Dennet], and mention my wish" (15:650–51). Hawthorne's advice suggests that he may have already called on Tappan and Dennet himself—or that he may have been thinking of calling on them. He would not likely have missed their shop at 114 Washington Street—Tappan and Dennet was located in a row of publisher/booksellers, between Little, Brown at 112 Washington Street and William Crosby (and the Boston Circulating Library) at 118 Washington Street. Sophia Hawthorne also mentioned the publisher, noting in a 23 March 1843 letter to her mother that, on the stage back from Boston to Concord, she and her husband and the other passengers "took up Mr. [Theodore] Parker at Tappan and Dennet's." (Parker was going to deliver a lecture at the Concord Lyceum—a lecture that would later be termed "good and interesting.") Sophia wrote as if Tappan and Dennet's were a familiar location. Perhaps Sophia had seen Tappan and Dennet's before—perhaps she and her husband had called on his publisher during their stay in Boston in late October 1842 (8:363). It is certainly plausible that Charles Tappan and/or Charles F. Dennet then discussed with Hawthorne the firm's forthcoming book, *The Salem Belle*, and the book's author (who was then living at the same address as Tappan).[23]

And it would not have been at all surprising for Hawthorne to have taken an interest in a minor novel by a minor novelist. As Elizabeth Peabody wrote, "'He [Hawthorne] read a great many novels; he made an artistic study of them. There were many very good books of that kind that seem to be forgotten now.'"[24]

Even as Hawthorne would have heard of *The Salem Belle* through Lowell (certainly in *The Pioneer*, and perhaps in conversation), possibly through Peabody, and assuredly through his publisher, he could not have failed to learn about the novel from the numerous reviews that its first issue prompted. The reception of *The Salem Belle* therefore warrants consideration.

Hawthorne would very likely have read the reviews of the book in the Salem newspapers when he lived in Concord—these newspapers were regularly sent to him by his sister Maria Louisa.[25] The reviews of *The Salem Belle* in the *Salem Gazette*, the *Salem Observer*, and the *Salem Register* were all positive. After offering detail from the novel's introduction, the reviewer for the *Salem Gazette*, writing on 2 December 1842, stated, "The tale appears to be well wrought up, independently of its local interest, which ought to commend for it a ready sale in this vicinity." Again relying on the novel's introduction, the reviewer for the *Salem Observer* commented on 3 December 1842, "The author, in an interesting style, introduces new scenes and hitherto unknown actors in that fatal [Salem witchcraft] tragedy, which so deeply stains the history of New England"; this reviewer then excerpted a passage regarding the rescue from imprisonment of Mary Lyford (aka Mary Graham), the innocent young woman accused of witchcraft. And the reviewer for the *Salem Register*, writing on 5 December 1842, began, "We are indebted to the author for a copy of this excellent little book" and went on to feature the review from the Boston *Evening Bulletin*, which echoed the assertion of the novel's introduction that the witchcraft delusion may serve as a warning to readers regarding possible present delusions. The *Evening Bulletin* reviewer added, "The *Salem Belle* is a simple and beautiful tale, and is beautifully written. The characters are well portrayed, and that of Mary Graham is sweetly drawn. We cheerfully commend this work to our readers."

Hawthorne's interest would likely have been piqued by any one of the reviews of *The Salem Belle* in the Salem newspapers; it may well have been increased by reviews and notices of the novel in the Boston newspapers, which he might have seen at the Concord Athenaeum.[26] Without having read the novel, the reviewer for the *Daily Atlas* remarked on 1 December 1842, "We have not had time to examine [the work's] merits, but its subject is one of deep interest, and well adapted to supply the materials of romance." Similarly, the reviewer for the *Bay State Democrat* opined on the same date, "A careful investigation into the history of the times will show that the witchcraft delusion was but an engine set in motion by priestcraft, to destroy its opponents. How far this volume goes towards setting the matter in its true light, we are unable to say; it is, however, worthy of attention, and has the appearance of an attractive tale." The reviewer for the *Evening Mercantile Journal* had read the work; he or she reported, also on 1 December 1842, "The scene is laid in Salem, in the days of witchcraft, and [*The Salem Belle*] gives a graphic and interesting view of the state of society at that period when Delusion spread her thick mist over New England." The reviewer for the *Daily Evening Transcript* focused on the novel's heroine, stating, on 2 December 1842, "The belle, herself, though not one of the ancient witches, was a bewitching creature, and married without 'witchcraft' to a lover who, unlike Othello, had shared with her many a perilous adventure"; this reviewer added, "The book has a sober moral, showing that true religion has no affinity with superstition and skepticism."[27] And the reviewer for the *American Traveller* offered a fuller assessment, which appeared on 9 December 1842; part of this appraisal read:

> This story is well and movingly told, and presents the whole horror of the time in that strong and true light, which can only be done with a masterly hand. We consider it the duty of the community to possess themselves fully with the history of past delusions, in order more effectively to guard against the many to which the times are periodically exposed. That whole nations like individuals may run mad, is peculiarly true of the Anglo-Saxon race,— and the history of past excesses will prove the strongest guard for the future. It is happy when the knowledge can be obtained with pleasure, as well as profit, as in this instance. The lovers of a well told tale will find a rich feast in The Salem Belle.

The "interesting view," "sober moral," and "masterly hand" were not recognized by everyone—three reviewers for Boston newspapers offered negative assessments. The reviewer for the *Boston Post*, writing on 5 December 1842, considered the work to be dull and anachronistic, and concluded:

> In a word, the whole thing is a humdrum failure—the trickeries of the bewitched—the behaviours of the supposed witches—and even the accusation and condemnation of the heroine herself, are told without the least power. The story wanders here and there without object, and finally winds up like a nursery tale. We would advise the writer to study well the art of novel writing ere another attempt. We were vexed at having wasted our time over such a hodge podge of stuff, developing little or no talent and less tact.

Furthermore, the reviewer for the *New England Puritan*, writing on 9 December 1842, argued:

If parents wish their children to acquire a taste for novel reading, so that they may be ready to devour every fictitious work that comes in their way, with all the poison it may contain, this is a good work for them to commence with. The moral bearings of the work are just enough to exclude all qualms of conscience, and give it the completest influence in the formation of such a taste.

Finally, the reviewer for the *Boston Recorder*, writing on 30 December 1842, acknowledged the "elegant and captivating style" of this "exciting tale of witchcraft times," but criticized the substance:

we cannot help thinking that [*The Salem Belle*] bears too severely upon the motives of some of the eminent divines—Cotton Mather in particular—who were subjects of that dreadful witchcraft delusion, and who were active promoters of the shocking measures which were instituted in their imagined conflict with Satan. The impression which the author of this tale leaves upon the reader's mind is, that the witchcraft delusion was rather an artifice of wicked men, and that its main evils were the result of diabolical frauds, in which some of the clergy were but too easily duped and led to participate.

This reviewer closed by stating,

We are aware that the true history of Salem Witchcraft has not yet been written; but we are not prepared to believe, that its real characteristics are developed in the narrative of the "Salem Belle."

Even if Hawthorne read only a few of the Boston newspaper reviews of *The Salem Belle*, he would have learned something about the work—and perhaps if he read enough of the reviews to see the difference of opinion expressed, he would have been interested to judge for himself whether the work offered "a rich feast" or "poison."[28]

Hawthorne might have encountered reviews of *The Salem Belle* in New York newspapers, as well. The *New York Tribune* reflected the largely positive response to the novel: "The style of this little book is easy and graceful, and the incidents of the tale possesses [*sic*] variety and no little interest." But the minority negative view would also have been represented. Tappan and Dennet had sent a copy of *The Salem Belle* to the *Congregational Observer*, which merged with the *New-York Evangelist*, and this latter paper criticized the book for its censure of the Puritans: "We must say we have read this book with pain and dislike. . . . Those writers who directly or indirectly would stigmatize the faith of the Puritans, never tell us that other men believed and acted in like manner."[29] Hawthorne would not have been wholly unsympathetic to this defense of the Puritans.

Of the magazine reviews of *The Salem Belle*, a paragraph in the *Knickerbocker* might have engaged Hawthorne's attention—according to the reviewer here, the novel was "an agreeable and entertaining, but not particularly powerful story." But sure to have won Hawthorne's attention were the fuller reviews of the novel in three other magazines—*The Pioneer*, *Sargent's New Monthly Magazine*, and the *Boston Miscellany*—to all of which Hawthorne had a significant link.

As mentioned, the review of *The Salem Belle* in *The Pioneer* appeared in the first number—the one that Sophia Hawthorne, on 4 January 1843, reported to Maria Louisa Hawthorne that Lowell had sent to the Hawthornes (15:667)—the one that included "The Tell-Tale Heart" and Lowell's review of Hawthorne's *Historical Tales for Youth*. The review of *The Salem Belle* appeared thirteen pages after Poe's tale and one page after Lowell's review of Hawthorne.

After stating that *The Salem Belle* was written by "a young merchant of this city," Lowell went on to note the novel's anachronisms, and then he offered his most interesting comments on the work:

> The story is one of love, and is pleasingly told. The main interest turns upon the famous witchcraft delusion of 1692, and the danger incurred by the heroine, who becomes involved in the persecution levelled at every one suspected of dealing in the black art, and is rescued by her lover, and carried off to Virginia, on the day previous to that appointed for her death on the scaffold.

It is that last phrase, "her death on the scaffold," that would have especially awakened Hawthorne's interest. Friend George B. Loring later recalled,

> The indictment, the sentence, the sheriff's return, which brought many an innocent accused to the scaffold in the dark days of the witchcraft delusion were preserved in the court-house near [Hawthorne's] dwelling. The hill on which the sad tragedy was enacted, and whose wind-stricken trees shivered and shrunk where the gallows once stood, overlooked his town and was the favorite spot of his morning walk.

Furthermore, Hawthorne had written about Gallows Hill in his 1835 short story "Alice Doane's Appeal"—"I have often courted the historic influence of the spot"—a spot, he wrote, "where guilt and phrenzy consummated the most execrable scene, that our history blushes to record"

(11:267). And he imagined the sad procession up Gallows Hill of those accused of witchcraft:

> And thus I marshalled them onward, the innocent who were to die, and the guilty who were to grow old in long remorse—tracing their every step, by rock, and shrub, and broken track, till their shadowy visages had circled round the hill-top, where we [he and his two auditors] stood. I plunged into my imagination for a blacker horror, and a deeper woe, and pictured the scaffold— (11:279)

Hawthorne mentioned "the ridge of Gallows-Hill where . . . he [Time] and Cotton Mather hung the witches," in the 1838 piece "Time's Portraiture" (11:331), and he stated in his 1842 children's book *Famous Old People*, "The place of execution was a high hill, on the outskirts of Salem; so that many of the sufferers, as they stood beneath the gallows, could discern their own habitations in the town." And Grandfather later comments, "the innocent dead could not be restored to life; and the hill where they were executed, will always remind people of the saddest and most humiliating passage in our history" (6:78–79). Additionally, Hawthorne would later write about the witches' "place of execution on Gallows Hill" in the 1849 sketch "Main-Street" (11:74). And he mentions "Gallows Hill" in *The Scarlet Letter* (1:8). For Hawthorne, it was precisely the scaffold on that hill outside Salem—that site of the climax of the witchcraft tragedy—that was so exceptionally vivid in imagination. He was sure to have been caught by Lowell's writing, in his review of *The Salem Belle* in *The Pioneer*, about an innocent young woman's anticipated "death on the scaffold" for witchcraft.

And perhaps he would have been especially responsive to this review since he had just read in the same issue of *The Pioneer* both Poe's "The Tell-Tale Heart," and Lowell's comment, in his review of Hawthorne's *Historical Tales for Youth*, that the author of this collection, "a man of acknowledged genius," "has woven the softening halo of romance around the iron visages of the puritans, and intertwined the gentle flowers of love and poesy with the self-inflicted crown of thorns which encircled their gloomy and sallow brows." Perhaps he would have been particularly attentive to Lowell's wish that he "not let his labors for the youthful deprive us of his instructions for the more mature, for we all need him, old as well as young."[30] Very likely already interested in reading *The Salem Belle* when he encountered the first number of *The Pioneer* in early January 1843, Hawthorne would probably have developed an even greater interest in that book after he read the Lowell review. And that interest would have only grown when Hawthorne came upon another review of *The Salem*

Belle—a review perhaps written by Epes Sargent—in the February 1843 issue of *Sargent's New Monthly Magazine*.

Sargent—whom Hawthorne later termed "a friend of mine" (16:273)—was planning his magazine in the fall of 1842 and requested a contribution from the celebrated tale-writer. On 21 October 1842, Hawthorne responded by sending "The Old Apple-Dealer" (and recommending the writing of his townsman, Henry David Thoreau) (15: 656–57). Sargent published Hawthorne's sketch in the first issue of his magazine, that of January 1843. In the following month, Hawthorne mentioned magazine editors Epes Sargent and Henry Tuckerman in "The Hall of Fantasy" (in Lowell's second issue of *The Pioneer* [10:636]), and Sargent published Hawthorne's tale "The Antique Ring" in the second issue of *Sargent's New Monthly Magazine*. (Notably, a passage in this latter piece concerns the "dark red circle, resembling the effect of intensest heat," which the ring leaves upon the breast of its deceitful possessor [11:347].) Six pages after the conclusion of "The Antique Ring" appears praise for *Twice-Told Tales*—and three pages later appears a review of *The Salem Belle*. Hawthorne would not have missed it.[31]

This paragraph on *The Salem Belle* notes the book's "glowing colors" and its "unaffected and agreeable" "style." It mentions, perhaps following the review in *The Pioneer*, that the novel is the author's "first production," and "wanting in terseness and vigor." What is most important, however, is the review's assertion of highest regard: "The closing chapters of the book are calculated to awaken a deep, and sometimes thrilling interest." It is the climax of those very chapters, the confession of Trellison on the scaffold, that, as will be argued, Hawthorne borrowed and transformed for the climax of the closing chapters of *The Scarlet Letter*. The "deep . . . sometimes thrilling interest" of the ending of *The Salem Belle* contributed to Hawthorne's eliciting such interest for the ending of his masterpiece.

And surely Hawthorne's interest in *The Salem Belle* would have increased when he read another review of the book, published in the *Boston Miscellany*. This review, perhaps written by editor Henry T. Tuckerman, appeared in the February 1843 issue. Hawthorne, who had praised the January 1842 issue of the *Boston Miscellany* (15:598) and contributed "A Virtuoso's Collection" to the May 1842 issue (15:619), was subsequently considered as a possible editor of that journal, to replace editor Nathan Hale Jr. (8:357; 15:644–45). However, at the end of 1842, Tuckerman was selected as the new editor. As noted, for his 1843 piece "The Hall of Fantasy," Hawthorne included editors Sargent and Tuckerman (10:636). Unfortunately, Tuckerman was able to edit his journal for only two issues. The review of *The Salem Belle* was included in the second of these issues.

Given Hawthorne's notable connection with the *Boston Miscellany*, it is highly likely that he would have seen this late review. And in light of his friendship with editor Tuckerman—who referred to Hawthorne in 1846 as "a brother whom to know is to love"—Hawthorne's reading the review becomes even more probable.[32]

The *Boston Miscellany* review of *The Salem Belle* is critical of the novel, but not of its subject:

> This little story possesses some local interest. It is from an anonymous source. The object of the author is to illustrate the extraordinary delusion which resulted in the sacrifice of so many victims of popular superstition, under the name of witches. The period to which the tale refers, abounds in materials for the novelist, and, in judicious and gifted hands, might be rendered fearfully interesting. The present attempt is of a more humble order, and contains some evidence of want of practice or ability in the author. To those, however, who find amusement in such fictions, it will afford entertainment.

It seems plausible that Hawthorne might have read these lines as an invitation—could those "judicious and gifted hands" be his own? The remainder of the review seems to intensify that invitation:

> In the preface it is justly observed that "the elements of delusion always exist in the human mind." The simple narrative of "Salem Witchcraft," however, (as related, for instance, by Upham,) appears to us, far more impressive, than any but a truly powerful delineation of the subject, in the form of a drama, romance or tale.

It is true that Hawthorne had been influenced by Upham's work on witchcraft, the 1831 *Lectures on Witchcraft*—had included mention of it in "Alice Doane's Appeal" (11:267)—had even recommended Upham's autograph to a collector (15:260–61). Yet also Hawthorne saw "Rev. Mr. Upham"—who had refused to marry a man and the woman whom the man had seduced—as a "hardened" man (23:194–95), and as a gossiper with regard to the institutionalization of Jones Very and the poverty of the Hawthornes.[33] Most critically, Hawthorne apparently thought that Upham's witchcraft study could be improved upon: Hawthorne wrote about his own possible historical study of witchcraft to Evert A. Duyckinck on 10 October 1845:

> As to the history of Witchcraft, I had often thought of such a work; but I should not like to throw it off hastily, or to write it for the sole and specific

purpose of getting $500. A mere narrative, to be sure, might be prepared easily enough; but such a work, if worthily written, would demand research and study, and as deep thought as any man could bring to it. The more I look at it, the more difficulties do I see—yet difficulties such as I should like to overcome. Perhaps it may be the work of an after time. (16:126–27)

Hawthorne never wrote this history of witchcraft, but he may well have continued to think of "a truly powerful delineation of the subject, in the form of a drama, romance or tale"—a work that might be "far more impressive" than Upham's study. Hawthorne had been working on tales about witchcraft since his career began, as his sister Elizabeth reported—and apparently he had burned the tales of witchcraft that did not satisfy him.[34] Early Hawthorne tales of witchcraft that were published include "The Hollow of the Three Hills," "Alice Doane's Appeal," and "Young Goodman Brown." It would not be surprising if Hawthorne's early ambition to write about witchcraft had endured. And when Nathaniel Hawthorne discovered in 1849 that Charles Wentworth Upham was, in fact, his archenemy in the painful Salem Custom-House debacle—the key opponent to his keeping his position as Surveyor—then perhaps Hawthorne's sense of literary rivalry with the writer of *Lectures on Witchcraft* significantly deepened. And although *The Scarlet Letter* is plainly a novel about adultery, witchcraft does discreetly inform that theme.

But to return—when reading the *Boston Miscellany* review of *The Salem Belle* in February 1843, Hawthorne would surely have been curious to read this so divergently received novel about the Salem witchcraft era. He would have wanted to make his own determination. And he might well have wanted to understand why this work about a most cherished subject was "of a more humble order"—and what it would take to create that "truly powerful delineation."

In summary, Hawthorne would have learned of *The Salem Belle* from James Russell Lowell, perhaps from Elizabeth Palmer Peabody, and certainly from publisher Tappan and Dennet; and he would surely have learned about the novel from reviews of the work—especially the three reviews that appeared in magazines with which Hawthorne had a strong connection, *The Pioneer*, *Sargent's New Monthly Magazine*, and the *Boston Miscellany*. Also, Hawthorne might have learned of the novel's author from Lowell or Peabody—and in all probability, he learned of Ebenezer Wheelwright from Tappan and Dennet. In light of his increasing knowledge of *The Salem Belle* and his keen interest in the Salem witchcraft period depicted in that novel, Hawthorne would surely have wished to read the work. He might have bought a copy of the book, but perhaps he was given a copy by his publisher Tappan and Dennet—as Julian Hawthorne wrote, "Some volumes [Hawthorne] bought; but most of them came either as gift copies from their authors, or from Ticknor and Fields, and other publishers." If Hawthorne owned a copy of the book in Concord, then he would have had that copy in Salem, for he took all his books from Concord to Salem in 1845.[35] Perhaps, alternatively, Hawthorne read *The Salem Belle* at the Concord Athenaeum or borrowed the book from a friend. Finally, we cannot know precisely how he read *The Salem Belle*. But clearly he had reason to read it. And he would later have reason to be reminded of it.

In the summer of 1847, Hawthorne was once again living in Salem, at 18 Chestnut Street (16:193, 196 n); he had begun his tenure in the Salem Custom House the previous year. Sophia, Una, and Julian were with the Peabodys in Boston. (Hawthorne and his family would move to 14 Mall Street in September 1847 [16:213 n].) Not inclined to write very much during the summer and not spending time with his wife and children in Salem, Hawthorne had there chiefly his position at the Custom House to occupy him, and, presumably, occasional visits to his mother and sister on Herbert Street. Perhaps, with "eyes wandering up and down the columns of the morning newspaper" (1:8), he would have come across a notice in the 22 July 1847 issue of the *Salem Register*:

> "The Salem Belle." Messrs. W. & S. B. Ives, 232 Essex street, have for sale a new edition of The Salem Belle, a tale of Love and Witchcraft, in the year 1692—recently published by John M. Whittemore, Boston. It makes a neat little volume of 238 pages.

Perhaps, too, Hawthorne might have seen the advertisements for the new edition of *The Salem Belle*, squibs that appeared between 19 July and 7 August 1847 in the *Salem Register*, the *Salem Observer*, and the *Salem Gazette*. These advertisements had been placed in these newspapers by booksellers Henry Whipple (at 190 Essex Street) and W. and S. B. Ives (at 232 Essex Street). Hawthorne could easily have returned home from the Custom House by way of the Essex Street bookshops and thereby encountered the reissue of *The Salem Belle*. Alternatively, when Sophia Hawthorne returned from Boston, she might have borrowed a copy of *The Salem Belle* for her husband from her friend Mary Foote, from whom she had borrowed books for him before.[36] That Hawthorne read this book about which he would have repeatedly heard is clear from the parallels between Ebenezer Wheelwright's first novel and his own.

The correspondences between *The Salem Belle* and *The Scarlet Letter* involve primarily details of plot and setting in the final third of both works, and secondarily details of language. Before proceeding to the correspondences, however, we should review very briefly the characters and plot of *The Salem Belle* prior to the final third of the narrative.

Based on a manuscript about a "remarkable legend" (iii)—a document sent by one "J.N.L." (vi)—the story of *The Salem Belle* concerns a beautiful young woman, Mary Lyford (known at first as Mary Graham), at the time of the Salem witchcraft delusion. Mary is the unrevealed granddaughter of the late hidden regicide, General William Goffe, and the sister of young James Lyford, a student at Harvard College.[37] Two young men, also students at Harvard, are competing for Mary's affections—the devoted Walter Strale and the egotistical Trellison. Rebuffed by Mary, the angry Trellison takes advantage of the witchcraft hysteria by accusing Mary of witchcraft—with the support of a young servant woman, whom he would evidently pay. Believing the testimony of Trellison and the servant girl, Reverend Samuel Parris initiates proceedings that will lead to the arrest of Mary Lyford.

Three passages in the final third of *The Salem Belle* anticipate passages in the final third of *The Scarlet Letter*: James's effort, in the forest, to persuade Mary to escape; the presence of the escape ship in the town harbor; and the confession of Trellison at the scaffold. It is important to add that no other work that we know that Hawthorne would have been likely to read prior to writing *The Scarlet Letter* offered the equivalent of these three anticipative passages.

The first of the correspondences involves Mary's meeting with her brother James in a forest retreat, a meeting that anticipates Hester's meeting with Arthur in the forest. Mary and James Lyford visit that retreat, "the borders of a little stream in the forest" (172), and she confides to her brother her sorrow regarding Trellison's conspiracy against her (evident here in the voices of demonic temptation that she and James hear, arranged by a confederate of the vengeful Trellison) and her discouragement regarding everyone's suspicion of her guilt. James seeks to offer his strength, cautioning "dear Mary, do not sink under this load of sorrow" (173) and promising "deliverance" (174). But in despair, Mary replies, "Ah! my brother, I would that such a hope could send its reviving influence to my heart, but I have the most gloomy anticipations and painful forebodings of the result" (174). And she speaks of the appeal of life after death. James persists: "Why speak so mournfully, dear Mary? This world is not yet a desert, which no flower of hope nor green beauty of summer can adorn" (174). Mary hears the voices, and then (as quoted earlier), "The wind sighed mournfully along, as if in sympathy with the sadness which had fastened deeply on the minds of brother and sister" (175). They both hear the diabolical song, but James says, "Time will soon disclose all; meanwhile, have courage, my dear sister" (176). He promises that he and her beloved, Walter Strale, will protect her, and he advises that "immediate flight is necessary" (176).

This passage recalls Hester's meeting Arthur near the stream in the forest. He confides in Hester his sorrow regarding his guilt and his false performance of his duties, and his general discouragement. Hawthorne writes, "one solemn old tree groaned dolefully to another, as if telling the sad story of the pair that sat beneath, or constrained to forebode evil to come" (1:195). Arthur wonders, "Must I sink down there, and die at once?" (1:196), and Hester offers encouragement, "Heaven would show mercy, hadst thou but the strength to take advantage of it" (1:196). Arthur responds, "Be thou strong for me! Advise me what to do" (1:196). Determined to help the weakened minister, long tormented by the vengeful Chillingworth, she asks, "Is the world then so narrow? Doth the universe lie within the compass of yonder town, which only a little time ago was but a leaf-strewn desert . . .?" (1:197). Hester suggests escape to the wilderness or to Europe, but Arthur says, "I am powerless to go" (1:197). Then, "fervently resolved to buoy him up with her own energy" (1:198), Hester rouses him to flee, concluding "Up, and away!" (1:198).

There is a notable inversion—an innocent woman generally considered guilty (in *The Salem Belle*) becomes a guilty man generally considered innocent (in *The Scarlet Letter*). But strong correspondences are evident, as well. The forest setting, the expressive wind and tree, the communion of a determined character with a despairing one who is the object of great vengeance, the determined character's emboldening the despairing one, the final resolution to escape—all suggest a resonance between the noted passages in *The Salem Belle* and *The Scarlet Letter*. And additional corresponding passages in the two novels may be observed.

Mary Lyford is arrested, tried, and convicted; an escape is planned, and Walter Strale designs it. Mary is to be broken out of prison by William Somers (a long-time admirer of General Goffe), with the help of James Lyford, and Walter Strale disguised as Satan, and she is to be taken on board a vessel in the harbor. Ebenezer Wheelwright's presentation of an escape ship in *The Salem Belle* anticipates Nathaniel Hawthorne's presentation of an escape ship in *The Scarlet Letter*.

In *The Salem Belle*, it is "a little schooner" named the "Water Witch" that appears in Salem harbor (203). (Here Wheelwright may be acknowledging a debt to Cooper.) The vessel is commanded by Captain Ringbolt.

He regularly offers a variety of choice articles to the women of the town, but his source for these goods is questionable: "How he obtained his merchandise was sometimes a mystery; but the Salem ladies were careful not to inquire too curiously into the matter" (204). His suspicious dealings—implicitly with an illicit trade, perhaps involving piracy—is well tolerated by the Puritans: "It was rather wonderful, however, that so much charity was extended towards this gentleman [Captain Ringbolt], considering the very strict morals of the Puritans, and the rigid honesty with which they were accustomed to discharge their pecuniary obligations" (204). William Somers, the associate of James Lyford and William Strale, meets with Captain Ringbolt on board the schooner to arrange secret passage for Mary and James Lyford, Strale, and his own wife and child and himself.

In *The Scarlet Letter*, it is "a ship" that lies in Boston harbor, "one of those questionable cruisers, frequent at that day, which, without being absolutely outlaws of the deep, yet roamed over its surface with a remarkable irresponsibility of character," a "vessel . . . recently arrived from the Spanish Main" (1:215). "Hester Prynne," Hawthorne writes, "could take upon herself to secure the passage of two individuals [Arthur Dimmesdale and herself] and a child [Pearl], with all the secrecy which circumstances rendered more than desirable" (1:215). During the holiday, the captain and crew come to watch the festivities. Hawthorne comments, "It remarkably characterized the incomplete morality of the age, rigid as we call it, that a license was allowed the seafaring class, not merely for their freaks on shore, but for far more desperate deeds on their proper element. The sailor of that day would go near to be arraigned as a pirate in our own" (1:233). And he adds, "the Puritan elders, in their black cloaks, starched bands, and steeple-crowned hats, smiled not unbenignantly at the clamor and rude deportment of those jolly seafaring men" (1:233). The depiction of the Puritans' tolerance for the piratical in *The Salem Belle*—presumably an ironic commentary on the Puritans' intolerance for others—appears again in *The Scarlet Letter* as incisive critique.

Although Mary Lyford's escape on board ship is effected successfully, Hester learns that Chillingworth booked passage on the ship on which she and the minister and Pearl intended to voyage, and then Reverend Dimmesdale confesses all and dies. Still, the presence in both books of an escape ship in the harbor, an attempt to secure secret passage on this ship, and Puritan indulgence of the ship's piratical men suggests Hawthorne's continued reliance on Ebenezer Wheelwright's work. Furthermore, the parallels between *The Salem Belle* and *The Scarlet Letter* continue: we may compare Trellison's confession on the scaffold with Dimmesdale's confession on the scaffold—the two events bear a significant resemblance.

Realizing that Mary Lyford is going to be executed on the scaffold on the basis of his false accusation of witchcraft, a miserable Trellison determines that he will "follow her to the scaffold, and there avow his guilt, and invoke every power within his reach, to save her from the threatened doom" (192). Reverend George Burroughs—a distinguished man of the "sacred profession" (195)—and four others falsely accused are executed on the scaffold on 19 August 1692; Mary Lyford is scheduled for execution there on 20 August. Trellison writes her a letter in which he confesses, and he plans that he would indeed "vindicate her at the scaffold, though it might cost him his life" (199–200). On the morning of the appointed day, the crowd is gathered to watch "another act in the tragedies of the times" (226). Trellison stands near the "scaffold"—"the spot" (226)— watching for the "procession" (227). Just past "the hour of twelve," the sheriff announces to "the multitude" that Mary Lyford has escaped (227), and while the sheriff lectures the surprised crowd, "Trellison mounted the scaffold" (228). His face, formerly "the livid hue of death," shows a "flush of emotion" (228). "Every eye in that immense assemblage," we are told, "was fixed upon him" (228). With "a calm and clear voice," Trellison "gave utterance to the feelings which moved his inmost soul" (228). He acknowledges that God had turned back "a tide of guilt and horror," and he cries out, "Hear me, magistrates and men, and ye ministers of an insulted God! hear me, old age, middle life and youth!" Then he declares Mary's innocence and his own guilt: "the maiden who has this day escaped death, was guiltless of the crime for which she was condemned to die. . . . [i]t was this hand that brought down the threatened ruin upon that child of innocence and love" (229). Trellison attests to the mercy of God, who prevented another tragedy and who did not seek vengeance on the truly guilty. And after Trellison confesses, he steps down from the scaffold and "passed through the spell-bound and awe-struck multitude" (230). After he disappears into the forest, "[a]n unbroken silence reigned for a few moments through all that vast assembly, and the first words that were spoken, were an expression of thankfulness that the innocent maiden had escaped" (230). Yet some townspeople do not believe Trellison's confession; they attribute it to the sorcery of the accused Mary Lyford.

In *The Scarlet Letter*, as the "procession" comes toward the "scaffold," where Hester Prynne stands, "all eyes were turned towards the point where the minister was seen to approach among them" (1:250–51). Reverend Dimmesdale walks slowly, and his face has "a deathlike hue" (1:251). He pauses near the scaffold and calls Hester and Pearl to him— Chillingworth warns him against despoiling his "sacred profession"—but, with Hester's support, the minister approaches the "scaffold" and "ascend[s] its steps" (1:253). And so comes the "closing scene" of this "drama of guilt and sorrow" (1:253). Clearly, "some deep life-matter . . . was now to be laid open to [the people]." "The sun," we are told, is "but little past its meridian" (1:254). With a "high, solemn, and majestic" voice, Dimmesdale cries out, "People of New England! ye, that have loved me!—ye, that have deemed me holy!—behold me here, the one sinner of the world!" "At last," he says, he is standing on "the spot" where he should have stood seven years ago (1:254). Then he diminishes Hester's sin in contrast to his own: her scarlet letter is "but the shadow of what he bears on his own breast" (1:255). And he reveals the physical stigma that he bears. While "the gaze of the horror-stricken multitude was concentrated on the ghastly miracle; . . . the minister stood with a flush of triumph in has face" (1:255). A dying Dimmesdale acknowledges that "God knows; and He is merciful" for having allowed him to endure afflictions and thus atone for his sin (1:256). And when the minister dies, "[t]he multitude, silent till then, broke out in a strange, deep voice of awe and wonder" (1:257). But some of the townspeople are not persuaded by the minister's confession and do not see the mark on his breast; they say that he was only offering a parable suggesting that we are all sinners (1:259).

The differences are plain—Trellison sought forgiveness for what amounted to attempted murder while Dimmesdale sought forgiveness for adultery; Trellison lived while Dimmesdale died—but the numerous correspondences are distinct as well. In both passages in *The Salem Belle* and *The Scarlet Letter*, a guilty man perceived to be innocent ascends the scaffold at noon and speaks to the townspeople, denying or diminishing a woman's sin, confessing his own sin, and acknowledging God's mercy, thereby prompting silence, speech, and—among some—disbelief.

Although *The Salem Belle* and *The Scarlet Letter* are clearly two very different works, the parallels are sufficient to allow us to infer once again Hawthorne's transformative borrowing. The passages in *The Salem Belle* regarding James Lyford's effort, in the forest, to persuade Mary to escape; the presence of the escape ship in Salem harbor; and Trellison's scaffold confession—with regard to plot, setting, and sometimes language—find important correspondences in the passages in *The Scarlet Letter* concerning Hester Prynne's effort, in the forest, to persuade Arthur Dimmesdale to escape; the presence of the escape ship in Boston harbor; and the minister's scaffold confession. The rush of action from forest to harbor to scaffold in the final third of *The Salem Belle* recurs in the final third of *The Scarlet Letter*; the original sequence helped to provide direction and energy to the close of Hawthorne's novel. *The Salem Belle* was one source in his catalog of secret sources, a remarkable matching thread for his narrative fabric.

The focus on witchcraft in *The Salem Belle* is manifest, of course, in *The Scarlet Letter*. Hawthorne explicitly treated witchcraft there by including Mistress Hibbins, an historical figure executed for witchcraft in 1656, and by liberally mentioning tales of the Black Man and his dreaded book. (Indeed, Hester's honoring for seven years her vow to Chillingworth not to reveal that he is her husband is akin to a bondservant's honoring for seven years his vow to his master—but in this case, Hester's master is characterized as an agent of the devil.) Additionally, Hawthorne wrote of the children of the Puritans of the 1640s—those who would be adults in 1692—as "the most intolerant brood that ever lived" (1:94), who "wore the blackest shade of Puritanism, and so darkened the national visage with it, that all the subsequent years have not sufficed to clear it up" (1:232). The tragedy to come haunted his depiction of the earlier period in Puritan history.

Still, Hawthorne did not tell the story of Salem witchcraft. With regard to *The Salem Belle*, he selected elements, with a broader focus. Even as Hawthorne linked William Hathorne, his Quaker-persecuting ancestor, with William's son John Hathorne, the unrepentant Salem witch-trial judge (1:9–10), he linked the persecutions committed by the two men, and these acts inform the persecution of Hester Prynne and Arthur Dimmesdale. Hawthorne would not be limited by one historical event in his writing *The Scarlet Letter*—conflating several events, he contended for his own "license" (1:33), the moonlight effect of his imagination, to create a meeting of "the Actual and the Imaginary" (1:36).[38] He dealt with the thematics of the Salem witchcraft trials and their aftermath—guilt, punishment, atonement, redemption—and to that extent, at least, he created "a truly powerful delineation" "far more impressive" than Upham's. Valueing his artistry—"poesy," to use Lowell's word—he borrowed from Wheelwright's novel even as he shed some of its historical details. He diminished the witchcraft context of the climactic scaffold scene of *The Salem Belle* as he completed *The Scarlet Letter*, preserving some of the setting and action, some of the language, and, most importantly, the concern with guilt publically unburdened. And he thereby maintained the "deep . . . sometimes thrilling interest" of his source's climax.

Hawthorne acknowledged at the outset of *The Scarlet Letter* his ancestors' sins, and added, "I . . . take shame upon myself for their sakes" (1:9–10). It is Trellison's climactic taking shame upon himself, regardless of specific context, that proves so important to Hawthorne as he imagines

Dimmesdale's taking shame upon himself. Doubtless he associated Dimmesdale's confession with memorable confessions he'd read or read about—those of Samuel Sewall, Samuel Johnson, Jervase Helwyse, notorious criminals, Adam Blair, and the narrator of "The Tell-Tale Heart." But Trellison's confession, in plot, setting, and language, is closest of all to Dimmesdale's. And Trellison's confession is the only one that is part of a series of passages corresponding to passages in *The Scarlet Letter*. Hawthorne's deft allusion to the exciting close of *The Salem Belle* strengthens his rendering of his final scaffold scene; Trellison's painful scaffold confession intensifies Dimmesdale's own. Hawthorne's use of *The Salem Belle* for *The Scarlet Letter* reminds us of the dye of the original thread, the trace of the coloring that still remains, and Hawthorne's extraordinary skill in modulation.

Just as Hawthorne diminished the emphasis on murder when he adapted Poe's "The Tell-Tale Heart" and reduced the suggestion of the erotic when he adapted Lowell's "A Legend of Brittany," he lessened the concern with Salem witchcraft when he adapted Wheelwright's *The Salem Belle*. And in this last case, he again diminished the emphasis on murder—Trellison had striven for the public execution of the woman who had rejected him; Dimmesdale had only committed adultery. Hawthorne both borrowed and subtilized; he effectively muted the colors in his literary threads. We may wish to modify the earlier noted judgment of David S. Reynolds: the careful apportionment of Hawthorne's literary source materials in a unified artistic structure is one of the author's highest achievements.

The critical three passages in *The Salem Belle* reveal Hawthorne's transformation—a creative attenuation or spiritualizing that we have seen also in Hawthorne's reliance on Poe's "The Tell-Tale Heart" and Lowell's "A Legend of Brittany." What remains to be considered for *The Salem Belle* is the important consequence of the identification of its long-unknown author, Ebenezer Wheelwright.

As already posited, Hawthorne may well have learned of Ebenezer Wheelwright as the author of *The Salem Belle* through James Russell Lowell or Elizabeth Palmer Peabody, and certainly through Tappan and Dennet. If he did not know the author before he read the book, he would surely have been interested in knowing the author's identity after he had finished the work. Once he did learn that Ebenezer Wheelwright had written *The Salem Belle*, Hawthorne might have thought of his own Boston Custom House days, when he would have encountered many Boston merchants. He might also have thought of his good friend Franklin Pierce—perhaps he knew that Pierce's wife, Jane Appleton Pierce, had lived with the Wheelwrights in Newburyport before she and Franklin were married. However, in view of Hawthorne's extensive knowledge of Puritan history, he would most likely—and most significantly—have thought of Ebenezer Wheelwright's famous ancestor, his great-great-great-great-grandfather, John Wheelwright. The association would have been especially likely given Hawthorne's propensity to think in terms of the abiding presence of one's Puritan progenitors—that of William Hathorne and John Hathorne for himself; that of Matthew Maule (in *The House of the Seven Gables*) for Holgrave.[39]

The relevance of John Wheelwright to *The Scarlet Letter* is great. He was, in fact, one of the leading figures in the Antinomian Controversy. And that controversy is unquestionably critical to *The Scarlet Letter*. Hawthorne mentions "an Antinomian," among others, "to be scourged out of the town," when he discusses the public persecutions by the Puritans (1:49–50). And twice he mentions the most celebrated figure in the Antinomian Controversy, Anne Hutchinson. Early on, he describes the rosebush outside the prison from which Hester Prynne and her daughter Pearl emerge—perhaps, he speculates, "it had sprung up under the footsteps of the sainted Ann Hutchinson, as she entered the prison-door" (1:48). And later he compares Hester with Anne Hutchinson (if Hester had not given birth to Pearl): "Then, she might have come down to us in history, hand in hand with Ann Hutchinson, as the foundress of a religious sect. She might, in one of her phases, have been a prophetess. She might, and not improbably would, have suffered death from the stern tribunals of the period, for attempting to undermine the foundations of the Puritan establishment" (1:165).

The connection between John Wheelwright and Anne Hutchinson was a notable one: they were the two preeminent Antinomian leaders. Both defied Puritan authorities, and both were punished. Furthermore, John Wheelwright was married to Mary Hutchinson—Anne Hutchinson was his sister-in-law.[40]

The classic study of the Antinomian Controversy and *The Scarlet Letter* is Michael Colacurcio's essay, "Footsteps of Ann Hutchinson." Stating that Hawthorne's novel "is neither allegory nor *roman à clef*," Colacurcio examines the relationship between Hester Prynne and Anne Hutchinson, and that between Arthur Dimmesdale and John Cotton. The former relationship is clear—Hawthorne asserts it himself—and Colacurcio examines the parallel between a woman's spiritual freedom and her sexual freedom. The latter relationship, between Dimmesdale and Cotton, is clear, as well, but further consideration is necessary. It is true that, like Dimmesdale, Cotton was a highly learned minister who led the Boston church with John

Wilson and who served as pastor to the passionate woman who so challenged Puritan strictures. Colacurcio develops additional correspondences
between Dimmesdale and Cotton; his argument is strong.[41] But Hawthorne's reliance on *The Salem Belle* suggests, by way of the novel's
author, Ebenezer Wheelwright, that Colacurcio's argument is incomplete.
We may readily see this by consulting John Winthrop's *The History of
New England from 1630 to 1649*—the invaluable journal that Hawthorne
read and on which he relied.[42]

Winthrop introduces John Wheelwright immediately after he introduces Anne Hutchinson, in an entry for 1636, stating, "There joined with
her in these [Antinomian] opinions a brother of hers, one Mr. Wheelwright, a silenced minister sometimes in England." Winthrop asserts that
although John Cotton and John Wheelwright said that they rejected the
Antinomian idea that sanctification (works) cannot evidence justification
(redemption), they held to "the indwelling of the person of the Holy
Ghost [in a justified person]." Proposed as a minister for the Boston
church, to join John Cotton, Wheelwright was rejected by Cotton. (The
editors of the current edition of Winthrop's work state that Cotton was
protecting fellow minister John Wilson.) Wheelwright defended himself
and accepted a pastoral position at "Mount Woollaston, now Braintree."
Winthrop subsequently writes that Wheelwright was accused of sedition
for a sermon (his Fast-Day Sermon of 19 January 1637) in which he at-
tacked other ministers for preaching a covenant of works (as opposed to a
covenant of grace), and notes that Wheelwright was found guilty of sedition and contempt. Winthrop recounts the election of the Legalists (including himself as governor), and he observes that Wheelwright was
asked to retract his controversial views, but he refused. "[S]ome reconcil-
iation" took place among John Cotton, John Wheelwright, and John
Wilson; however, later, at an important meeting of the Boston church
leaders, John Cotton agreed with the authorities on the expression of doc-
trinal matters—"but Mr. Wheelwright did not." Winthrop goes on to ex-
plain that when Wheelwright continued to "justify his sermon," the
church authorities banished him. Anne Hutchinson was then interrogated
regarding her biweekly lectures, which conveyed Antinomian views, and
she, too, was banished. She initially planned "to take water, with Mr.
Wheelwright's wife and family, to go to Pascataquack [Wheelwright's
settlement, soon to become Exeter, New Hampshire]; but she changed her
mind." Cotton later acknowledged his error in having supported the Antinomians.[43]

Winthrop is pleased with the consequence of the banishment of John
Wheelwright and Anne Hutchinson; in 1639, he writes:

By this time there appeared a great change in the church of Boston; for whereas, the year before, they were all (save five or six) so affected to Mr. Wheelwright and Mrs. Hutchinson, and those new opinions, as they slighted the present governour and the pastor, looking at them as men under a covenant of works, and as their greatest enemies; but they are bearing all patiently, and not withdrawing themselves, (as they were strongly solicited to have done), but carrying themselves lovingly and helpfully upon all occasions, the Lord brought about the hearts of all the people to love and esteem them more than ever before.

Winthrop later mentions Anne Hutchinson's death at the hands of Indians, and John Wheelwright's written confession of his error and his wish for forgiveness: the banished minister wrote, "I confess that herein I have done very sinfully, and do humbly crave pardon of this honoured state." Winthrop includes Wheelwright's second letter, which limits his error, and he acknowledges that Wheelwright was allowed to return, that his banishment came to an end.[44]

What warrants particular comment regarding the aforementioned detail about John Wheelwright in Winthrop's *History* is that, from beginning to end, Anne Hutchinson and John Wheelwright are closely linked—they threatened the doctrine and authority of the Boston church with their shared Antinomian views, and they refused to retract these views. Accordingly, they were both punished. John Cotton, who had been a supporter of Hutchinson and Wheelwright, finally sided with the church authorities— as Hawthorne wrote drily in his early essay, "Ann Hutchinson," "Mr. Cotton began to have that light in regard to his errors, which will sometimes break in upon the wisest and most pious men, when their opinions are unhappily discordant with those of the Powers that be" (23:70). Cotton confessed to not recognizing the errors of others and went unpunished; Wheelwright, from his banishment, confessed to his own error. John Wheelwright and Anne Hutchinson seriously violated Puritan standards and endured similar punishments, and Wheelwright confessed his sin. To this extent, John Wheelwright and Anne Hutchinson—more strongly than John Cotton and Anne Hutchinson—resemble Arthur Dimmesdale and Hester Prynne. Ebenezer Wheelwright's Antinomian ancestor is the missing man of *The Scarlet Letter*.

In summary, then, even as Hester Prynne is explicitly associated with Anne Hutchinson, Arthur Dimmesdale is implicitly associated with both John Cotton and John Wheelwright. And the identification of the author of *The Salem Belle*, Ebenezer Wheelwright, has helped us come to this view. That is to say, what Colacurcio terms "some complex, Road-to-Xanadu association that lies somewhere behind [*The Scarlet Letter*]" importantly complements his own contextual argument.[45]

Hawthorne would surely have found John Wheelwright an appealing figure. He would have respected, one imagines, Wheelwright's fidelity to the "covenant of grace"—Anne Hutchinson's "inner light"—suggestive of what Hester Prynne and Arthur Dimmesdale said of their love: "What we did had a consecration of its own" (1:195). Of course, Hester had done many good works, but it was a sense of inwardness—"the grace of God within us" rather than "the grace of God towards us" (to use John Cotton's formulation)—that had guided her and the minister in their love.[46] Even as Hawthorne referred to "the sainted Ann Hutchinson" (1:48), he would have been admiring of John Wheelwright's defiance of the Puritan authorities and his holding to his conscience. And Hawthorne would have been responsive to Wheelwright's eventual confession of his sin.

Of distinct significance would have been Wheelwright's punishment: banishment. For when Hawthorne began to write *The Scarlet Letter*, he had just suffered his own banishment—from the Salem Custom House.[47] Both John Wheelwright and Nathaniel Hawthorne were proud men who had been forced out. The austere and buffeted John Wheelwright—perhaps more than the accommodating and relatively safe John Cotton—would have especially engaged Hawthorne's imagination.

And the disobedience of John Wheelwright and Anne Hutchinson, and their expulsion from the new settlement, would surely have intrigued Hawthorne. Their story would probably have seemed a Puritan echo of the story of Adam and Eve.

Clearly, the tale of the Garden of Eden permeated Hawthorne's work, from *Fanshawe* to *The Marble Faun*—there is even an 1843 short story titled "The New Adam and Eve." And, as noted in chapter 2, the Fall importantly links "A Legend of Brittany" and *The Scarlet Letter*. The disobedience and expulsion of John Wheelwright and Anne Hutchinson fit a larger pattern in Hawthorne's writing. We may infer that by relying on a source, *The Salem Belle*, whose anonymous author, Ebenezer Wheelwright, was a descendant of John Wheelwright, and by twice mentioning Anne Hutchinson, Hawthorne was subtly underscoring the Edenic thematics of *The Scarlet Letter*. In Hawthorne's novel, Wheelwright and Hutchinson represented "the world's first parents," who "were driven out" (1:90). Inasmuch as Arthur Dimmesdale was partly suggested by John Wheelwright, we may wonder whether the minister's initials, *A.D.*, suggest not only "Adultery," but also "Adam." Appropriately, then, genetic criticism leads back to Genesis.[48]

And, certainly, the most celebrated work concerning Adam and Eve, after the Bible, was Milton's *Paradise Lost,* about which Andrew Marvell had written, in "On Mr Milton's 'Paradise Lost,'"

> Thou hast not missed one thought that could be fit,
> And all that was improper dost omit:
> So that no room is here for writer's left,
> But to detect their ignorance or theft.[49]

Writing *The Scarlet Letter,* a masterpiece that suggests, both overtly and covertly, the story of the Garden of Eden, Hawthorne was evidently challenging Marvell's judgment. There clearly was room left, and, partly through skillful allusion, Hawthorne assumed it.

Perhaps Hawthorne would have tried to read into *The Salem Belle* Ebenezer Wheelwright's awareness of his ancestor John Wheelwright. Plainly Ebenezer Wheelwright did know of his distant forefather. On 10 October 1867, Ebenezer Wheelwright wrote, "Myself, my two brothers, & three sisters, are of the eighth generation in a direct line from John Wheelwright." And, responding on 23 October 1872 to John A. Vinton's reference to his own work on the Antinomian Controversy, Ebenezer Wheelwright wrote, "so far as Mr. Wheelwright & Mrs. Hutchinson are concerned, it seems desirable that those matters should be set right."[50]

Wheelwright himself had tried to set those matters right—in 1867, he featured in the *Panoplist* John Wheelwright's Fast-Day Sermon, as well as his own comments on the Antinomian Controversy. He faulted Anne Hutchinson and John Wheelwright for their views, and John Winthrop for his harsh treatment of the two Antinomians. Pertinently, Ebenezer Wheelwright saw the persecution of the Antinomians as related to that of the supposed witches in Salem: "the violence with which they [the Antinomians] were persecuted in Boston belongs to the same class of delusions, which about sixty years later were developed in the bloody scenes of Witchcraft."[51]

Perhaps the persecution of Mary Lyford in *The Salem Belle* could have been taken to suggest the persecution of Anne Hutchinson, or even that of John Wheelwright. And Ebenezer Wheelwright's laudatory comments about George Burroughs, who was executed at the scaffold for wizardry in 1692—comments anticipating Hawthorne's own favorable remarks on Burroughs in his 1849 sketch "Main Street" (11:76–77)—might have recalled to Hawthorne that George Burroughs worked for John Wheelwright in Wheelwright's later years.[52]

In any case, by virtue of its subject and its author's most renowned ancestor, *The Salem Belle* would probably have invited from Hawthorne a conflation of the Salem witchcraft trials and the Antinomian Controversy, two of the most notorious instances of Puritan persecution. One of these may indeed be seen as a type of the other. Hawthorne would probably have highly prized the anonymity of the author of *The Salem Belle* since through that author, whose name was known to so very few, he could privately allude to Anne Hutchinson's "brother"—and, figuratively, his own. The very hiddenness of the allusion would have further linked Hawthorne with his secretive minister. And like Dimmesdale's secret, the covert allusion—by way of Ebenezer Wheelwright to John Wheelwright—could one day be ascertained.

Finally, then, in the case of *The Salem Belle*, it is not just the original thread that is so important to recover, but also the maker of that thread, whose ancestry leads to an earlier, historical thread—and then a biblical one. Even as *The Salem Belle* helped Hawthorne write the ending of *The Scarlet Letter*, it also linked his novel to the beginning of Puritan history in America—and to the begining of the story of man.

4

The Matter of Form

THIS FINAL CHAPTER WILL FOCUS ON THE PATTERN OF THREADS IN *The Scarlet Letter*—it will attend more to formal traditions and conventions, and less to specific source passages. The theme of sin and abiding guilt—evident in "The Tell-Tale Heart," "A Legend of Brittany," and *The Salem Belle*—is reflected in *The Scarlet Letter* in a structure involving Christian judgment. This chapter will argue that *The Scarlet Letter* offers a symmetrically framed Sun of Righteousness, Christ come in judgment, and a critical chiastic expression of that judgment.

The form of *The Scarlet Letter* has been amply studied. The novel has been variously understood to involve four, five, six, and seven sections.[1] A matter about which there seems little dispute, however, is that, as F. O. Matthiessen has observed, the novel's "symmetrical design is built around the three scenes on the scaffold of the pillory."[2] The first scaffold scene, involving the condemned Hester and her infant Pearl, balances the third scaffold scene, involving the confessing minister, Hester, and Pearl. These two scaffold scenes frame the central scaffold scene, wherein the guilt-ridden Arthur Dimmesdale stands on the scaffold with Hester and Pearl at night. What warrants elaboration is the presence of the midday sun—or its midnight equivalent—in each of these scaffold scenes.

In the first of these scenes, Hester stands on the scaffold beneath "the hot, midday sun burning down upon her face, and lighting up its shame; with the scarlet token of infamy on her breast" (1:63), the scarlet letter *A*, indicating the judgment of adultery. Hawthorne ironically reinforces the association of the sun and its judgment when John Wilson lectures the unresponsive Hester "in the unadulterated sunshine" (1:65). In the last scaffold scene, the minister, Hester, and Pearl stand on the scaffold beneath "The sun, but little past its meridian" (1:254)—a sun that "shone down upon the clergyman" (1:254) while "God's judgment on a sinner" (1:255) is again revealed: the *A* upon Dimmesdale's breast, again the judgment of adultery. When some people doubt Dimmesdale's guilt, Hawthorne acknowledges "proofs" of that guilt "clear as the mid-day sunshine on the scarlet letter" (1:259).

The middle scaffold scene offers an extremely bright meteor at midnight—a meteor of "powerful . . . radiance" (1:154). It would appear that, for this meteor, Hawthorne may have borrowed and modified another existing thread. In all likelihood, Hawthorne, an avid reader of newspapers, came upon the *Salem Tri-Weekly Gazette* on Saturday, 6 November 1847, where he would have noticed on the first page a long paragraph titled "Intelligence Office" (engaging because of his March 1844 sketch titled "The Intelligence Office")—and he would have read in the adjacent right column a short untitled paragraph:

> A very brilliant Meteor was seen last evening just before ten. Its course was from South to North, and passed very near the Pleiades. The light was so bright for the moment, as to light up the street. It left a bright train behind it.[3]

Perhaps Hawthorne had seen this meteor himself—in any case, he would surely have read this piece about it. Probably relying on this item, Hawthorne wrote in *The Scarlet Letter* that the meteor "showed the familiar scene of the street, with the distinctness of mid-day"—that it produced "the noon of that strange and solemn splendor" (1:154). The terms "midday" and "noon" intimate that Hawthorne's meteor serves as the midday sun. And taking the form of the letter *A*, the sun-like meteor also yields the judgment implicit in that letter—adultery.

The sun in the three scaffold scenes suggests a judgmental divine presence. And the association of sun and divinity was not anomalous for Hawthorne. He wrote in his 1837 sketch "Sunday at Home," "so long as I imagine that the earth is hallowed, and the light of heaven retains its sanctity, on the Sabbath—while that blessed sunshine lives within me—never can my soul have lost the instinct of its faith" (9:21). Additionally, when sending sunflowers as consolation to mourning neighbors, Hawthorne also sent the message, "the sunflower is a symbol of the sun, and . . . the sun is a symbol of the glory of God."[4]

The framing of the middle scaffold scene by the first and last scaffold scenes is reinforced in *The Scarlet Letter* by the framing of the scene by symmetrical language. A sample of such language will clarify the pattern:

First half of *The Scarlet Letter*, forward

[one of the flowers of a wild rose-bush] may serve . . . to symbolize some sweet moral blossom, that may . . . relieve the darkening close of a tale of human frailty and sorrow. (1:48)

distil drops of bitterness into her heart (1:84–85)

Sometimes . . . venerable minister or magistrate. . . . Again . . . some matron. . . . Or, once more . . . young maiden. . . . (1:87)

"O, I am your little Pearl!" answered the child. (1:97)

to the mansion of Governor Bellingham (1:100)

"one of those naughty elfs or fairies, whom we thought to have left behind us . . . in merry old England" (1:110)

taking his hand in the grasp of both her own (1:115)

a man . . . emerging from the perilous wilderness, beheld the woman, in whom he hoped to find embodied the warmth and cheerfulness of home (1:118)

. . . he gathered herbs . . . and dug up roots. . . . (1:121)

kindly, though not of warm affections (1:129)

"But wilt thou promise," asked Pearl, "to take my hand, and mother's hand, to-morrow noontide?" (1:153)

The great vault brightened. . . . It showed the familiar scene of the street, with the distinctness of mid-day, but also with the awfulness that is always imparted to familiar objects by an unaccustomed light (1:154)

Second half of *The Scarlet Letter*, backward

[a herald's wording of a device on an engraved escutcheon] might serve for a motto and brief description of our now concluded legend, so sombre is it, and relieved only by one ever-glowing point of light gloomier than the shadow:—"ON A FIELD, SABLE, THE LETTER A, GULES." (1:264)[5]

drop into her tender bosom a germ of evil (1:219–20)

For instance. . . . hoary-bearded deacon. . . . Again. . . . old dame. . . . Again. . . . youngest sister. . . . (1:217–19)

. . . answered the child. . . . "And I am thy little Pearl!" (1:211)

"to the house of yonder stern old Governor" (1:207)

"one of the fairies, whom we left in our dear old England" (1:206)

holding her mother's hand in both her own (1:180)

. . . he used to emerge . . . from the seclusion of his study, and sit down in the fire-light of their home, and in the light of her nuptial smile (1:176)

He gathered here and there an herb, or grubbed up a root. . . . (1:175) "kind, true, just, and of constant, if not warm affections" (1:172)

"Thou wouldst not promise to take my hand, and mother's hand, to-morrow noontide!" (1:157)

. . . the meteor kindled up the sky, and disclosed the earth, with an awfulness that admonished Hester Prynne and the clergyman of the day of judgment. (1:156)[6]

The intensely bright meteor that yields midday—the midnight equivalent of the sun, which offers judgment upon the guilty minister—is amply framed by both the visual and the verbal.

Critically, the scene in which this sun-like meteor appears is repeatedly linked to the Last Judgment. The connection to the Last Judgment is anticipated by Dimmesdale's response to Pearl that he will hold her hand, and her mother's, "At the great judgment day!" (1:153). He adds that "Then, and there, before the judgment-seat, thy mother, and thou, and I, must stand together!" (1:153). Thus, through Dimmesdale, Hawthorne alludes to Romans 14:10—"we shall all stand before the judgment seat of Christ"—and 2 Corinthians 5:10—"we must all appear before the judgment seat of Christ." The connection to the Last Judgment is evident again in Hawthorne's rendering of the meteor's effect: "They [the minister, Hester, and Pearl] stood in the noon of that strange and solemn splendor, as if it were the light that is to reveal all secrets, and the daybreak that shall unite all who belong to one another" (1:154). Hawthorne then discusses the Puritan belief in "meteoric appearances" "as so many revelations from a supernatural source" (1:154). And he refers to the meteor's warning Hester and Dimmesdale "of the day of judgment," and Roger Chillingworth's seeming to be "the arch-fiend," ready "to claim his own" (1:156).

In the eschatological context that Hawthorne creates—an earthly approximation of the Day of Judgment—the sunlike meteor seems an emblem of Christ come in judgment. And presumably the judgmental sun in the other scaffold scenes is such an emblem as well. The judgment in each case, the letter *A*, is a sign of Christ's recognition of the minister's guilt for adultery. In this regard, we should recall that *The Scarlet Letter* was almost called *The Judgment Letter* (16:308). But we should also note that Hawthorne would later write that he did not wish to see Christ at the Last Judgment portrayed as "inexorable" (14:214–15).[7]

The framed meteor, appearing in the central section of *The Scarlet Letter*, causing (like the sun) what seems to be "mid-day" or "noon," and serving as an emblem of the judgmental Christ, suggests a notable literary convention. *The Scarlet Letter*, a novel honoring a providential atonement, seems itself written in a providential form—that is, it offers symmetrical language framing a significant midpoint, a midpoint associated with the noonday sun, "the Sun of righteousness" —a biblical image taken to mean, in a Christian reading, Christ come in judgment:

> For, behold, the day cometh, that shall burn as an oven; and all the proud, yea, and all that do wickedly, shall be stubble: and the day that cometh shall burn them up, saith the Lord of hosts, that it shall leave them neither root nor branch. But unto you that fear my name shall the Sun of righteousness arise with healing in his wings. (Malachi 4: 1–2)

Art historian Erwin Panofsky has traced the development of "the Sun of righteousness" from both pagan and Christian origins to its articulation in the late Middle Ages by Pierre Bersuire:

> Further I say of this Sun [viz, the "Sun of righteousness"] that He shall be inflamed when exercising supreme power, that is to say, when He sits in judgment, when He shall be strict and severe . . . because He shall be all hot and bloody by dint of justice and strictness. For, as the sun, when in the center of his orbit, that is to say, at the midday point, is hottest, so shall Christ be when He shall appear in the center of heaven and earth, that is to say, in Judgment. . . . In summer, when he is in the Lion, the sun withers the herbs, which have blossomed in the spring, by his heat. So shall Christ, in that heat of the Judgment, appear as a man fierce and leonine; He shall wither the sinners and shall destroy the prosperity of men which they had enjoyed in the world.

Panofsky goes on to discuss Albrecht Dürer's famous 1498/99 engraving of the Sun of Righteousness: a Christ with eyes of flame, who is seated upon a lion and holding a sword in his right hand and a set of scales in his left hand.[8] Ernst H. Kantorowicz has considered the Sun of Righteousness to be suggested in the sixteenth canto of Dante's *Purgatorio* in its reference to "Two Suns." Alastair Fowler sees the Sun of Righteousness, the *Sol Iustitiae*, (and the *Sol oriens*, the rising sun) in the central stanza of John Donne's "Nuptial Song," and he observes the Sun of Righteousness as Phoebus "in the central position of sovereignty" in John Milton's "Lycidas." John Carey sees the image of the Sun of Righteousness in the "greater Sun" of Milton's "Nativity Ode." And Fowler writes that the image of the Sun of Righteousness is intimated by the ascent of Christ in a chariot at the textual center of *Paradise Lost*. Douglas Brooks extends the argument; he finds "the Christian notion of the *Sol Iustitiae* or Sun of justice (Christ come in judgment described in terms of the midday sun)" at the center of Daniel Defoe's novel *Robinson Crusoe*.[9]

Defoe's novel was one of those books for which Hawthorne, as a boy, "acquired a great fondness," and it became a part of his library. In subsequent years, his young son Julian pretended to read it (8:407). Later, Julian and sister Una play-acted Crusoe's story—what Julian Hawthorne termed "our autobiography."[10] It is of note that Tappan and Dennet sold the E. C. Biddle children's edition of *Robinson Crusoe* in 1842 and 1843 and that the reviews of the book appeared immediately previous to reviews of *The Salem Belle* in the *Boston Evening Gazette* and the *Boston Miscellany*. But regardless of any possible association of the two books, Hawthorne, when preparing to write his first novel in 1849, would probably have turned to an old favorite that was, in fact, the first novel written in English—an inevitable part of any "artistic study" of novels. We may be encouraged in sensing his interest in Defoe by observing that in June of 1848 Hawthorne borrowed from the Salem Athenaeum Defoe's *Captain Singleton* and in June of 1849 Defoe's *Roxana*.[11] Of course, other works besides *Robinson Crusoe* were written with a providential form; we cannot claim more than is warranted for Defoe's classic. However, we can note that there is a formal affinity between *Robinson Crusoe* and *The Scarlet Letter*. And we can note that even as Hawthorne borrowed and transformed threads for his literary fabric, he also borrowed and transformed the design for that fabric.

Douglas Brooks shows that *Robinson Crusoe* has the symmetrical design typical of the providential form: "Adventures with Xury / Brazil // Island // Brazil / Adventures with Friday." And, relying on E. M. W. Tillyard and Frank H. Ellis, he points to the symmetrical verbal patterning in the pre-island chapters and the post-island chapters. And at the center of the island section, and of the novel as a whole, is that critical moment when Crusoe discovers Friday's footprint—the moment of the Sun of Righteousness. Brooks sees the footprint as "a telling test of the strength of Crusoe's religious faith." He notes, "In Christian iconography the foot symbolizes humility and human fallibility; e.g., Ps. 94: 18: 'When I said, My foot slippeth; thy mercy, O Lord, held me up.' In other words, the footprint should be understood by Crusoe as a warning against self-sufficiency and a reminder of God's Providence."[12] We may add that Crusoe acknowledged what he termed "my ORIGINAL SIN," his opposing his father's "excellent Advice" to accept his "middle State."[13]

As Brooks maintains, the warning footprint occurs "halfway through the novel," with notable markers. Defoe writes, in the paragraph before that concerning the footprint, "this was also about half Way between my other Habitation, and the place where I had laid up my Boat." And Defoe states, "It happen'd one Day about Noon going towards my Boat, I was exceedingly surpriz'd with the Print of a Man's naked Foot on the Shore."

The focus on "Noon" emphasizes the centrality of the passage. And Brooks asserts, "there can be little doubt that Defoe alludes to the identification of the midday sun with the *Sol iustitiae* and the consequent interpretation of noon as a time of trial and judgment." Furthermore, Brooks observes, Crusoe "went up to a rising ground to look farther"—Defoe thereby acknowledges his working within "the iconographical tradition of elevation at the centre," indicative of "cosmic kingship."[14]

Initially, Crusoe fails the test, but over time, his faith grows. Crusoe comes to conclude "that God had appointed all this to befal me"; he comes to see that not only his suffering, but his prevailing, was providential. Indeed, as Brooks notes, Crusoe later states, "I frequently sat down to my Meat with Thankfulness, and admir'd the Hand of God's Providence, which had thus spread my Table in the Wilderness."[15]

Even as both *Robinson Crusoe* and *The Scarlet Letter* offer symmetrical action and language, both novels offer a significant midpoint (the appearance of a footprint or the letter *A*), occurring at noon, involving the implicit appearance of the sun—or the explicit appearance of a sun or sun equivalent—signifying the Sun of Righteousness. "Cosmic kingship" is suggested by an elevation—whether a hill or a scaffold—and the king implied is Christ, who has come in judgment. Though very different in myriad ways, the novels *Robinson Crusoe* and *The Scarlet Letter*—both of which do, in fact, concern Original Sin, Divine Providence, and spiritual redemption—may be considered as homologous texts, distinct instances of providential form.[16]

Another instance of the providential form may be elaborated, and this American. Poe's novel *The Narrative of Arthur Gordon Pym*, directly influenced by Defoe's *Robinson Crusoe*, embodies such a form.[17] Although there is no evidence to suggest that Hawthorne read Poe's novel, its structural affinity with *The Scarlet Letter* should be noted.

The novel's providential form may be delineated briefly. Symmetrical events frame the center: most conspicuously, the destruction of a boat, the *Ariel*, by a ship, the *Penguin*, and the rescue of Arthur Gordon Pym and Augustus Barnard; the confinement of Pym in the hold of the ship *Grampus*; and the attack of the mutineers, in the first half, appear in reverse order in the second half with the attack of the Tsalalian natives, the confinement of Pym by the landslide, and the imminent destruction of Pym's canoe by the (encoded) *Penguin* and the rescue of Pym and Dirk Peters. The symmetry of events is reinforced by a symmetry of language. Such phrases as "were hurrying us to destruction" (*Collected Writings* 1:60), "of ultimate escape" (*Collected Writings* 1:60), "a loud and long scream or yell" (1:60), "drowned some thirty or forty poor devils" (1:64), and "death or captivity among barbarian hordes; . . . a lifetime dragged out in sorrow and tears" (1:65) in the first half of the novel are reflected in the second half by such phrases as "being put to death by the savages, . . . dragging out a miserable existence in captivity among them" (1:185), "killed, perhaps, thirty or forty of the savages" (1:187), "screaming and yelling for aid" (1:187), "of ultimate escape" (1:198), and "were still hurrying on to the southward" (1:204). *Pym*'s symmetry calls attention to its critical center. And at this center—in the middle of the middle chapter (chapter 13)—Pym's friend Augustus Barnard dies of his wounds. Poe writes,

> *August* 1. A continuance of the same calm weather, with an oppressively hot sun. . . . We now saw clearly that Augustus could not be saved; that he was evidently dying. We could do nothing to relieve his sufferings, which appeared to be great. About twelve o'clock he expired in strong convulsions, and without having spoken for several hours. (1:142)

The well-framed "oppressively hot sun" at "twelve o'clock," occurring at the midpoint of Poe's novel, represents the Sun of Righteousness. Pym's trial is the death of his friend Augustus—or, to speak of an allegorical meaning, Poe's trial was the death of his brother Henry (who did, in fact, die on August 1). That Pym/Poe successfully endured the trial is implied by the transcendent vision at the book's end—the white "shrouded human figure," suggesting Christ in Revelation. The providential form of the work enhances the providential theme, illustrated by the recurrent deliverance of Pym and intimated by Poe's reference in the novel to "the special interference of Providence" (1:62).[18]

Accordingly, the form of *Pym* anticipates the form of *The Scarlet Letter*. Both works feature symmetrical events and phrases framing a significant midpoint—the death of Augustus or the letter *A*. Associated with this midpoint in *Pym* is "the oppressively hot sun" at noon that represents the Sun of Righteousness; similarly, linked to the midpoint in *The Scarlet Letter* is the sun-like meteor that turns night to day—specifically, to "mid-day," "noon"—and that represents the same image, the Sun of Righteousness. The trial in *Pym* is the loss of the brother-like friend; the trial in *The Scarlet Letter* is the hidden sin of the guilt-ridden minister. Providentially, it would seem, Pym finds a new brother in the formerly savage Dirk Peters, and he will be reunited with Augustus/Henry in the afterlife, as promised by the final coded vision of Christ come to prophesy the New Jerusalem. Dimmesdale is permitted to atone for his sin and to confess it publicly, thereby finding salvation and, perhaps, eventual reunion with Hester in the afterlife. Though one story is set on nineteenth-century shipboard and on a remote island in the South Seas, and the other is set in seventeenth-century Boston, the two works have a shared structure. The imagination of Poe and that of Hawthorne had an even greater affinity than we have formerly recognized. Hawthorne and Poe did share a common literary heritage, the providential form, which constitutes an important part of the design of two of their major works. In both *Pym* and *The Scarlet Letter*, "the Sun of righteousness" does "arise with healing in his wings."[19] According to Christian belief, man is redeemed from Original Sin by the Covenant of Grace, attained through Christ's sacrifice. It is fitting, then, that *The Scarlet Letter*, a narrative about Original Sin and redemption, is overseen by an emblem of a providential Christ. Hawthorne's tale of the unfortunate lovers is, after all, a tale of the Fortunate Fall.

Even as the brilliant meteor serves as the providential Sun of Righteousness in Hawthorne's novel, the significant midpoint is the letter that it forms—"an immense letter,—the letter A" (1:155). The symmetrical visual and verbal patterning of *The Scarlet Letter*, already discussed, frames a vital central chiasmus—a figure that warrants further inquiry.

The word "chiasmus" is drawn from the name for the Greek letter X, "chi." The figure of chiasmus involves symmetrical inversion—crossover—the pattern *ABBA*. (It had hitherto been known as "commutatio" and "antimetabole.") Chiasmus has been amply treated with regard to classical literature, the Old and New Testament, and British and American literature.[20] It has also been discussed specifically in terms of *The Scarlet Letter*.

In 1973, Raymond Benoit focused on the phrase "A letter,—the letter A" (1:178) in chapter 15 of Hawthorne's novel, "Hester and Pearl"; he saw the letter as "one limb spirit and one limb matter, with Pearl, herself a symbol, the connecting link between these two." In 1990, Jon B. Reed noted the same instance of chiasmus in *The Scarlet Letter*, stressing the ambiguity of the letter. In 1995, Matthew Gartner speculated that perhaps the chiastic structure of the Book of Esther importantly influenced the structure of *The Scarlet Letter*.[21] This latter view may be valid, but many other chiastic models could have served. And we should observe that the chiastic pattern that Benoit and Reed address is found elsewhere. For instance, there is the language in "The Custom-House" introduction, "This rag of scarlet cloth . . . assumed the shape of *a letter*. It was the capital *letter A*" (1:31; emphasis added here and below). And there is the language of the sexton to the minister at the close of chapter 12: "But did your reverence hear of the portent that was seen last night? *A* great red *letter* in the sky,—the *letter A*" (1:158). The three noted instances serve to underscore the well-framed central chiastic phrase in chapter 12, describing the appearance of the meteor to Dimmesdale:

> We impute it, therefore, solely to the disease in his own eye and heart, that the minister, looking upward to the zenith, beheld there the appearance of *an* immense *letter*,—the *letter A*,—marked out in lines of dull red light. (1:155)

The significant midpoint with which the Sun of Righteousness is linked—its judgment of the guilty minister—is the letter *A*, chiastically expressed.

And the phrase "looking upward to the zenith" calls attention to the centrality of this passage, itself framed by the nearby previous passage in which the minister "cast his eyes towards the zenith" (1:154) and the imminent one in which the minister "gazed upward to the zenith" (1:155). The notable proximity of the central *A* to the *z* of the repeated word "zenith" may call to mind Hawthorne's biblical range, from Original Sin to Last Judgment, as well as Christ himself, "Alpha and Omega, the beginning and the end, the first and the last" (Rev. 22:13).

As chiasticist Max Nänny has thoroughly and ably demonstrated, chiasmus is sometimes ornamental and sometimes functional. In the case of *The Scarlet Letter*, the central chiasmus is clearly functional. The chiastic phrase at the center of the novel—"an immense letter,—the letter A"—suggests the verbal symmetry of the entire novel. *The Scarlet Letter* is folded; its reading involves its unfolding. The evident verbal balance throughout (suggested by the chiastic pattern *ABBA*) nicely underscores the thematic balances—those between head and heart, law and love, sin and redemption, justice and mercy, providence and free will. If there is an innovation in the spatial chiasmus of Hawthorne's novel, it is that the outer elements—the rose of the first chapter and the red letter of the last chapter—relate so closely to the central phrase. We seem to find here a noteworthy correspondence—even as the scarlet letter on Dimmesdale's chest is said to emerge from the remorse in his heart (1:258–59), so, too, do the rose in the beginning and the red letter *A* at the end emerge from "an immense letter,—the letter A, marked out in lines of dull red light" at the heart of the novel.

Temporally, the central chiastic phrase relates to the changing characters. Inasmuch as the inversion of chiasmus indicates an *X*, that central phrase reflects the crossing paths of the protagonists. There is the changing position of Hester and Chillingworth over seven years—her rising, his falling: "She had climbed her way, since then, to a higher point. The old man, on the other hand, had brought himself nearer to her level, or perhaps below it, by the revenge which he had stooped for" (1:167). Her ascent and his decline reveal the chiastic X. There is also the changing position of Hester and Dimmesdale over seven years—the respected minister standing high above the guilty woman in the first scaffold scene (1:64–69), the increasingly-respected woman holding up the guilty minister in the final scaffold scene (1:255–57)—he who has finally "step[ped] down from a high place" (1:67).[22]

Accordingly, the central chiastic phrase "an immense letter,—the letter A" is not only the powerful divine judgment upon the guilty minister, but also the controlling figure for both textual space and narrative time in the novel. Its resonance is rich, both morally and formally.

Notably, a central chiasmus may be found in other classic American works of Hawthorne's time. Edgar Allan Poe's "The Tell-Tale Heart" (again), Henry David Thoreau's *Walden*, and Harriet Beecher Stowe's *Uncle Tom's Cabin* illustrate the pattern well.

"The Tell-Tale Heart," so critical an influence on chapter 10 of *The Scarlet Letter*, offers a chiastic center concerning the old man's "Evil Eye." The "ray . . . upon the vulture eye" and the "ray . . . upon the damned spot" frame that center, a center that describes the provoking eye itself: "It was *open—wide, wide open*" (*Collected Works* 3:794–95; emphasis added). Poe's chiastic *X* marks "the spot." His chiasmus intensifies the horrific image of the "Evil Eye" and effectively serves to emphasize the centrality of that image to the story. And perhaps the double ds of "wide, wide" serve, as David Ketterer has noted regarding the double ds of "The Fall of the House of Usher," as Poe's signature, "Eddy."[23]

And Thoreau's 1854 masterpiece *Walden* features a chiastic center, as well. We may be directed there by Thoreau's remarking that, having repeatedly sounded Walden Pond, he found that "the number indicating the greatest depth was apparently in the centre of the map." Charles R. Anderson leads us to the center, too:

> At the very heart of the book lies Walden Pond, the central circle image. All paths lead into this chapter, "The Ponds"; all lines of meaning radiate from it. Here Thoreau found his ideal Self in that symbol of perfection which was the exact opposite of all those imperfections he had inveighed against in the life of society. The other ponds form a ring around Concord . . . the circle of his endless saunterings. At their center lies Walden, and at its center Thoreau glimpses the end of his quest.

Thoreau writes about Walden Pond, at the center of "The Ponds," with a subtle chiasmus:

> It is a soothing employment, on one of those fine days in the fall when all the warmth of the sun is fully appreciated, to sit on a stump on such a height as this, overlooking the pond, and study the *dimpling circles* which are incessantly inscribed on its otherwise invisible surface amid the reflected skies and trees. Over this great expanse there is no disturbance but it is thus at once gently smoothed away and assuaged, as, when a vase of water is jarred, the trembling circles seek the shore and all is smooth again. Not a fish can leap or an insect fall on the pond but it is thus reported in *circling dimples*, in lines of beauty, as it were the constant welling up of its fountain, the gentle pulsing of its life, the heaving of its breast. (emphasis added)

The chiastic phrases not only clarify the formal center of the work, but also delicately frame what may perhaps be "the end of his quest." The "trembling circles" becoming smooth are infinitely emblematic. They seem to suggest, among other possibilities, human consciousness attaining calm.[24]

Finally, in view of the Christian significance of Hawthorne's central chiasmus—it is the judgment on the minister by the Sun of Righteousness, Christ—we may consider a final instance of central chiasmus that also offers a Christian resonance, an instance appearing in Stowe's 1852 classic, *Uncle Tom's Cabin*. The work offers at its center (the beginning of the second volume of two volumes) a chiastic conversation. Little Eva has just heard from Tom about the death by starvation of a slave woman's baby, and, stricken, she refuses to be taken for a ride in her carriage:

> "Tom, you needn't get me the horses. *I don't want to go*," she said.
> "Why not, Miss Eva?"
> "*These things sink into my heart*, Tom," said *Eva*,—"*they sink into my heart*," she repeated, earnestly. "*I don't want to go*," and she turned from Tom, and went into the house.[25] (emphasis added)

Assuredly, this is no secular chiasmus. While indicating the center of the narrative, the *ABBA* pattern clearly frames Little Eva—Evangeline, the bearer of the good news of the redemption of the world through Christ. The chiasmus honors Eva's loving Christian spirit. And, indeed, in this case, the *X* may be the cross. Unmistakably, Hawthorne's central chiasmus in *The Scarlet Letter* concerns judgment and Stowe's in *Uncle Tom's Cabin*, love. But the judgment and the love are specifically those of Christ. And we may well wonder whether the central chiasmus in *The Scarlet Letter*—"an immense letter,—the letter A" (1:155)—also suggests the cross. In this regard, we might remember that, over time, Hester's "scarlet letter had the effect of the cross on a nun's bosom" (1:163).[26]

By virtue of the central chiasmus in each work, *The Scarlet Letter*, "The Tell-Tale Heart," *Walden*, and *Uncle Tom's Cabin* are akin. While Hawthorne, Poe, Thoreau, and Stowe are diverse writers, whose works are examined and taught in divergent ways, the formal relatedness of these works suggests a greater affinity than heretofore recognized. And, assuredly, there are a number of other examples of central chiasmus in American literature—examples warranting identification and interpretation. In this regard, Poe's canny chiastic statement, made in his comic short story "X-ing a Paragrab," may be aptly employed here: "*X*, everybody knew, was *an unknown quantity;* but in this case . . . there was *an unknown quantity* of *X*" (*Collected Works* 3:1375; emphasis added).

Even as Hawthorne creatively transformed previous work for *The Scarlet Letter*—including "The Tell-Tale Heart," "A Legend of Brittany," and *The Salem Belle*—he also borrowed and reshaped formal conventions—including the Providential form and the central chiasmus. Thus, Hawthorne both hid and revealed. Even as *The Scarlet Letter* is made up of various knowable matching threads, muted for aesthetic concerns, those threads are stitched in a knowable design—evident, to varying degrees, in other literary works as well. To borrow again from Hawthorne regarding the scarlet letter, the "skill of needlework" in his masterpiece is indeed "wonderful"—but the "art" is not "forgotten" (1:31).

Conclusion

"Picking out the threads"—and the pattern of threads—of *The Scarlet Letter* does help us to recover "a now forgotten art." Careful consideration of "The Tell-Tale Heart," "A Legend of Brittany," *The Salem Belle*, and the relevant critical formal traditions does clarify Hawthorne's method of composition. Working within the conventions of the providential form and a central chiasmus, Hawthorne fashioned a narrative repeatedly informed by catalogs of related narratives, which he adapted for his purposes. All three narrative sources studied here concern sin and guilt. And even as one of the three specifically supports the preeminent narrative in *The Scarlet Letter*, that of the Fall and its consequences, another may be linked to the Fall through the life of its author's most famous ancestor. And even while (as others have noted) Hawthorne softened the supernatural detail, spiritualized the historical background, and apportioned the subversive imagery in *The Scarlet Letter*, he also modulated his literary influences. In the interest of an aesthetic wholeness—once termed literary "keeping"—he subdued the physical violence of "The Tell-Tale Heart," tempered the sexual suggestiveness of "A Legend of Brittany," and diminished the witchcraft-trial context of *The Salem Belle*. Yet Hawthorne's aesthetics of attenuation may be recovered; indeed, it seems part of the job of Hawthorne scholarship to reveal the colors that Hawthorne allowed to fade in the literary threads that he borrowed.

As we reread the middle scaffold scene, where Pearl is united with her mother and father, and "The three formed an electric chain" (1:153), we may well think not only of the girl who embodies the scarlet letter, but also of the novel *The Scarlet Letter*—united with its growing family of sources, charged by its relatedness. Probably, like Dimmesdale, who was so anxious about acknowledging his child, Hawthorne was anxious about ac-

110

knowledging his novel's origins. Nonetheless, although he did not, like the minister, reveal his secret, he did offer sufficient detail to permit his secret to be found. Indeed, it seems highly appropriate that he mentions in *The Scarlet Letter* Shakespeare's great source-book, the Holinshed *Chronicles* (1:105). We may consider a modification of Hawthorne's moral in *The Scarlet Letter*: "Be true! Be true! Be true! Show freely to the world, if not your sources, yet some traits whereby these sources may be inferred!" (1:260).

Assuredly, other American writers also hinted at their sources. We may remember Washington Irving's mentioning at the close of "Rip Van Winkle" "a little German superstition about the Emperor Frederick *der Rothbart*, and the Kypphauser mountain," probably thereby indirectly suggesting the source for his tale, "Peter Klaus the Goatherd," which appeared before the Rothbart legend in a volume of Otmar's folktales.[1] And there is, too, in Poe's "The Murders in the Rue Morgue," the revealing response of Dupin to his friend's theory that the unknown murderer is an escaped madman: "In some respects . . . your idea is not irrelevant" (*Collected Works* 2:558). After all, Poe was relying in that story, in part, on a newspaper source titled "Humorous Adventure—Picking Up a Madman." Poe's detective story invites detection of its own sources—retracing Poe's steps—engaging in "the processes of resolution," which are "the processes of invention or creation" "conversed" (*Collected Works* 2:527).[2] So, too, *The Scarlet Letter*—a detective story of sorts, involving a mysterious birth rather than mysterious deaths—invites the reader to retrace Hawthorne's steps, to resolve his creation into its original elements—to unimagine what has been imagined—to complete the larger symmetry of writing and reading.

There is a great pleasure in our working backward to a work's origins. In part, it is the thrill of discovery. In part, it is the satisfaction of deeper understanding. But there is yet more. The renowned scholar of religion and mythology, Mircea Eliade, once wrote:

> Since the sacred and strong time is the *time of origins*, the stupendous instant in which a reality was created, was for the first time fully manifested, man will seek periodically to return to that original time.[3]

The recovery of literary origins may well involve a recovery of that "sacred and strong time," and therefore a sense of renewal—a sense of our own creative possibility—a sense that we, too, may try great things. The scholarly endeavor may well involve its own exhilarating "eternal return."

Readers of American literature will readily recall, in this context of the time of origins, F. Scott Fitzgerald's rendering, near the end of *The Great Gatsby*, Nick Carraway's reverie about Long Island and the moment of American origins. The classic passage begins,

> And as the moon rose higher the inessential houses began to *melt away* until gradually I became aware of the old island here that flowered once for Dutch sailors' eyes—a *fresh, green* breast of the new world.[4] (emphasis added)

The wonder of that imagined moment of discovery is extraordinary—and it may only increase for us with the discovery of this passage's literary origins—in "Rip Van Winkle":

> At the foot of these fairy mountains the voyager may have descried the light smoke curling up from a village, whose shingle roofs gleam among the trees, just where the blue tints of the upland *melt away* into the *fresh green* of the nearer landscape.[5] (emphasis added)

Fitzgerald was evidently celebrating the glorious promise of beginnings—not only the beginning of the European settling of America, but also the beginning of American romantic fiction. Enjoying both beginnings—borne back into historical and literary pasts—we may share with Fitzgerald a new sense of possibility.

Study of literary origins will endure. At its best, such study does not lessen an author's reputation but, rather, shows that author's transformative artistry—and thus increases his or her reputation. Discovery reveals creation. Attention to the threads of *The Scarlet Letter* reveals that which we so resolutely seek—Hawthorne at his needle. And, of course, by recovering his creating, we recognize more fully the work he created. But also, we may develop a stronger sense of our own power of creation. If by writing *The Scarlet Letter* Hawthorne sought to "complete his circle of existence by bringing him into communion with it" (1:4), so, too, may we come full circle, brought into communion with our own imaginative potential.

Appendix:
A Bibliographical Overview

I HAVE MENTIONED IN THE PRECEDING CHAPTERS NUMEROUS SCHOLARLY studies of the origins of *The Scarlet Letter* that relate to my findings, but there are yet other studies of these origins that also warrant acknowledgment. The first of these, however, was a distinctly false start.

A Boston correspondent for the *Salem Register*, who was identified only as "M," asserted soon after *The Scarlet Letter* was published that there was an actual Hester Prynne, "heroic and beautiful," who had helped her mother, sister, and brother escape from an attack by Seminole Indians in Florida. A week after this letter was published, the *Salem Register* offered a correction, stating, in part, "The name of the heroine of the Florida escape was *Perrine*, and not *Prynne*, as our Boston correspondent supposed." Although "M" initially defended his claim, he eventually conceded his error: "I was wrong in regard to the name Prynne.—It should be Perrine." (Slightly modified, and attributed to "X," the letter asserting the false claim appeared again in the *Louisville Daily Journal*. The *Literary World* mentioned the *Louisville Daily Journal*'s claim [crediting it to the nonexistent *Louisville Gazette*] in its column "Facts and Opinions.")[1]

Despite this inauspicious beginning, the history of the study of the genesis of *The Scarlet Letter* has been fascinating and provocative, and some of the strongest contributions have importantly enhanced understanding of Hawthorne's novel. The present bibliographical overview is included to facilitate the continuing examination of the origins of Hawthorne's greatest work. Included in this consideration are studies that concern relevant backgrounds, sources, and allusions.

Of note early on are George Parsons Lathrop's 1876 comparison of *The Scarlet Letter* to John Bunyan's *Pilgrim's Progress*, Henry James's 1879 comparison of *The Scarlet Letter* to John G. Lockhart's *Adam Blair*—a comparison also made earlier in two reviews—Julian Hawthorne's 1884 identification of settings in *The Scarlet Letter* with actual sites in Boston, and Thomas Wentworth Higginson's 1888 linking of Hawthorne's use of multiple perceptions and explanations with William Austin's use of the same technique. An anonymous author suggested, in a 1902 newspaper piece, "Tragedy in Tale of Love," that Eliza Wharton's life was distorted by Hannah Foster in *The Coquette*, but may have been a critical element of *The Scarlet Letter*. In 1904, Paul Elmer More maintained that the weird in Poe and Hawthorne grew out of a tradition that may be traced from the Puritans through Cotton Mather, Michael Wigglesworth, and Jonathan Edwards to Philip Freneau, Charles Brockden Brown, Washington Irving, and William Cullen Bryant: it is "the peculiar half vision inherited by the soul when faith has waned and the imagination prolongs the sensations in a shadowy involuntary life of its own."[2]

In 1920, Pauline Carrington Bouve posited that the original of Hester Prynne may have been Puritan spinster Elizabeth Payne. In 1926, Elizabeth Lathrop Chandler wrote "A Study of the Sources of the Tales and Romances Written by Nathaniel Hawthorne before 1853," wherein she discussed, among other matters, the sections of Hawthorne's American notebooks that helped to prompt *The Scarlet Letter*. Chandler mentioned now-familiar passages on insincerity (1837), vengeance (1838), penance (1838), the moral and physical effects of crime (1842), and Hawthorne's daughter Una (1849). Citing more fully passages from Hawthorne's journals concerning Una, as well as passages from *The Scarlet Letter* concerning Pearl, son Julian Hawthorne elaborated on the influence of his sister Una on his father's rendering of Pearl, in a 1931 essay, "The Making of 'The Scarlet Letter.'" He noted, aptly, "Mere abstract musings or unaided invention might not have created a figure so alive and undeniable." Randall Stewart's introduction and notes for his 1932 edition of the American notebooks furnish further commentary on entries related to Hawthorne's first novel; his essay "Hawthorne and *The Faerie Queen*" suggested the novel's debts to Spenser.[3]

In 1932, "Books Read by Nathaniel Hawthorne, 1828–1850" appeared, a useful reference work concerning books borrowed from the Library of the Salem Athenaeum (a piece later succeeded by Marion L. Kesselring's 1949 "Hawthorne's Reading, 1828–1850"). Also in that year, G. Harrison Orians discussed Hawthorne's reliance on "the theological sin of witchcraft" in his fiction. In 1934, Arlin Turner completed his remarkable dissertation, "A Study of Hawthorne's Origins," in which he considered the originals of the characters in "The Custom-House" and Hawthorne's method of developing a series of scenes in his first novel. The appendix, "Hawthorne's Reading," is another valuable reference tool, as is a similar effort, Austin Warren's 1935 essay, also titled "Hawthorne's Reading." Many of Turner's findings appeared in print in his 1936 article, "Hawthorne's Literary Borrowings," and his 1940 work, "Hawthorne's Method of Using His Source Materials."[4]

Edward Dawson argued for *The Journal of John Winthrop* and Felt's *Annals* as important sources for *The Scarlet Letter* in his 1937 dissertation, "Hawthorne's Knowledge and Use of New England History: A Study of Sources." Of particular note is that Dawson linked several Hawthorne passages—including a passage in the 1838 short story "Endicott and the Red Cross" concerning "a young woman with no mean share of beauty, whose doom it was to wear the letter A on the breast of her gown"; an entry in the *American Notebooks* regarding a colonial woman who always had "to wear the letter A, sewed on her garment, in token of her having committed adultery" (1844/45); and related passages in *The Scarlet Letter*—to Felt's *Annals*, wherein it is stated that an adulterer must wear "a capital A, two inches long, cut out of cloth coloured differently from their clothes, and sewed on the arms, or back parts of their garments so as always to be seen when they were about." Dawson also contended for the influence of Cotton Mather's *Wonders of the Invisible World* and *Magnalia Christi Americana*.[5]

In 1940, J. Chesley Matthews posited a Dantesque character to a description of Reverend Dimmesdale. In 1946, Jane Lundblad noted the gothic elements of *The Scarlet Letter*. Focusing on Chillingworth, F. O. Matthiessen, in his 1941 book *American Renaissance*, and Darrel Abel, in his 1953 article "The Devil in Boston," found a Miltonic element in *The Scarlet Letter*, and W. Stacy Johnson, in his 1951 essay "Hawthorne and *The Pilgrim's Progress*," found a Spenserian one. Also in 1951, Vernon Loggins linked the brother-sister incest of Hawthorne's Manning ancestors, Rousseau's *Julie; ou, La Nouvelle Héloise*, and Hawthorne's first novel, a point later expanded by Leslie Fiedler. James J. Lynch, in the following year, recounted varying views of the sources of Hawthorne's knowledge of witchcraft. William Bysshe Stein argued, in his 1953 book *Hawthorne's Faust*, that *The Scarlet Letter* was drawn from the Faust myth. (Roy Harvey Pearce cautioned, however, "Where all is Faust, Hawthorne is imminently in danger of being lost.") Although Hubert H. Hoeltje's interesting 1954 essay, "The Writing of *The Scarlet Letter*," considered the Custom House controversy, it did not elaborate any important new sources. But Alfred S. Reid's 1955 book, *The Yellow Ruff and "The Scarlet Letter,"* the first book-length work devoted to the origins of *The Scarlet Letter*, offered various sources (alleged, questionably, to be the "principal sources") relating to the murder of Sir Thomas

Overbury, a crime to which Hawthorne refers twice in his novel (1:127, 221).[6]

In 1955, Marvin Laser asserted Hawthorne's use of Thomas C. Upham's psychology in *The Scarlet Letter*; in 1956, Robert Stanton noted Hawthorne's ironic modification of the pilgrimage of John Bunyan's Christian. Walter Blair offered a discussion of sources, including some for *The Scarlet Letter*, in the "Hawthorne" chapter of *Eight American Authors*. In 1958, Pat M. Ryan Jr. implied the effect of Kotzebue's play *Lover's Vows* on dialogue in the novel, and Robert L. Brant observed Hawthorne's allusion to Andrew Marvell's "The Unfortunate Lover" at the close of the book. And in 1959, Charles Ryskamp wrote one of the classic source studies, "The New England Sources of *The Scarlet Letter*." This work effectively shows Hawthorne's grounding in Puritan history and develops his borrowing in *The Scarlet Letter* from Caleb Snow's *History of Boston*, as well as from John Winthrop's *History of New England* and Cotton Mather's *Magnalia Christi Americana*. Ryskamp acknowledged the need to recognize not only Hawthorne's respect for the facts of history, but also his regard for the spirit of a time; he quoted fittingly from Hawthorne's 1846 review of William Gilmore Simms's *Views and Reviews in American History* regarding the need in literature for "the magic touch that should cause new intellectual and moral shapes to spring up in the reader's mind" (23:240).[7]

In 1960, Charles Boewe and Murray G. Murphey identified models for Hester Prynne in Goodwife Mendame of Duxbury, who wore an "AD" for adultery; Hester Craford, who was whipped for fornication; and Mary Latham, who was sentenced to death for adultery. The following year, Edward H. Davidson noted Hawthorne's alteration of Puritan history, his imbuing the 1640s with the more severe ethos of the 1690s. The 1963 edition of *Eight American Authors* featured J. Chesley Mathews's bibliographical supplement. In the same year, Grace Pleasant Wellborn argued for Hawthorne's debt to plant lore in *The Scarlet Letter*. Then Jessie Ryon Lucke suggested that the use of the phrase "holy family" for a slave family in Cuba, a term appearing in Mary Peabody Mann's novel *Juanita*, influenced Hawthorne's depiction of Hester and Pearl as Madonna and child. Austin Warren wrote of Hawthorne's use of Cotton Mather as a model for Arthur Dimmesdale;[8] Francis E. Kearns inferred Hawthorne's reliance on Margaret Fuller for Hester Prynne; and Peter Schwarz explored further Hawthorne's borrowing from the Faust myth.

Thomas F. Walsh, in 1966, found that the language used to describe Dimmesdale's Election Sermon was consonant with the language of actual election sermons and of Edward Johnson's *Wonder-Working Providence*.

Julian Smith posited Salem merchant Richard Saltonstall Rogers as a model for Chillingworth. Nicholas Canaday Jr. then suggested a possible source in Dante's *Purgatorio* for the "sweet moral blossom" in the first chapter of *The Scarlet Letter* (1:48). And Ernest W. Baughman studied Dimmesdale's public confession in the context of public confession in Puritan times. In 1968, Hena Maes-Jelinek challenged Alfred S. Reid's view that Roger Chillingworth is similar to William Chillingworth, arguing instead that Francis Cheynell, spiritual tormentor of William Chillingworth, is a closer match. And John C. Stubbs, who seems not to have known the Brant attribution to Marvell for the final wording in *The Scarlet Letter*, proposed, not altogether convincingly, a paragraph from Sir Walter Scott's novel *Waverly* as a source.

Michael Davitt Bell assessed Hawthorne's use of the historical romance in 1971, with some attention to the author's reliance on Governor Bellingham and Governor Winthrop. Richard Harter Fogle noted correspondences between Lord Byron's *Childe Harold* and *The Scarlet Letter*, including the key phrase "electric chain."[9] Walter Blair revised and expanded his "Hawthorne" essay for *Eight American Authors*, and B. Bernard Cohen published an excellent new reference tool in "Hawthorne's Library." J. D. C. Masheck also offered an illuminating piece on the presence of Samuel Johnson's confession in *The Scarlet Letter*. Gerald R. Griffin provided a study concerning the story "The New England Village" (attributed to Hawthorne) and *The Scarlet Letter*; however, the attribution was challenged by the Centenary Edition editors (11:406–7). Mukhtar Ali Isani suggested, in 1972, that Roger Chillingworth's tormenting Arthur Dimmesdale corresponds with William Prynne's tormenting Bishop Laud. Robert E. Todd noted mythic and biblical elements in Hawthorne's treatment of Hester Prynne, and Betty Kushen identified the scarlet letter with the cross. Kent P. Wentersdorf observed Hawthorne's indebtedness to the history and lore of witchcraft. And Michael J. Colacurcio wrote the valuable study, "Footsteps of Ann Hutchinson," in which he showed the relationship of Anne Hutchinson and John Cotton to Hester Prynne and Arthur Dimmesdale, noting Hawthorne's use of the original figures to investigate resistance to social restraint.

In 1973, Robert and Marijane Osborn confirmed and elaborated the Brant linking of Marvell's "The Unfortunate Lover" with the "herald's wording" at the end of *The Scarlet Letter*. In the following year, Hans Abrahamsson suggested Hester's relationship to the biblical Esther, and Dorothea Kehler found in Hawthorne's first novel an allusion to Shakespeare's *Richard II*. And, in 1975, Louis Owens contended for Hawthorne's having borrowed detail for Dimmesdale and Hester from the characters Walter and Phoebe in James K. Paulding's story, "The Dumb Girl," while Mona Scheuermann linked Chillingworth and Dimmesdale with Caleb Williams and Falkland of William Godwin's novel *Caleb Williams*, and Max. L. Autrey suggested that Roger Chillingworth was drawn from Dr. Chillingworth in James Malcolm Ryder's novel *Varney the Vampire*.

Allusions in *The Scarlet Letter* to Psalms, Proverbs, Song of Solomon, and Ecclesiastes were suggested by Robert Geraldi in 1976. And in a 1977 article (and again in his book in 1987), Frederick Newberry mentioned as works that inform *The Scarlet Letter* not only Cotton Mather's *Magnalia Christi Americana* and John Winthrop's *History*, but also William Howes's *Every Day Book* (regarding the church calendar), Clarendon's *History of the Rebellion* and Guizot's *History of the English Revolution* (regarding the Cromwell period), Sir Walter Scott's novels *Ivanhoe* (concerning the Templars) and *Woodstock* (concerning Oxford), and the Book of Acts (concerning the description of Dimmesdale's voice). Studies bearing on the origins of *The Scarlet Letter* concluded in the 1970s with Stephen Nissenbaum's admirable consideration of the impact of Hawthorne's loss of his Custom House job on the novel, Ronald J. Gervais's treatment of Catholic influences in Hawthorne's narrative, Paula K. White's evaluation of the presence of Puritan theories of history in the work, Donald Darnell's investigation of the role of emblem books on *The Scarlet Letter*, Richard Harter Fogle's suggestion of correspondences between the work of the British Romantics and Hawthorne's writing (including the aforementioned Byron-Hawthorne parallel), and Hyatt H. Waggoner's own confirmation of the Brant discovery of the Andrew Marvell source for the final line of the novel.[10]

In 1980, Arlin Turner published his excellent biography of Hawthorne. The chapter about Hawthorne's dismissal from the Custom House noted, among other matters, the writer's debt to a letter to the editor in the *Boston Post* for his image of himself as the decapitated Surveyor. The chapter on *The Scarlet Letter* discussed the historical Surveyor Pue, the originals of the officials in the Custom House, those who had forced Hawthorne from the Custom House, and the novel's links to some of Hawthorne's tales. Helen Wyatt Ferguson completed her dissertation, "Nathaniel Hawthorne and Charles Wentworth Upham: The Witchcraft Connection"; chapter 6 traced Hawthorne's use of witchcraft in *The Scarlet Letter*. Also, O. M. Brack Jr. ably related Dimmesdale's confession in the marketplace to Samuel Johnson's confession at Uttoxeter. Furthermore, Gloria C. Ehrlich returned to the link earlier offered by Loggins and Fiedler—the incest of brother Nicholas Manning and sisters Anstiss and Margaret Manning with the adultery of Dimmesdale and Hester Prynne—and she elaborated Hawthorne's Manning ancestry fully. Earl R. Hutchison Sr. unpersuasively suggested that Hester Prynne was drawn from the mythological Hetaira Phryne. J. Jeffrey Mayhook treated Hawthorne's novel with regard to heraldry, John G. Bayer with regard to the oral tradition, and Carlanda Green with regard to Dante. Dorena Allen Wright, in 1982, argued that "the chief inspiration for Pearl's part in Dimmesdale's conversion" came from "the vision of the Other World" in Dante's *Divine Comedy* and the anonymous poem *Pearl*. And Nina Baym argued that the inspiration for Hester Prynne was Hawthorne's mother Elizabeth Clarke Manning Hathorne; *The Scarlet Letter* provided Hawthorne's "real tribute to [his mother], and to her influence."[11]

Two years later, Sarah I. Davis elaborated further the parallels between Anne Hutchinson and Hester Prynne, and those between John Cotton and Arthur Dimmesdale. However, Nina Baym supplemented her 1982 study by noting that as a would-be reformer whose perceived error precluded her success, Hester Prynne "cannot but refer to George Sand" rather than Anne Hutchinson.[12] Also in 1984, Sargent Bush Jr. proposed a Salem newspaper source for the prison rose in chapter 1 of *The Scarlet Letter*, and Mona Scheueurmann suggested a link between Hawthorne's novel and early American novels of seduction. Gloria C. Ehrlich published a book that included her Manning work, *Family Themes and Hawthorne's Fiction: The Tenacious Web*. And Philip Young offered, in *Hawthorne's Secret: An Untold Tale*, his own exploration of the presence of the Manning incest in *The Scarlet Letter*, providing documents regarding the original crime.

David Van Leer suggested an Emersonian character to *The Scarlet Letter* in the 1985 *New Essays on "The Scarlet Letter,"* and editor Michael J. Colacurcio offered, in the same volume, a reconsideration of Hawthorne's use of Governor Bellingham and Governor Winthrop. In the following year, Jonathan Arac construed *The Scarlet Letter* as Hawthorne's response to the growing slavery debate, and James Walter observed several affinities between Hawthorne's novel and Dante's *Purgatorio* and *Paradiso*. Furthermore, Thomas Pribek proposed Hawthorne's debt to Francis Baylies for William Blackstone's riding on a bull; Hugh J. Dawson showed that Hawthorne varied his Custom House eagle from the actual carving; and Laurie N. Rozakis developed the Bouve argument, positing Hawthorne's reliance for Hester Prynne on Elizabeth Payne (or Pain). In 1987, Frederick Newberry amplified on a story found in Winthrop and mentioned in 1985 by Colacurcio—the adulterous behavior of a seventeenth-century minister from Maine, Reverend Steven Batchellor—and he also introduced an account of the branding of the minister's wife, Mary

Batchellor, with the letter A for adultery. Reiner Smolinski mentioned the Steven Batchellor case, too, and noted parallels between the death of Arthur Dimmesdale and "the Puritan model," the death of John Knox, as related in Thomas M'Crie's *Life of Knox*.[13]

Amy Schrager Lang considered Hawthorne's use of the Puritans' rendering of Anne Hutchinson. Hugh J. Dawson observed Christian iconography in *The Scarlet Letter*, and Leland S. Person suggested that Hawthorne's language at the beginning of the novel regarding the author's imagined reader was anticipated by his language in one of his love letters to Sophia Peabody. (See also Person's 1988 book, *Aesthetic Headaches*.) Susan Swartzlander indicated Hawthorne's probable reliance for "The Custom-House" introduction on Charles Wentworth Upham's *Lectures on Witchcraft* with regard to treatment of John Hathorne.

Thomas Woodson, in 1988, argued that Hawthorne based Dimmesdale on his nemesis Charles W. Upham, and T. Walter Herbert Jr. explored Hawthorne's modeling Pearl on his daughter Una. David S. Reynolds, in his pioneering work *Beneath the American Renaissance*, related *The Scarlet Letter* to reform movements, sensational literature, and popular humor. He is strongest on sensational literature: "Featuring a likable criminal, oxymoronic oppressors, a reverend rake, scaffold scenes, and sadistic women, [*The Scarlet Letter*] was a meeting ground for key stereotypes from the sensational press." Of special note is that Reynolds paid particular attention to the Salem murder case, which, he argued, influenced Hawthorne's depiction of Chillingworth.[14]

Luther S. Luedtke, in 1989, perceived an Oriental passion in Hester Prynne, perhaps related to Hawthorne's reading in travel literature, and Gabriele Schwab considered *The Scarlet Letter* as critically influenced by the witchcraft theme, and treated Anne Hutchinson as consonant with the witch stereotype. Jean Fagan Yellin asserted that Hawthorne drew on antislavery feminism in his portrayal of Hester, but that the heroine eventually turns from this ideology to that of the Angel in the House. She also argued that Hawthorne avoided the issue of slavery in his major romances because of both his aversion to reformers and his racism. David C. Cody focused on "The Custom-House" introduction, contending that Hawthorne worked within the tradition of palingenesis—the raising of the dead—a metaphor for his artistic process. J. Edward Schamberger discussed Salem architecture and proposed that the Bellingham mansion has an analogue in the Downing-Bradstreet House and that the stucco of the Bellingham mansion has an affinity with that of the Sun Tavern. He also investigated the history and significance of the actual Custom House. Evan Carton analyzed Dimmesdale and Pearl in terms of Hawthorne and Una. And Edward

Wagenknecht, in his 1989 biography of Hawthorne, offered a brief overview of the sources of *The Scarlet Letter*.[15]

At the beginning of the final decade of the twentieth century, John Gatta and Evans Lansing Smith contended, reasonably, that *The Scarlet Letter* is indebted to the Book of Revelation. Douglas Anderson considered the importance for Hawthorne's novel of not only the writings of John Winthrop, but also the tales of the Minotaur—fables of human loneliness, anger, and despair. Elizabeth Aycock Hoffman returned us to Rousseau's *Julie, où la nouvelle Héloise* as a source for *The Scarlet Letter* and, in a Foucauldian context, introduced magazine articles of Hawthorne's time that concerned power relations in prisons. Advancing the view that Hawthorne may have associated the Puritans with the Whigs of his own time, Janet Gabler-Hover suggested in her rhetoric-focused volume an 1838 magazine piece, "Mr. Forrest's Oration," as a possible influence, as well as an 1827 piece about rhetorician James Rush. She also compared Hester and Dimmesdale to Dante's Francesco and Paolo and discussed the relevance of the Quintilian principle.

In 1991, Shari Benstock discussed the Virgin Mary in Hawthorne's novel. Eileen Dreyer postulated Hawthorne's borrowing for *The Scarlet Letter* from a passage in Thomas Broughton's *An Historical Dictionary of All Religions* concerning William Chillingworth on the relation of repentance to confession. She comments, "[Hawthorne's] reading gave him ideas which he worked into his stories loosely, without undue concern for historical accuracy, so long as the effect his borrowing achieved was satisfactory." Alfred H. Marks maintained that Hawthorne's reading of Johann Ludwig Tieck's story "The Elves" influenced his writing of *The Scarlet Letter*—in particular, that Mary's daughter Elfrida helped suggest Hester's Pearl. Emily Miller Budick briefly noted a resonance between Pue and Poe, *The Scarlet Letter* and "The Purloined Letter." In his reading of *The Scarlet Letter*, Sacvan Bercovitch offered occasional hints of origin—as, for example, Rufus Choate's address "The Importance of Illustrating New England History by a Series of Romances" and Ralph Waldo Emerson's view of individualism.[16] Gillian Brown argued that Hawthorne's treatment of Hester and Pearl at the novel's end implies a trust in the progress of property laws for women. And Jennifer Fleischner contended that the resolution, in *The Scarlet Letter*, of the conflict of private and public concerns through faith is related to Hawthorne's approach to the issue of slavery.

Not particularly helpful is James C. Keil's 1992 study, contending that Hawthorne's extensive reading and drawing on that reading in the early part of his career may have been a form of sexual sublimation. But Richard O'Keefe offered a provocative "probable supposition" that Hawthorne's list (in "The Custom-House" introduction) of soon-to-be-forgotten Salem merchants was influenced by Emerson's list (in the poem "Hamatreya") of long-deceased Concord leaders. Interesting in this connection is Emerson's praise for the introduction to *The Scarlet Letter*—it was "*absolutely* perfect in *wit*, in *life*, in *truth*[,] in *genial spirit & good nature & . . .* there [is] nothing equal to it in the language."[17] Haipeng Li wrote about Hawthorne's awareness of the folk art of embroidery and this art's influence on his composing *The Scarlet Letter*. And Toni Morrison published her influential study *Playing in the Dark*, which asserts the Africanist presence in American literature.

Arguing for Chillingworth's sexual impotence, Claudia Durst Johnson claimed, in 1993, "In the text of *The Scarlet Letter*, Hawthorne makes an oblique reference to the issue of impotence" by mentioning the Overbury case—we may recall Reid here—since Overbury's enemy, the Countess of Essex, divorced her husband on the grounds of his impotence. Furthermore, T. Walter Herbert proposed that the sexual problematics of the novel derive from the flawed domestic ideal that Hester nonetheless eventually advocates. Carol M. Bensick found "a precedent for Dimmesdale's bachelorhood" in Cotton Mather's reference, in *Magnalia Christi Americana*, to the unmarried minister of Newbury, Thomas Parker—who is pressured to marry by John Wilson. Bensick also discussed, in another essay, a link between *The Scarlet Letter* and Hawthorne's editorial comment regarding Bunyan in the June 1836 issue of the *American Magazine of Useful and Entertaining Knowledge* (the phrases "laugh, rather than tremble" [in the novel] and "smile, instead of shuddering" [in the magazine]). Christopher D. Felker treated as wonder-cabinets the writings of Cotton Mather and Nathaniel Hawthorne, with some reference to *The Scarlet Letter*, especially "The Custom-House." Will and Mimosa Stephenson recurred to Henry James's comparison of Hawthorne's novel to Lockhart's *Adam Blair*, maintaining, in light of parallels of plot and character, that "it seems likely Hawthorne wrote [*The Scarlet Letter*] in active dialogue with [*Adam Blair*]." And Caroline M. Woidat built on the Morrison thesis, writing that "Hester's plight becomes conflated with that of the African-American other seemingly absent from the text" and that Hawthorne offered in his novel "a case for a gradualist approach to slavery."[18]

In 1994, Jenny Franchot published her study of antebellum Catholic influence in America, *Roads to Rome*; chapter 13, "The Hawthorne Confessional," critiques incisively the pro- and anti-Catholic elements of the novel. Samuel Coale drew attention to mesmerism in Hawthorne's fiction, relating it to, among other things, the scarlet letter and the gaze. And Arnold G. Tew explicated Hawthorne's reference to "P. P., Clerk of this

Parish" (1:3), showing that mention of the humorous rendering of Bishop Gilbert Burnet by Alexander Pope and John Gay allows Hawthorne a comic veil for his anger and offers a suggestion of "seduction and ministerial lust." In the following year, Mara L. Dukats developed Morrison's argument further, stating that "the 'invisible mediating force' (Morrison, *Playing in the Dark,* 46) behind Hester is the Africanist presence, as formulated by Morrison."[19] Recalling Hans Abrahamsson's linking of Hester and Esther, Matthew Gartner propounded parallels between *The Scarlet Letter* and the Book of Esther with regard to characters, plot, theme, and form. Susan Elizabeth Sweeney offered a personal treatment of the Catholic leitmotif in Hawthorne's novel. And the present writer assessed Hawthorne's reliance on Poe's "The Tell-Tale Heart" in *The Scarlet Letter.* (The essay constitutes an intermediate draft of chapter 1 of this book.)

Warranting particular attention is Deborah Gussman's 1995 article, "Inalienable Rights: Fictions of Political Identity in *Hobomok* and *The Scarlet Letter.*" Although the differences between Lydia Maria Child's novel (1824) and Hawthorne's are emphasized, similarities are noted, as well. Some of those mentioned are that both novels are historical works addressing and modifying the ideal of republican citizenship, both are validated by imagined documents, and both delineate "subversive female characters" who are "passionate" and defy "significant social and religious taboos." We may pursue additional correspondences between the two works. In both novels, a woman (Mary Conant, Hester Prynne) who believes that her partner (Charles Brown, Roger Chillingworth) is drowned at sea enters an illicit union (an interracial one with the Indian Hobomok, an adulterous one with the minister Dimmesdale), a union that yields a child (Charles Hobomok Conant, Pearl) who eventually lives abroad, receives a legacy or bequest, and achieves personal success or happiness. Furthermore, both novels touch on antinomianism, the unpardonable sin, free will and determinism, and witchcraft, as well as Isaac Johnson's burial ground. And the critical Byronic phrase cited by Richard Harter Fogle— "electric chain"—appears in *Hobomok,* also. Despite Hawthorne's stating that "I do abhor an Indian story" (10:429), it is certainly possible that *Hobomok,* Child's novel of Salem, was one of the threads of *The Scarlet Letter.*[20]

In 1997, John Gatta wrote further of the Catholic influence on Hawthorne's depiction of Hester: he noted acutely that the comparison of Hester to Mary at the book's opening suggests that "sacred love can indeed coexist with sin . . ." and he judged that by the book's end, "Hester does fulfill a prophetic office of revelation and mediation between humanity and godly love." Laura Hanft Korobkin offered a political rather than a religious context: acknowledging Puritan sources, she focused on the Fugitive Slave Law and on Hester's representing the contemporary reader, who must decide whether to obey the law. In 1998, Samuel Coale developed further his argument regarding the relation of the scarlet letter and the gaze to mesmerism, and Thomas R. Mitchell asserted his view that *The Scarlet Letter* was importantly shaped by Hawthorne's relationship with Margaret Fuller: he writes, "Through Hester, Hawthorne, on one level at least, continues his now-distant dialogue with Fuller and attempts to represent, if not actually to solve, the riddle of Fuller and their relationship." Also, in 1999, Dan McCall reconsidered Hawthorne's debt in *The Scarlet Letter* to J. G. Lockhart's *Adam Blair* and Ralph Waldo Emerson's *Nature*. Elmer Kennedy-Andrews briefly discussed source studies for *The Scarlet Letter* and excerpted works on Hawthorne's novel that feature a historical approach—Michael J. Colacurcio, "'The Woman's Own Choice'"; Larry J. Reynolds, "*The Scarlet Letter* and Revolutions Abroad"; Jonathan Arac, "The Politics of *The Scarlet Letter*"; and Michael David Bell, "Arts of Deception." In 2000, Patricia Crain reconsidered the Marvell source for the end of Hawthorne's novel and the historical locations on which Hawthorne relied, noting that the site of the house of Anne Hutchinson became that of the building of the publisher of *The Scarlet Letter*, Ticknor and Fields.[21]

The origins of *The Scarlet Letter* will inevitably continue to be discussed and clarified; the present bibliography offers a survey of a discipline's work-in-progress. As arguments are added, rejected, accepted, refined, we can only come closer to a fuller understanding of the hue and texture of each thread in Hawthorne's fabric, and of the "subtle interconnectedness" of these myriad threads. Sophia Hawthorne once wrote, "The day will come when there will be pilgrimages for a thread of a shirt which Nathaniel wore in babyhood."[22] The hyperbole is forgivable, and it does anticipate a reality—that scholarly pilgrims have long sought, and will long seek, for a thread of the fabric that Nathaniel made.

Notes

1. Unless otherwise stated, the writing of Nathaniel Hawthorne (and occasionally Sophia Hawthorne) is quoted from *Centenary Edition of the Works of Nathaniel Hawthorne*.

2. Stanton, "Hawthorne, Bunyan, and the American Romances," 165; Turner, "Needs in Hawthorne Biography," 43.

3. Wagenknecht, *Nathaniel Hawthorne*, 84.

4. Ripley, Review of *The Scarlet Letter*, 158; Stephen, *Hours in a Library*, 1:186; Reid, *Yellow Ruff*, 116–17; David S. Reynolds, *Beneath the American Renaissance*, 268.

CHAPTER 1. A TALE BY POE

I am pleased to note that an earlier version of this chapter appeared in the Autumn 1995 issue of *Studies in American Fiction*.

1. For sources for Chillingworth in the three identified clusters, consider the following scholarly works. Regarding Milton's *Paradise Lost*, see Stewart, Introduction, lii–liii; Matthiessen, *American Renaissance*, 305–8; and Abel, "Devil in Boston." Regarding Bunyan's *Pilgrim's Progress*, see Matthiessen, 273, and David E. Smith, *John Bunyan*, 62–66. Regarding versions of Faust, see Stein, *Hawthorne's Faust*. For Cheynell's torment of Chillingworth, see Maes-Jelinek, "Roger Chillingworth," and for Prynne's torment of Laud, see Isani, "Hawthorne and the Branding." For comment on Godwin's *Caleb Williams*, consult Scheuerman, "Outside the Human Circle"; for discussion of Rymer's *Varney the Vampire*, see Autrey, "Source." Reid considers the murder of Sir Thomas Overbury (*Yellow Ruff*), and David S. Reynolds treats the murder of Captain Joseph White (*Beneath the American Renaissance*, 250–51). A possible literary source for Chillingworth that does not fall into any one of the three clusters is Edmund Spenser's *The Faerie Queen*, characters from which may have suggested the doctor's appearance (Stewart, Introduction, lii–liii; "Hawthorne and *The Faerie Queen*," 200–201). A possible historical source is one of Hawthorne's Salem enemies, Richard Saltonstall Rogers (Julian Smith, "Hawthorne and a Salem Enemy").

2. Scholars have tried to date the composition of "The Hall of Fantasy" by attending to Hawthorne's comments on his contemporaries in the first version of that story. Harold P. Miller, considering when Henry Wadsworth Longfellow returned to the United States from England, suggested the time of composition as November 1842 ("Hawthorne Surveys," 228). Buford Jones, focusing on the time of Bronson Alcott's return from Europe, viewed the story as written "between 1 September and 20 October" ("Hall of Fantasy," 1430). The editors of the first volume of Hawthorne's letters, also noting Longfellow's return, asserted that "The Hall of Fantasy" was "probably written in October or early November" of 1842 (*Centenary Edition*, 15:662 n). John J. McDonald, attending to Hawthorne's knowledge of Longfellow's return, posits the time of composition as "16 November to 17 December 1842" ("Old Manse Period Canon," 23).

Poe quoted Hawthorne's comment about him from "The Hall of Fantasy" in the *Saturday Museum* biography, published on 25 February 1843 and 4 March 1843; see Pollin, "Poe's Authorship," 165.

3. Quotations from Edgar Allan Poe's work are cited in the text with short titles.

4. Ripley, Review of *The Scarlet Letter*, 158–59. For the quoted excerpts in the novel, see Cameron, "Literary News." For a portion of the review, see Ripley, "[Gothic, the Supernatural, the Imagination]." For Ripley's mixed evaluation of Poe, see his Review of *The Works of the Late Edgar Allan Poe*.

5. Turner, "Hawthorne's Literary Borrowings," 558; Beebe, "Fall of the House of Pyncheon"; Millicent Bell, *Hawthorne's View*, 81, 182; Pfister, *Production of Personal Life*, 43–44. Alfred H. Marks contended that Hawthorne satirized Poe in "Egotism; or, the Bosom Serpent" ("Two Rodericks and Two Worms"). Arlin Turner suggested that Hawthorne satirized Poe in "P's Correspondence" (*Nathaniel Hawthorne*, 159), though Poe's notice of the work does not indicate that he saw himself in it (*Collected Writings* 3:88–89).

6. Lowell's fiancée Maria White wrote to Caroline King on 4 October 1842, "James has gone to Portland today to engage John Neill [Neal] as a contributor [to *The Pioneer*] and will go this week to Concord to see Hawthorne and obtain his services." See Maria White Lowell to King. (Published by permission of the Schlesinger Library, Radcliffe Institute, Harvard University.) For a description of the manuscript of this letter, see Loewentheil and Edsall, *Poe Catalogue*, 56. Caroline King was later the author of *When I Lived in Salem*. Perhaps Lowell visited the Hawthornes by himself at this time; certainly he did visit them with Maria on 2 November. (See Maria White Lowell to Sarah Shaw.) Further consideration of Lowell's time at the Hawthornes and the Lowell-Hawthorne relationship is offered in chapter 2.

7. Writing in his review of Thomas Middleton's plays of the feeling of "*bodily remorse*" after one commits murder, James Russell Lowell states in a footnote, "This *bodily* feeling is painted with a terrible truth and distinctness of coloring in Hood's 'Dream of Eugene Aram,' and with no less strength by the powerful imagination of Mr. Poe, in his story of the 'Tell-tale heart,' on page 29 of the present number" ("Plays of Thomas Middleton," 37 n). (Poe later acknowledged this praise—see *Letters*, 1:221.) Poe mentions Thomas Hood's "The Dream of Eugene Aram" in August 1845 (*Collected Writings* 3:202); he also mentioned Edward Bulwer-Lytton's *Eugene Aram* in December 1835 (*Complete Works* 8:95) and April 1841 (*Complete Works* 10:132). Hawthorne reviewed Hood's *Poems* in May 1846, though without treating

"The Dream of Eugene Aram" ("Simms's *Views and Reviews*; Hood's *Poems*," 23:239–41). Although Hood's poem has an affinity with "The Tell-Tale Heart" and *The Scarlet Letter*, parallels are not strong enough to suggest its having served as a source.

8. James Russell Lowell, ed., *Pioneer*, inner wrappers of second issue.

9. In writing "The Tell-Tale Heart," Poe also relied on Charles Dickens's "The Clock-Case: A Confession Found in a Prison in the Time of Charles the Second" for the placement of the chair over the buried body and the murderer's difficulty in looking in the eye of his victim (Krappe, "Possible Source"; *Collected Works* 3:790). And he referred to a variety of biblical verses with several of the phrases in the story (including Psalms 113:6 and Phillipians 2:10 with "I heard all things in the heaven and in the earth" [*Collected Works* 3:792]; Exodus 20:21, Deuteronomy 4:11, and 5:22 with "thick darkness" [*Collected Works* 3:793]; and John 13:1 with "The old man's hour had come!" [*Collected Works* 3:795]). All citations to the Bible here and hereafter are to the King James Version.

10. See *Appendix*, 31–62. Webster's speech was reprinted in his *Speeches and Forensic Arguments*, 450–89.

11. Mellow, *Nathaniel Hawthorne*, 291; Moore, *Salem World*, 165–66.

12. Reference to the weapon that killed Joseph White was not made in the first appearance of the notebook entry in the Hawthorne edition (8:155) because the copytext was Sophia Hawthorne's version of the notebook, and she must have deleted the phrase (8:155; see also 8:701). She apparently shared a sensitivity regarding the White murder with Caroline King, who destroyed her own writing on the subject because it was "indiscreet" (*When I Lived in Salem*, 9). The full notebook entry was first published in Nathaniel Hawthorne, *Hawthorne's Lost Notebook*, 42.

One wonders if Hawthorne knew that the ship *Mary and Eliza*, which his father Nathaniel Hathorne had commanded in 1804, had been owned by Joseph White. (See Hoeltje, "Captain Nathaniel Hathorne," 346.)

13. George Parsons Lathrop, *Complete Works*, 3:9; David S. Reynolds, *Beneath the American Renaissance*, 251; Matthiessen, *American Renaissance*, 214–15; Moore, *Salem World*, 164.

14. Interesting Hawthorne-Webster links might be added. Hawthorne referred to the Whig view of Webster as "a disreputable character" in 1838 (15:230) and termed him "a majestic brute" in 1845 (8:258). Still, Hawthorne served as recording secretary of the Salem Lyceum when Webster spoke about the United States Constitution in 1848 (16:244–45), and historian and Whig leader William H. Prescott appealed for Webster's assistance regarding Hawthorne's imminent loss of his position at the Salem Custom House in 1849. Forwarding Prescott's letter, Webster wrote to William M. Meredith, secretary of the treasury, "I suppose it will be for the best to leave Mr. Hawthorne where he is, for the present" (See Cameron, "New Light," 4, and Mellow, *Nathaniel Hawthorne*, 296). But according to J. C. Derby, Webster wrote to Prescott, "How can you, a Whig, . . . do such a thing, as to recommend the continuance in office, of a man of the politics of Hawthorne?" (Derby, *Fifty Years*, 327). For a comparison of Hawthorne's negative view of Webster (allegedly revealed in "The Great Stone Face") with his wife's positive view, see Julian Hawthorne's *Nathaniel Hawthorne and His Wife*, 1:476–81. For a listing of several letters by Sophia Hawthorne touching on Daniel Webster, see McDonald, "Guide," 282–83. For a treatment of the

possible relationship of *The Scarlet Letter* to the Fugitive Slave Law, notoriously supported by Daniel Webster, see Korobkin, "Scarlet Letter of the Law."

15. Arlin Turner's doctoral dissertation, "Study of Hawthorne's Origins," provided the second and third of these Hawthorne links to *Macbeth*, 68–69. Turner also notes a passage in Hawthorne's *The Marble Faun* that is suggestive of the sleepwalking scene. A connection between "Young Goodman Brown" and *Macbeth* is suggested by Frank Davidson, "Young Goodman Brown," 69. An excellent discussion of "The Tell-Tale Heart" and *Macbeth* is offered by Wilbur, "Poe," 6–8.

16. Julian Hawthorne, *Hawthorne Reading*, 122.

17. Gross, "Poe's Revision," 18–20; Regan, "Hawthorne's 'Plagiary,'" 284–92; McKeithan, "Poe and the Second Edition," 257, 262–68.

18. For Poe's toast, see Thomas and Jackson, *Poe Log*, 243. For Poe's library, see Stoddard, *"Put a Resolute Hart to a Steep Hill,"* 26.

19. Park Benjamin had been editor of the *New England Magazine* and publisher there of fifteen Hawthorne stories; however, Hawthorne may have been irritated because Benjamin had broken up his collection "The Story-Teller" (see "Fragment, to Elizabeth P. Peabody," 18:89; see also Adkins, "Early Projected Works," 132–33). For further background on Benjamin, see Hoover, *Park Benjamin*; for additional considerations of Hawthorne and Benjamin, see Turner, "Park Benjamin," and Gilkes, "Hawthorne." During different portions of Poe's stay in New York City in 1837 and 1838, Benjamin was assisted by Charles Fenno Hoffman, Robert Montgomery Bird, and Robert M. Walsh (Chielens, *American Literary Magazines*, 19).

20. Benjamin, Review of *The Token* (1838), 487; Review of *The Token* (1837), 407. For the review of the 1837 *Token*, see Idol and Jones, *Nathaniel Hawthorne, Contemporary Reviews,* 15. For the anticipation of Hawthorne's essay on Fessenden, see Benjamin, "Thomas Green Fessenden." Lowell may have had Benjamin's original comment in mind when he referred to Hawthorne as "a man of acknowledged genius," Review of *Historical Tales for Youth*, 42. Benjamin's expression of admiration for Hawthorne in 1837 seems to anticipate Herman Melville's famous dedication to *Moby-Dick* (1851): "IN TOKEN OF MY ADMIRATION FOR HIS GENIUS, This Book is Inscribed TO NATHANIEL HAWTHORNE" (*Writings*, 6:vii).

21. Other items in the *American Monthly Magazine* of this period also merit mention. For example, the April 1837 issue included Park Benjamin's review of Thomas Green Fessenden's satirical poem *Terrible Tractoration* (previously reviewed by Hawthorne in the *American Magazine of Useful and Entertaining Knowledge* [23:230–34]), and the December 1837 issue featured William Austin's short story, "Martha Gardner; or, Moral Re-action" (considered by Brook Thomas to have an affinity with *The House of the Seven Gables* [*Cross-examinations of Law and Literature*, 51–52]).

22. Regarding Poe's employment goal, see Thomas and Jackson, *Poe Log*, 79. For the description of the *New-England Farmer*, see McCorison, "Thomas Green Fessenden," 14.

23. See [Advertisement for Bowles & Dearborn]; [Boston Map]; and the Boston directory for 1827. The Bowles & Dearborn bookshop is discussed by Mary E. Phillips (*Edgar Allan Poe*, 1:295–99), but with erroneous information regarding Poe's supposed trip to London before his stay in Boston. Bowles & Dearborn published the *United States Literary Gazette* and the *Christian Examiner*, as well as various books.

The printer of Fessenden's *New England Farmer's Almanack, for 1828* was John B. Russell, later the printer of the first edition of Hawthorne's *Twice-Told Tales*.

24. Thomas and Jackson, *Poe Log*, 83.

25. It is interesting to note that Hawthorne's future sister-in-law, Elizabeth Palmer Peabody, had stayed with the Fessendens in 1822—his future wife Sophia Peabody had written, "I am *very* glad to hear you are at Mr. Fessenden's where you are so pleasantly situated." See Sophia Hawthorne to Elizabeth Palmer Peabody, 2 November 1822. (Published by permission of the Berg Collection of English and American Literature, The New York Public Library, Astor, Lenox and Tilden Foundations.)

26. See Kopley, "*Very* Profound Under-current," 148–49; and *Narrative of Arthur Gordon Pym of Nantucket,* xxv, 239 n.

27. For Longfellow's advice in his 19 March 1843 letter to Hawthorne, see Longfellow, *Letters,* 2:519. Poe's other contributions to *The Pioneer* were "Lenore" (February 1843) and "Notes upon English Verse" (March 1843), where he offered scansion of Longfellow verses. Hawthorne's positive attitude toward Poe in early 1843 may be suggested by his responsiveness to Poe's invitation to contribute a story and a portrait to the *Stylus.* On 17 April 1843, both Lowell and Sophia Hawthorne reported Hawthorne's acceptance of the invitation (Poe, *Complete Works* 17:142; Sophia Hawthorne to Maria Louisa Hawthorne, 17 April 1843). See also her letter to her mother, Mrs. Elizabeth Palmer Peabody, 20 April 1843.

28. The dating of Hawthorne's beginning work "in earnest" on *The Scarlet Letter* is offered by Larry J. Reynolds in "*The Scarlet Letter* and Revolutions Abroad," 57. A discussion and listing of the obituaries of Poe and memorial pieces about Poe appearing in the year after his death are provided by Pollin, "Posthumous Assessment."

29. The variorum edition of Poe, edited by T. O. Mabbott, *(Collected Works)* offers the 1850 *Works* text of "The Tell-Tale Heart," with variants from the *Pioneer* and *Broadway Journal* texts of the story identified at the base of the page. None of the material quoted here varies from the *Pioneer* text except for the word "Death," which was, in *The Pioneer*, "death." (See James Russell Lowell, *Pioneer,* 30.) Mabbott does not list the lower-case variant.

30. Another Poe work that might have reinforced for Hawthorne the idea of the revelatory heart is the "Marginalia" installment in the January 1848 issue of *Graham's Magazine*, which gave the title of the unwritable true autobiography as "My Heart Laid Bare" (*Collected Writings* 2:322–23). Poe writes that "The paper [of this autobiography] would shrivel and blaze at every touch of the fiery pen" (*Collected Writings* 2:323); Hawthorne writes in "The Interior of a Heart" that Dimmesdale, confessing obliquely from the pulpit, had thought that "the only wonder was, that they [his congregants] did not see his wretched body shrivelled up before their eyes, by the burning wrath of the Almighty!" (1:143–44).

31. For a formal link between "The Tell-Tale Heart" and *The Scarlet Letter,* see chapter 4.

It is interesting to recall Edward Stone's observation ("More on Hawthorne and Melville," 66) that Herman Melville wrote in *Moby-Dick,* "For all men tragically great are made so through *a certain morbidness*" (Melville, *Writings,* 6:74; Stone's emphasis) even as Hawthorne had written in chapter 10 of *The Scarlet Letter,* "Yet Mr. Dimmesdale would perhaps have seen this individual's character more perfectly, if *a certain morbidness*, to which sick hearts are liable, had not rendered him suspicious of all mankind" (1:130; Stone's emphasis). It is certainly possible that Melville was influenced by this Poe-permeated chapter of Hawthorne's novel. Furthermore, Starbuck's looking at the sleeping Ahab, that "Terrible old man!" whose closed eyes looked toward the "tell-tale" (6:235), may recall to us Poe's "The Tell-Tale Heart." And the association of *Moby-Dick* with Poe's tale becomes even stronger when we note that the monomaniacal Ahab—linked (by "half-slouched hat" [6:161] and swinging cabin light [6:235]) with the evil-eyed, guilty Jonah (6:43–45)—speaks of dismemberment (6:168).

Another debt to Poe's "The Tell-Tale Heart" seems present in chapter 11 of Frederick Douglass's 1845 *Narrative of the Life of Frederick Douglass*. Douglass writes of an angry Master Hugh Auld, "He raved, and swore" (73), recalling Poe's writing, as the narrator of "The Tell-Tale Heart," "I raved—I swore!" (*Collected Works* 3:797). Furthermore, Douglass writes that by "working steadily," he was able to allay suspicion of his imminent flight north—indeed, his master "thought I was never better satisfied with my condition than at the very time during which I was planning my escape (74). Similarly, Poe's narrator asserts, "I was never kinder to the old man than during the whole week before I killed him" (*Collected Works* 3:792). Douglass was living in Lynn, Massachusetts, when Poe's tale appeared in *The Pioneer* in January 1843. He was, of course, involved in Boston's abolitionist movement, as was the editor of *The Pioneer*, James Russell Lowell. Douglass probably read Poe's work and later alluded to it as he wrote his own story. This is not so surprising for, as J. Gerald Kennedy has pointed out, Poe and Douglass shared a defiant attitude toward paternalistic authority. (See "Trust No Man," 228.)

32. For the comment on Hawthorne's "prevailing method of expanding each idea," see Turner, "Hawthorne's Methods," 305; for elaboration of this view regarding *The Scarlet Letter*, see 307, 309–12.

33. Abel, "Immortality vs. Mortality," 570.

34. That Matthew Maule's descendant Holgrave was the murderer of Judge Pyncheon has been argued in Cox, "'Who Killed Judge Pyncheon?'"

35. Thornton, "Hawthorne, Poe, and a Literary Ghost," 151–52.

CHAPTER 2. A POEM BY LOWELL

1. For further information on the historical and literary connections, consult the following references. For Nathaniel Manning, see Loggins, *Hawthornes*, 87–95, 278–79; Fiedler, *Love and Death,* 229–30; Ehrlich, *Family Themes,* 35–37; and Young, *Hawthorne's Secret*, 124–27, 165. For Michael Wigglesworth, see Claudia Durst Johnson, *Understanding "The Scarlet Letter,"* 57–64. For Rousseau's Saint-Preux, see Loggins, *Hawthornes,* 279–83; Fiedler, *Love and Death,* 228–29; and Hoffman, "Political Power," 18. With regard to Lockhart's Adam Blair, see Sir Nathaniel, Review of *The Scarlet Letter*, 52; James, *Hawthorne*, 111–13; and Stephenson and Stephenson, *"Adam Blair."* And for Paulding's Avery, see Owens, "Paulding's 'The Dumb Girl.'" John Cotton has been effectively put forth by Michael Colacurcio ("Footsteps of Ann Hutchinson," 462–66, 485– 94). (See chapter 3 for more on the Antinomian Controversy.) Charles Wentworth Upham, a former minister

who became Hawthorne's political enemy, has also been suggested as an influence on Hawthorne's creation of Dimmesdale (Woodson, "Hawthorne, Upham, and *The Scarlet Letter*"), but Hawthorne's sympathetic treatment of his fictional minister tends to argue against this view.

2. Smolinski, "Covenant Theology," 223; Thomas F. Walsh, "Dimmesdale's Election Sermon"; Newberry, *Hawthorne's Divided Loyalties*, 191.

3. For the date of publication of *A Year's Life*, see Blanck and Winship, *Bibliography of American Literature*, 6:23–24. For Lowell's comments to Longfellow on *A Year's Life*, see James Russell Lowell, *Letters*, 1:98–99. For a discussion of reviews of *A Year's Life*, see McFadyen, "The Contemporaneous Reputation of James Russell Lowell" (23–35).

4. Barrett to Lowell, 31 Mar. 1842. Published by permission of the Houghton Library, Harvard University.

5. For the unworkable agreement, see Tucker, "James Russell Lowell and Robert Carter," 191. For further information on the early demise of Lowell's *Pioneer*, see his letter to Poe of 24 March 1843 (*Complete Works* 17:138–39); as well as Scudder, *James Russell Lowell*, 1:107–8; Sculley Bradley, Introduction, xxiv–xxvi, and his "Lowell, Emerson, and *The Pioneer*"; Howard, *Victorian Knight-Errant*, 129–34; Martin Duberman, *James Russell Lowell*, 52–53; and Lease, "Robert Carter."

6. James Russell Lowell, *Letters*, 1:71–72.

7. For discussion of the source for "A Legend of Brittany," "Les Trois Moines Rouges," see Charles Oran Stewart, *Lowell and France*, 23–26. For Lowell's reading French in his boyhood and youth, see 9–10. See also James Russell Lowell, *Letters*, 1:6. The Houghton Library holds the Charles Sumner copy of the 1840 *Chants Populaires* and a Lowell copy of the 1860 edition. By the time he was writing "A Legend of Brittany," Lowell certainly knew Sumner: when Lowell and his *Pioneer* co-editor Robert Carter took action against their publishers Leland and Whiting in March 1843, they provided a bond signed by lawyers Sumner and George S. Hillard (Howard, *Victorian Knight-Errant*, 130). It is relevant to note that Lowell drew from a book of Breton legends for his 1861 poem "The Washers of the Shroud"—a book that he had borrowed from Charles Eliot Norton (Pound, "Lowell's 'Breton Legend'").

8. "Les Trois Moines Rouges" was translated into English for me by Jill Landis, a Penn State graduate student in French.

9. For Irving's reliance on "Peter Klaus" for "Rip Van Winkle," see Pochmann, "Irving's German Sources," 489–97. For contemporary awareness of Irving's debt to "Peter Klaus," see "Peter Klaus: The Legend of the Goatherd—Rip Van Winkle."

10. Briggs to Lowell, quoted by permission of the Archives of American Art, Smithsonian Institution.

11. Blanck and Winship, *Bibliography of American Literature*, 6:25.

12. For the comment about Lowell's first meeting Hawthorne, consult Edward Everett Hale, *James Russell Lowell and His Friends*, 84. For the date of the wedding of Nathaniel Hawthorne and Sophia Peabody, see Mellow, *Nathaniel Hawthorne and His Times*, 175. For Sophia Peabody's early friendship with Maria White, see Mellow, 221, and Rose Hawthorne Lathrop, *Memories of Hawthorne*, 119. For the presence of Sophia Peabody and Maria White at the first class of Fuller's "Conversations," see Vernon, *Poems of Maria Lowell*, 10. For the date of that class, see von Mehren, *Minerva and the Muse*, 114.

13. Lowell asserts his early discipleship to Hawthorne in a letter to Hawthorne of 24 April 1851. (Quotation by permission of the Berg Collection of English and American Literature, The New York Public Library, Astor, Lenox and Tilden Foundations.) The letter is mentioned in Duberman, *James Russell Lowell*, 487 n.

14. Lowell, "The First Client," 230. "The First Client" was noted as Lowell's by E. E. Brown, 37–38; Underwood, *The Poet and the Man,* 22; Littlefield, "James Russell Lowell in 1842," xxv and xxix; and Cooke, *A Bibliography of James Russell Lowell,* 22. The short comic tale anticipates elements of both Poe's "The Man of the Crowd" and Melville's "Bartleby the Scrivener."

15. The reviews of *A Year's Life* are considered in McFadyen, "Contemporaneous Reputation," 23–35.

16. For the 4 October 1842 letter concerning Lowell's visiting Hawthorne, see Maria White Lowell to Caroline King. (The passage from this letter is published by permission of the Schlesinger Library, Radcliffe Institute, Harvard University.) See also chapter 1, note 6. Sophia Hawthorne made her statement about Lowell's offer to her husband in a letter to her mother, Mrs. Elizabeth Palmer Peabody, 28 February 1843. (Publication of the quoted passage from the letter of Sophia Hawthorne is by permission of the Berg Collection of English and American Literature, The New York Public Library, Astor, Lenox and Tilden Foundations.)

17. Publication of the quoted passages from the letters of Mary Peabody and Sophia Hawthorne is by permission of the Berg Collection of English and American Literature, The New York Public Library, Astor, Lenox and Tilden Foundations. The Mary Peabody letter, written after 2 October 1842, is mentioned in John J. McDonald, "Guide to Primary Source Materials," 272.

18. Publication of the quoted passage from the Maria Lowell letter (Lowell to Shaw, 4 Nov. 1842) is by permission of the Massachusetts Historical Society. Sarah Blake Sturgis Shaw was the beautiful and socially-conscious wife of the affluent Frank Shaw, who was a supporter of Brook Farm and a translator, for the *Harbinger*, of two novels by George Sand, *Consuelo* and *The Countess of Rudolstadt*. (See Milne, *George William Curtis,* 85; and Delano, *"Harbinger,"* 36). A long-time friend of Maria Lowell's, Sarah Shaw was also a friend of both Elizabeth Peabody and Sophia Hawthorne. She and her sister-in-law Anna Blake Shaw visited the Hawthornes in Concord in June 1843 (15:696, 697 n). Frank Shaw evidently later provided some financial support to the Hawthornes (16:201; see also Rose Hawthorne Lathrop [117]). The Shaws' son, Robert Gould Shaw, was killed in 1863 at Fort Wagner while leading the famous black regiment, the Massachusetts 54th. His sister, Josephine Shaw, married Lowell's nephew Charles Russell Lowell, who, in 1864, was also killed in the Civil War.

19. For the various datings of Hawthorne's composition of "The Hall of Fantasy," see chapter 1, note 2. I contend that Hawthorne completed the work after the Lowells' visit on 2 November 1842 because otherwise he would probably have handed the story to the editor of *The Pioneer* rather than mail it on 17 December. For Lowell's comment about Hawthorne's genius, see James Russell Lowell, Review of *Historical Tales for Youth*, 42. This comment may well allude to an earlier comment about Hawthorne's genius by Park Benjamin. (See chapter 1, page 27, and note 20.)

20. Lowell wrote to his partner Robert Carter on 19 January 1843, "Hawthorne should be paid, & Neal & Poe," and on 24 January 1843, "Tell H. [Hawthorne] why

we do not pay him immediately, & that I am personally responsible for the debt." (See Tucker, "James Russell Lowell," 204, 208.) Hawthorne wrote to Carter on 1 February 1843, "I did not intend to make a demand for immediate payment of my last contribution," but Sophia wrote to her mother more bluntly on 28 February 1843, "James Lowell owes us seventy dollars I believe. I am sorry for him but we want it" (15:669, 669 n). Sophia Hawthorne, in Boston, informed her husband of the failure of *The Pioneer*, and Nathaniel Hawthorne responded on 16 March 1843, "It is queer news that thou tellest me about the Pioneer. I expected it to fail in due season, but not quite so soon. Not improbably we shall have to wait months for our money" (15:678). Leon Howard states, "All told, it is doubtful whether the editors [of *The Pioneer*] paid out more than seventy-five dollars to their authors while their magazine was alive" (*Victorian Knight-Errant,* 133). For an elaboration of Lowell's debts after the failure of *The Pioneer*, see Bradley's introduction to the magazine (James Russell Lowell, *Pioneer*, xxv–xxvi) and Robert Carter's 29 March 1843 letter in Lease, "Robert Carter."

21. The Lowells' visit to the Hawthornes in Concord after the 3 March 1843 birth of Una is evident from Maria Lowell's 16 January 1845 letter to Sophia Hawthorne. The letter is included in Julian Hawthorne, *Nathaniel Hawthorne and His Wife*, 1:283–84; and furnished in facsimile in Lowell, Maria White, *Letter*. For the date of the wedding of James Russell Lowell and Maria White, see Scudder, *James Russell Lowell*, 2:132; and Duberman, *James Russell Lowell*, 68. For Lowell's inscription to Hawthorne in *Conversations on Some of the Old Poets*, see Scudder, 2:419, and Tucker, "James Russell Lowell and Robert Carter," 217. The inscription appears in the "List of Copies of the 'Conversations' to be given away by the Don." ("The Don" is Robert Carter.) Carter dated this list of twenty copies "Dec. 1844." For a facsimile of the list, see Hale, *James Russell Lowell,* 92–93. For Lowell's reference to Hawthorne's "right in any gathering of poets" in *Conversations*, see 119. For the second reference to Hawthorne in *Conversations*, see 212.

22. The Houghton Library holds several first editions of *Poems*: one is inscribed by Lowell to William Henry Channing and features an original handwritten sonnet; another is inscribed by Lowell to Ralph Waldo Emerson and also features an original handwritten sonnet; a third is inscribed to E. H. Bartol (daughter of Lowell's friend Cyrus Augustus Bartol, who was the successor to Lowell's father Charles Lowell as minister of Boston's West Church); and a fourth is inscribed from publisher John Owen to Henry Wadsworth Longfellow. The Berg Collection of the New York Public Library has three large-print copies of the first edition of *Poems*; two of these are inscribed by Lowell—one volume to his friend G. W. Richardson, and the other to Ann A. Gray. The Berg also holds a standard first edition of the volume, inscribed by Longfellow to Emmeline Austin Wadsworth. The *National Union Catalogue* notes the Harvard College Library copy, presented by John Owen. The catalogue for the Stephen H. Wakeman Sale lists a copy that Lowell inscribed to "C. E. Briggs," Charlotte Briggs, the daughter of Lowell's friend Charles F. Briggs. See item 810. This copy is now held by the American Antiquarian Society. The *Bibliography of American Literature* mentions this inscribed copy, as well as another inscribed copy at the University of Virginia. Eva M. Chandler, cataloguing assistant at the Special Collections Department of the University Library at the University of Virginia, adds that the inscribed copy was sold at auction (Swann Galleries, 21 Nov. 1974). The inscription is by Lowell's friend, Thomas Wentworth Higginson.

For information on Lowell's contract for the 1844 *Poems*, see note 33.

23. James Russell Lowell, "Ballad of the Stranger" (*The Token*, 136; *Uncollected Poems*, 27) and *Conversations*, 136.

24. The date of Hawthorne's writing "Egotism, or the Bosom Serpent" is offered in McDonald, "Old Manse Period Canon," 25. Lowell's figure for the desire for power, a serpent, appears in "A Legend of Brittany," *Poems*, 35, 44. Julian Hawthorne's judgment of his father's attitude toward a friend's work appears in *Hawthorne Reading*, 125.

25. Rufus Wilmot Griswold had solicited Hawthorne's contribution for *Graham's Magazine*, and Hawthorne had responded positively in his letter of 2 July 1843 (15:693–94). On 9 January 1844, Sophia Hawthorne wrote to her mother that Griswold had promised "five dollars per page, & the liberty of drawing for the money the moment the article was published, and the number of pages thus ascertained" (15:694 n; see also Rose Hawthorne Lathrop, *Memories of Hawthorne*, 69–73, and Sanborn, *Hawthorne and His Friends*, 31). For bibliographical information on "Earth's Holocaust," see 10:579. McDonald infers that Hawthorne had completed "Earth's Holocaust" by 9 January 1844 because of Sophia Hawthorne's stating, in the noted letter of that date, "My husband will dispatch a budget to Mr. Hillard's care, containing a paper which he is to send to Mr. Griswold, editor of 'Graham's Magazine'" (McDonald, "Old Manse Period Canon," 28; see also Rose Hawthorne Lathrop, 69).

26. For Poe's 19 October 1843 letter to Lowell, see *Letters*, 1:238. For Poe's 15 December 1846 letter to Eveleth, see *Letters*, 2:332. George W. Eveleth, a young correspondent of Poe's, had asked in a letter of 13 October 1846, "Also in 'Graham's' for March 1844, is the notice of Lowell's 'Legend of Brittany' by yourself?" (*Letters*, 8). Poe acknowledged his authorship in his 15 December 1846 response. Lowell may also have suspected that Poe had written the review: Lowell wrote to Poe on 6 March 1844 noting that he had inferred Poe's authorship in the "editorial matter (critical)" of *Graham's Magazine* but that Graham had denied Poe's hand (Poe, *Complete Works*, 17:160). If, as Dwight Thomas and David K. Jackson suggest, the March 1844 issue of *Graham's* appeared "before 22 February" (*Poe Log*, 452), then it is possible that Lowell was referring to Poe's review of *Poems*, a review that Poe had promised. (See *Letters*, 1:238.) If Lowell was referring to material in an earlier issue of *Graham's*, then his letter is still pertinent in that it indicates Lowell's inclination to try to identify Poe's authorship, an effort that he would likely have made again regarding the March issue, and surely successfully.

27. Poe, *Letters*, 1:238–39.

28. Some people in the Boston area would have been more than usually informed about the church organ when *Poems* was published because of a memorable lecture about the organ that Henry Russell Cleveland had given at the Odeon in Boston in the spring of 1841. (See the Hillard memoir in Henry Russell Cleveland, *Selection*, xxvi.) Although the lecture was never published, Cleveland's review of William Gardiner's *The Music of Nature*, appearing first in the *New York Review* and then in the memorial volume for Cleveland (who died in June 1843), featured considerable commentary on the organ, 157–97. While Hawthorne was reponsive to Lowell's church organ passage, he seems to have had some reservations about the music of the organ itself. In October 1863 he declined James T. Fields's invitation to attend the dedication of a new organ, writing, "I have no ear for an organ or a jews-harp, nor for any instrument

between the two" (18:605). And his narrator in the 1837 sketch "Sunday at Home" writes that if he were within the nearby church, the sound of the choir and "the massive melody of the organ" would fall "with a weight upon me" (9:24). But the narrator adds that, at a distance, the sound of choir and organ "thrills through my frame, and plays upon my heart-strings, with a pleasure both of the sense and spirit." He notes, as well, "Heaven be praised, I know nothing of music, as a science; and the most elaborate harmonies, if they please me, please as simply as a nurse's lullaby" (9:24).

29. The authorship of the *Tribune* review is not known; however, Lowell probably met with the *Tribune*'s editor, Horace Greeley, a year earlier. For Lowell's planned visit with Greeley in January 1843, see Tucker ("James Russell Lowell," 201). Greeley may have written the review.

30. Peterson, Review of *Poems, Ladies' National Magazine*, March 1844, 97. For Peterson's earlier short notice of *Poems*, see the February 1844 issue of the *Ladies' National Magazine*. The review of Lowell's *A Year's Life*, to which Peterson refers in his review of *Poems*, appeared in the April 1842 issue of *Graham's Magazine*. Peterson anticipated his March 1844 review's remarks on the church organ passage in "A Legend of Brittany" when he wrote to Lowell, on 10 January 1844, "I think, if one takes this portion of the poem, beginning with the festival day & that incomparable description of the music of a cathedral organ, that nothing can be found, in any American poet, at all approaching it." See Peterson to Lowell, and Prestwich, "Charles Jacob Peterson," 69–71. (This passage is published by permission of the Houghton Library, Harvard University.) George R. Graham later told Lowell that he would have paid $150 to publish "A Legend of Brittany" (Tucker, "James Russell Lowell," 219).

31. Review of *Poems, New Jerusalem Magazine*, 253–54; Review of *Poems, The Critic*, 152; Review of *Poems, Littell's Living Age*, 161–62.

32. Felton, Review of *Poems*, 288, 291. For further information on the "Five of Clubs," see Horace William Shaler Cleveland, *Social Life and Literature*, 39–44; and Hale, *James Russell Lowell and His Friends*, 61. Another positive appraisal that did not quote from "A Legend of Brittany" was offered in the anonymous Review of *Poems*, Portland *Transcript*: this piece mentioned that "A Legend of Brittany" has a "freshness and vigor of thought." A third such appraisal appeared in Review of *Poems*, the *Boston Recorder*, where the unidentified critic refers to "the slower and statelier march of the Sonnets, and the Legend of Brittany." (Neither of these two reviews is collected in McFadyen.) On the other hand, W. A. Davis criticized "A Legend of Brittany" in the March 1844 issue of the *Christian Examiner*, stating, "We would not rest our author's fame on this so common-place performance. Were this his only work, he would offer no claim to a notice here; he would occupy no lofty place in the ranks of the sons of song" (Review of *Poems*, 174). However, Chandler Robbins, pastor of the Second Church of Boston, wrote to Lowell on 23 November 1844, "The Editor of the Christian Examiner sent me your Poems to notice for that periodical—but rejected what I prepared, because they could not consent to praise them so highly." (Lowell later sent Robbins a copy of *Conversations on Some of the Old Poets* [Tucker, "James Russell Lowell," 217].) And others privately indicated favorable responses to Lowell's work. William Henry Channing, liberal minister and editor of *The Present*, thought highly of Lowell's featured poem: thanking Lowell for an inscribed copy of a first edition of *Poems*, Channing wrote on 27 February 1844, "In The Legend of Brittany, you

appear to me to have reached a much unexpected success, for the subject was a very difficult one. Your picture of all confiding love in Margaret is as true as exquisitely beautiful" (Channing to Lowell). And Lydia Maria Child, author and abolitionist, wrote on 25 December 1844 to Maria White (who would be Maria Lowell when she received the letter), "Remember me most affectionately to your *husband*. I have been reading over his last volume lately, and with fresh delight. It abounds with rare gems" (Child to Lowell). (Passages from the letters of Robbins, Channing, and Child are quoted by permission of the Houghton Library, Harvard University.)

Occasionally the church organ passage in "A Legend of Brittany" would be excerpted without a review—for example, *The Columbian* (of Hartford, CT) offered stanzas 41 and 42 ("The Organ") in its 2 March 1844 issue, with the brief introduction, "This powerful description of heavy organ music in a vast Cathedral, is by James Russell Lowell."

33. The contract for *Poems*, signed by Lowell and John Owen and dated 18 December 1843, stipulates that Lowell will receive "ten cents for every copy printed, & ten copies of each edition of five hundred copies" (Lowell and Owen, Contract). (Quoted with the permission of The Pierpont Morgan Library, New York. MA 648.) Accordingly, with 1,100 copies printed, Lowell would have earned at least one hundred dollars—perhaps one hundred and ten dollars—and received twenty copies of the book. For Poe's response to Lowell's letter about the sales of *Poems*, see *Letters*, 1:246.

34. For Griswold's excerpt of "A Legend of Brittany" in the eighth edition of *Poets and Poetry of America*, see 499. For the dating of the publication of this edition, see Blanck and Winship, *Bibliography of American Literature,* 3:290. Lowell denigrated an earlier edition of Griswold's anthology in August 1846, calling the volume, "Mr. Griswold's catacombs" (Tucker, *James Russell Lowell,* 226), but, nonetheless, he sought earlier that year the inclusion of Maria's poetry in Griswold's 1848 *Female Poets of America* (James Russell Lowell, *New Letters*, 16–17).

35. For Lowell's famous couplet on Poe, see *Writings*, 9:72. For Lowell on Poe's drinking, see Thomas and Jackson, *Poe Log*, 536. For Briggs on Poe and the *Broadway Journal*, see Thomas and Jackson, 542, 551, 554–55, 557. Poe does assert in this negative review that Lowell was an expert in "the poetry of *sentiment*," rather than the loftier poetry of "imagination" or "the passions"—but he does not clarify into which category "A Legend of Brittany" falls (*Complete Works* 13:168). For that work to be "the noblest poem, of the same length, written by an American," however, we may infer that Poe must have thought it to be, according to his own classification, one of the more elevated kinds of poetry.

36. The date of the availability of the tenth edition of *Poets and Poetry of America* is in Blanck and Winship, *Bibliography of American Literature*, 3:290. Griswold's comment on Lowell is in the tenth edition of *Poets and Poetry*, 485.

37. It is interesting to note that Griswold offered the primary text of the ballad "Bold Hawthorne," appearing in the October 1842 issue of *Graham's Magazine*. The work is about the involvement of Hawthorne's grandfather Daniel Hathorne, captain of the *True American*, in a sea battle. For Hawthorne's mention (in his 1853 autobiographical sketch) of the poem as it appeared in Griswold's *Curiosities of American Literature*, see 23:379. For analysis of Griswold's inaccurate text, see Dameron, *Bold Hawthorne*. It was also Griswold who first noted in print the existence of Hawthorne's

early romance, *Fanshawe*. Griswold's 1851 mention of this work that Hawthorne preferred to ignore may have been indebted to Samuel Griswold Goodrich, once editor of *The Token* and publisher of Hawthorne's early fiction. For discussion of Griswold's comment and its likely source, see Robinson, "Rufus Wilmot Griswold."

38. James Russell Lowell, *Writings*, 9:59.

39. The inscription is quoted with the permission of the Berg Collection of English and American Literature, The New York Public Library, Astor, Lenox and Tilden Foundations. This copy of the 1849 *Poems* is mentioned by Cohen, "Hawthorne's Library," 137. For the time of the publication of Lowell's 1849 *Poems*, see Blanck and Winship, *Bibliography of American Literature*, 6:31.

40. Lowell's response in his revision of "A Legend of Brittany" to C. C. Felton's criticism is considered by Arthur W. M. Voss, "Lowell's 'A Legend of Brittany." Lowell's admiration for Elizabeth B. Barrett was expressed in *Conversation on Some of the Old Poets*, 37. Barrett's assessment of "A Legend of Brittany" may be found in Browning and Browning, *Browning to His American Friends*, 353.

41. Hawthorne would have been writing the final three chapters of *The Scarlet Letter* between 15 January 1850 and 3 February 1850. According to his 15 January 1850 letter to James T, Fields, "there are three chapters still to be written of 'The Scarlet Letter.' " (16:305–6), and according to his 4 February 1850 letter to Horatio Bridge, "I finished my book only yesterday; one end being in the press in Boston, while the other was in my head here in Salem" (16:311–13). For an argument that Hawthorne inserted chapter 4 late in the composition of *The Scarlet Letter*, see Branch, "From Allegory to Romance." I am not persuaded by Branch's argument; I agree with Rita K. Gollin, who writes, "Branch's essay has the unintended effect of proving how tightly [the novel] is plotted," *American Literary Scholarship*, 32.

42. The Lowell letter to Duyckinck is quoted in Scudder, *James Russell Lowell*,1:283–84. This letter and the letter to Davis are cited in Duberman, *James Russell Lowell*, 488 n. It should be noted that Duyckinck turned Lowell down: "In answer to your friendly letter with the Hawthorne suggestion I am compelled to conclude that little could be done here in the way you propose. Hawthorne is known best among those whose purses are no larger than his own." Duyckinck then goes on to suggest that Lowell propose that Hawthorne publish his collected works with George P. Putnam and thereby gain the needed funds. The passage from the Lowell letter to Davis and that from the Duyckinck letter to Lowell are quoted by permission of the Houghton Library, Harvard University.

We do not know what success Lowell had with Davis or Furness or O'Sullivan. (However, for elaboration of the Lowell-Davis friendship through Lowell's letters, see Hallowell, "Episode.") We do know that the money that was raised in New England was given to George S. Hillard, who, on 17 January 1850, sent it to Hawthorne on behalf of "those who admire your genius and respect your character." (See Julian Hawthorne, *Nathaniel Hawthorne and His Wife*, 1:354–55.) Hawthorne responded on 20 January 1850, admitting his tears at reading Hillard's letter, and adding "There was much that was very sweet—and something too that was very bitter— mingled with that same moisture. It is sweet to be remembered and cared for by one's friends— some of whom know me for what I am, while others, perhaps, know me only through a generous faith—sweet to think that they deem me worth upholding in my poor walk through life. And it is bitter, nevertheless, to need their support" (16:309).

43. Unless otherwise stated, the lines from "A Legend of Brittany" will be quoted from the 1844 edition of James Russell Lowell's *Poems*.

44. The relationship between the unborn infant in "A Legend of Brittany" and the young Pearl in *The Scarlet Letter* would have been strong for Hawthorne—Sophia had had a miscarriage in February 1843, and Una was born in March 1844 (Mellow, *Nathaniel Hawthorne*, 219–20, 239–40). Notably, in his 24 March 1844 letter about Una to his friend George Hillard, Hawthorne was sensitive to the fact that the Hillards had lost an infant—he closed by saying, "next to a child on earth, it is good to have a child in Heaven" (16:24). The release of Margaret's unborn infant to heaven is made possible by its baptism; Ernest W. Baughman has suggested a related point—according to Puritan practice, Pearl could not have been baptized until both her guilty parents had confessed ("Public Confession," 547–48). Whether Hawthorne knew this fact is uncertain.

45. Another item in Hawthorne's catalog of sources is also relevant here. The title of the chapter in which Hester releases her hair, "A Flood of Sunshine" (1:199), and the phrase in that chapter, "the sunshine, pouring a very flood into the obscure forest" (1:203), may owe a debt to Henry Wadsworth Longfellow's *Kavanagh, A Tale* (1849): "Mr. Churchill took occasion to make known to the company his long cherished purpose of writing a poem called 'The Song of the Saw-Mill,' and enlarged on the beautiful associations of flood and forest connected with the theme" (130). Commenting on Longfellow's relevant reading, Kent P. Ljungquist writes that "Longfellow must have just seen [William Cullen] Bryant's 'The Saw-Mill. From the German of Kerner,' which appeared in the February 1848 *Graham's Magazine*" ("Little War," 56 n). Hawthorne's phrases "the margin of the brook" (1:207, 211, 214) and "the mossy trunk" (1:195, 207, 217, 239) in the forest episode are also found in the forest episode in Longfellow, *Kavanagh* (128, 130). Longfellow sent an inscribed copy of his 1849 novel *Kavanagh* to Hawthorne on 19 May 1849 (16:271), and Hawthorne wrote to Longfellow on 5 June 1849 that the book was "a true work of genius, if ever there were one" (16:269). For further comment on the connection between *The Scarlet Letter* and *Kavanagh*, see Woodson ("Hawthorne," 185–86). A possible parallel with the forest scene in *The Scarlet Letter* has been noted in Lockhart's *Adam Blair*; see Stephenson and Stephenson ("Adam Blair," 7).

It must be observed that the sympathetic sun of the forest—part of the "wild, heathen Nature of the forest, never subjugated by human law, nor illuminated by higher truth" (1:203)—is distinct from the judgmental noonday sun of the scaffold scenes.

46. Lowes, *Road to Xanadu*, 56, 480 n.

47. The relevant quatrain in "The Church" is:

> I love to hear the glorious swell
> Of chanted psalm and prayer,
> And the deep organ's bursting heart
> Throb through the shivering air.

See James Russell Lowell, *A Year's Life* (120).

48. James Russell Lowell's comment on balancing sense and spirit appears in *Conversations on Some of the Old Poets*, 78. His comment on Shelley and physical sensation appears in a letter to Maria Lowell's cousin Eliza Webb Lippitt in *New Letters*, 207. Lowell might have read Shelley's poem "Lines to an Indian Air" in the

Posthumous Poems of 1824. For variants given by Robert Browning, see his letter to Leigh Hunt, 266–67. The poem is later retitled "The Indian Serenade."

49. Crews, *Sins of the Fathers*, 146 n.

50. Ibid., 145–48.

51. The possibly sexual pun of "organ-pipe" has been mentioned by Michael Davitt Bell, "Arts of Deception," 49; and Pfister, *Production of Personal Life,* 138–39. It should be added that the phrase "organ pipes" appears, without double entendre, in Longfellow, *Kavanagh,* 169.

The argument developed here plainly speaks to a heterosexual love between unrelated partners in Hawthorne's novel, but there have been many other readings of sexuality in *The Scarlet Letter.* Focusing on Chillingworth and Dimmesdale, David Leverenz discusses homosexual rape (*Manhood,* 270–78); and T. Walter Herbert considers masturbation (*Dearest Beloved,* 190–98). Monika Elbert concurs with and elaborates on Leverenz's view ("Hester on the Scaffold," 246–48, 253). Scott S. Derrick ("Curious Subject") and Karen L. Kilcup ("Ourselves Behind Ourself") also comment on homosexuality in the novel, and Claudia Durst Johnson writes about both impotence and masturbation in that work ("Impotence and Omnipotence"). Considering the ancestral sex scandal in the Manning family, Leslie Fiedler (*Love and Death,* 229–30) and Philip Young (*Hawthorne's Secret,* 115–47) write about incest in *The Scarlet Letter.*

52. David B. Downing is perceptive when he writes that the passage about Dimmesdale's presentation of the Election Sermon "literally throbs with its densely charged presentation of the thematic heart of the novel" ("Swelling Waves," 23). And I agree that the minister's pleasure is complemented by pain—he does feel great guilt for his adultery and his silence. However, I do not agree that Dimmesdale has completely denied his sexual energies and failed to achieve any satisfaction (24). It may be that here Dimmesdale is not so much protected from "intimate contact" with Hester (21) as figuratively permitted it.

53. Briggs offers his judgment of "A Legend of Brittany" in a letter to Lowell, quoted in part in Scudder, *James Russell Lowell,* 1:120. Hawthorne wrote that the conclusion of *The Scarlet Letter* "broke [Sophia's] heart and sent her to bed with a grievous headache—which I look upon as a triumphant success!" (16:311). Sophia Hawthorne later wrote to her sister Mary Mann on 12 February 1850, "[*The Scarlet Letter*] is most powerful, & contains a moral as terrific & stunning as a thunder bolt. It shows that the Law cannot be broken" (16:313 n). Sophia also wrote to Hawthorne's sister, Maria Louisa, on 28 April 1850, "Nathaniel's fame is perfectly prodigious. In Boston I hear the full blast. Some say [*The Scarlet Letter*] is the greatest book that ever was written, & *unqualified* praise comes from the most fastidious highly cultivated & most gifted persons. Mr. Emerson told me the other day that the Introduction was *absolutely* perfect in *wit*, in *life*, in *truth*[,] in *genial spirit* & *good nature* and that there was nothing equal to it in the language—This was immense commendation from him who is never satisfied." (This passage is published with the permission of the Berg Collection of English and American Literature, The New York Public Library, Astor, Lenox and Tilden Foundations.) And Sophia wrote to her sister Elizabeth Peabody on 21 June 1850, "The questioning of its morality is of all criticisms the funniest—especially the notion some short sighted persons have about the author's opinion of the crime! When the whole book is one great tragic chorus of con-

demnation—when such horrible retribution follows, when even the retribution lives & breathes in Pearl from beginning to end" (Edwin Haviland Miller, *Salem Is My Dwelling Place*, 302).

54. Colacurcio, "Sense of an Author," 130.

55. Perhaps Hawthorne's repeatedly referring to his wife Sophia as "my Dove" (see, for example, 15: 290, 294, 295, 296, 299, 305, and 320) owes something to the same phrase in The Song of Solomon (2:14, 5:2, and 6:9).

56. Regarding the minister's not being "a disciple of true love," see Ernest Sandeen, *"Scarlet Letter,"* 428. On Dimmesdale's not regretting his passion, see 427. On his conscience and pride, and his redeeming his passion, see 433. On his appeal as a lover, see 435. Regarding love as "the deep force" of the novel, see 426.

57. For further treatment of the allusion, see Osborn and Osborn, "Another Look at an Old Tombstone"; Crain, *Story of A,* 202, 265–67 n.

58. Marvell, "The Unfortunate Lover," 27.

59. Male, *Hawthorne's Tragic Vision*, 99. Reinforcing the frequent use in *The Scarlet Letter* of the word "fallen" is the frequent use there of the word "lapse" (1:10, 40, 123, 213, 217, 251, 263) and its variants ("lapsed," 1:204; "elapse," 1:96; and "re-lapsed," 1:248). Even as "lapse" indicates passage or period (as in "lapse of time"), it also indicates error—indeed, Original Sin—hence the word, applicable to *The Scarlet Letter,* "postlapsarian." For an interesting essay on the Garden of Eden in Hawthorne, see William H. Shurr, "Eve's Bower."

60. Chillingworth may perhaps be identified as one of "the wicked" who "search out iniquities" in others (Psalms 64:2, 6). Hawthorne may have had the sixty-fourth psalm in mind since the Massachusetts Bay Colony is referred to in *The Scarlet Letter* as a place "where iniquity is dragged out into the sunshine" (1:54), a place where "iniquity is searched out" (1:62). I thank my daughter, Emily Kopley, for noting the verbal correspondences. Clearly, Chillingworth's searching out iniquities is providentially permitted.

61. For the second scaffold scene as an inversion of the crucifixion, involving Hester and Pearl as Mary and Mary Magdalene, and Arthur as a resistant Jesus, see Hugh J. Dawson, "Triptych Design," 13. For the third scaffold scene as a version of the Pietà, see Todd, "Magna Mater," 424; Gervais, "Papist among Puritans," 14; Dawson, 13; Newberry, *Hawthorne's Divided Loyalties*, 176; Evans Lansing Smith, "Re-Figuring Revelations," 100; and Gatta, *American Madonna*, 17–18. An interesting speculation on Hawthorne's comparison of Hester to the Madonna is offered by Jessie Ryon Lucke, "Hawthorne's Madonna Image," who notes that the family of a slave mistress and her children in Cuba was referred to as a holy family in the novel *Juanita*, by Sophia Hawthorne's sister Mary Peabody Mann. Lucke suggests that perhaps Sophia, who, like her sister, had visited Cuba, might have mentioned such terminology to her husband. For the fullest study yet of the relationship of Catholicism to Protestantism in nineteenth-century America, see Jenny Franchot's *Roads To Rome*, which features a chapter on *The Scarlet Letter*, "The Hawthornian Confessional," 260–69. For an autobiographical essay with treatment of Catholicism and *The Scarlet Letter*, see Sweeney, "Madonna."

62. It is noteworthy that, living in Salem at 14 Mall Street (near Forrester Street) in 1849 and 1850, the Hawthornes were very close to a Catholic Church, St. Mary's Church (at Mall and Forrester). As he planned and wrote *The Scarlet Letter*, Haw-

thorne would surely have seen the comings and goings of the St. Mary's parishioners. On 19 August 1849, Sophia Hawthorne wrote from the Mall Street house, "The children are watching the Catholics as they throng to church." (See Sophia Hawthorne to her mother, Mrs. Elizabeth Palmer Peabody. The passage is quoted with the permission of the Berg Collection of English and American Literature, The New York Public Library, Astor, Lenox and Tilden Foundations.) Hawthorne would probably have heard the Catholic congregants, as well: Julian Hawthorne wrote that the Mall Street house was "small and ill-placed in a narrow side-street, with no possibility of shutting out the noise of traffic and domestic alarms" (*Hawthorne and His Circle*, 5–6). Hawthorne would certainly have heard any church bells, too. It is notable that Joseph B. Felt wrote of Salem in 1845, "there are two organs, of small size, in the Crombie street and the Catholic churches" (*Annals of Salem,* 2nd ed.,1:504). Perhaps—especially during summer months when windows would have been open—Hawthorne, like Hester, heard something of the sounds from within the church. For the history of the Catholic Church in Salem, see Louis S. Walsh.

63. For Lowell's report on his conversation with Hawthorne and his own comment on the planned confession of Dimmesdale to a priest, see James Russell Lowell, *Letters*, 1:302.

An interesting issue to pursue with regard to the attitude of Lowell and Hawthorne toward Catholicism is the importance of the views of Lowell's fiancée Maria White and Hawthorne's wife Sophia Hawthorne. Maria White attended Ursuline Convent in Charlestown—indeed, she was one of the Protestant girls who hid and then escaped when the convent was burned by an angry mob (Maria White Lowell, *Poems*, 6–10). The infamous convent burning is well described by a former convent student, Louisa Goddard Whitney, in *Burning of the Convent*, and the event is ably examined by Billington, "The Burning of the Charlestown Convent"; Cohen, "Alvah Kelley's Cow"; Franchot, *Roads to Rome*, 135–54; and Schultz, *Fire and Roses*. Of particular interest is the fact that the mob suspected that a nun had been buried alive at the convent (Franchot, 139–40, 399 n; see also Schultz, 108) since Maria later wrote a poem, "Legend of the Brown Rosarie," which mentions a nun buried alive (Maria White Lowell, *Poems,* 77), and since James Russell Lowell's source for "A Legend of Brittany," "The Three Red Monks," concerns a young woman's burial alive. Surely Maria conveyed to James both her interest in Catholicism and her extraordinary experience in the besieged convent. Indeed, he alluded to the burning of the convent in *Conversations on Some of the Old Poets* (187).

While Sophia Hawthorne did not have a Catholic education, she did have a sympathy for Catholicism. This is intimated in a 28 February 1869 letter she wrote to her friend Mrs. Mary Hemenway: after describing a moving experience she had had in a Catholic church, she adds, "You need not fear that I shall become a Roman Catholic under all this influence. But I find I can do justice to that faith, instead of feeling above it." (This passage is quoted with the permission of the Phillips Library, Peabody Essex Museum, Salem, Massachusetts.) Sophia must have shared her thoughts about Catholicism with Nathaniel before he wrote *The Scarlet Letter*. It was probably she who placed "the sweet and lovely head of one of Raphael's Madonnas" in Hawthorne's study in the Old Manse (10:5; see also 8:324). Furthermore in a 3 May 1846 letter to Maria Louisa Hawthorne, Sophia refers to "the sweet Madonna who presided over my husband's study in Concord." And in a 2 December 1849 letter to Elizabeth

Palmer Peabody, Sophia notes, with regard to another image of the Madonna, that she and her husband saw "a peculiar beauty in the Mother of Christ." (These passages are quoted by permission of the Berg Collection of English and American Literature, The New York Public Library, Astor, Lenox, and Tilden Foundations.) It is interesting to note that Maria Lowell wrote to Sophia Hawthorne of her feelings for the Virgin Mary: "Mary is a type of all women, and I love the Catholic feeling that enshrines and appeals to her. It has its root in the very deepest principle of life," Rose Hawthorne Lathrop, *Memories of Hawthorne,* 119.

64. For further information on the *Boston Miscellany,* see Mott, *History of American Magazines,* 718–20, and Chielens, 70–73. Hawthorne was apparently considered as a possible editor of the magazine in the summer of 1842; see his 20 August 1842 letter to Robert Carter, 15:644–45.

65. James Russell Lowell, "Old English Dramatists," *Boston Miscellany,* April 1842, 145; *Conversations,* 133.

66. For Lowell on "the undying fires," see ibid.; the passage appears, slightly modified, in *Conversations,*132. Lowell's comment on Wordsworth's Ode appears in *Conversations,* 49–50. Lowell's treatment of the amaranth appears in "Old English Dramatists," April 1842, 146; this passage is included, lightly revised, in *Conversations,* 136–37.

67. James Russell Lowell, *Conversations,* 119.

68. For Lowell on Spenser, see James Russell Lowell, *Writings* 4:299; for Lowell's admiration of Hawthorne, see *New Letters,* 104.

CHAPTER 3. A NOVEL BY EBENEZER WHEELWRIGHT

1. For the connection of the forest scene in *The Scarlet Letter* to a passage in *The Faerie Queen,* see Randall Stewart, "Hawthorne and *The Faerie Queen,*" 203–4. For a link between that forest scene and a passage in *Adam Blair,* see Stephenson and Stephenson, *"Adam Blair,"* 7. For the link between the forest scene and a passage in *Kavanagh,* see chapter 2, note 45. For a possible parallel between conversation in the forest scene with dialogue in *Lover's Vows,* see Ryan, "Young Hawthorne," 246. Dorena Allen Wright offers a correspondence between Pearl at the brook and Matilda and Beatrice at the brook in the *Divine Comedy* ("Meeting at the Brook-Side," 116–18); Wright also suggests that Hawthorne may have read Frederick Madden's summary of the *Pearl* manuscript (115–16). David Van Leer posits the link between Emerson's *Nature* and *The Scarlet Letter* ("Hester's Labyrinth," 61–62), a connection mentioned again by Dan McCall, *Citizens of Somewhere Else,* 74–75. For the correspondence between Dimmesdale's writing his sermon and Mr. Pendexter's writing his, see Woodson, "Hawthorne," 185–86. For allusions to Bunyan in the forest meeting and Dimmesdale's return to Boston, see Stanton, "Hawthorne, Bunyan, and the American Romances," 156–58, 162–65. For correspondences between Dimmesdale's Election Sermon and previous Election Sermons and the Bible, see Smolinski, "Covenant Theology," 223; Thomas F. Walsh, "Dimmesdale's Election Sermon"; and Newberry, *Hawthorne's Divided Loyalties,* 191. Mark Van Doren (*Nathaniel Hawthorne,* 33, 107–8) and Leslie Fiedler (*Love and Death,* 231–32) have related Dimmesdale's confession to that of Samuel Johnson in Uttoxeter market. (For Haw-

thorne's rendering of his 3 July 1855 visit to Uttoxeter, see the 4 July 1855 entry in *The English Notebooks,* 21:219–29, reworked for *The Keepsake* and enlarged for "Litchfield and Uttoxeter" in *Our Old Home,* 5:120–39. For studies of Hawthorne's use of Johnson at Uttoxeter, see Masheck, "Samuel Jackson's Uttoxeter Penance"; and Brack, "Hawthorne and Johnson.") The confessions of criminals in *The Record of Crime in the United States* are referred to by David S. Reynolds, *Beneath the American Renaissance,* 252–53; the confession of Jervase Helwyse is mentioned by Reid, *Yellow Ruff,* 40–43; and the confession of Judge Samuel Sewall is noted by Baughman, "Public Confession," 542; and Claudia Durst Johnson, *Understanding "The Scarlet Letter,"* 140–41. For Adam Blair's confession, see Stephenson and Stephenson, *"Adam Blair,"* 3–4. The importance of Christian iconography regarding Dimmesdale's death is discussed by Edward Dawson, "Hawthorne's Knowledge," 13. A connection between the aftermath of Hawthorne's work and *Adam Blair* is offered by Stephenson and Stephenson, *"Adam Blair,"* 7–8. And, of course, the importance of Marvell's "The Unfortunate Lover" is considered by Brant, "Hawthorne and Marvell"; Osborn and Osborn, "Another Look"; and Crain, *Story of A,* 202, 265–67 n.

2. For Orians's comments, see "New England Witchcraft in Fiction," 61–62 and "Angel of Hadley in Fiction," 269. The handwritten attribution to Mrs. William Cleveland—Lucy Cleveland—is quoted by permission of the Phillips Library, Peabody Essex Museum, Salem, Massachusetts. For Michael David Bell's comments, see *Hawthorne and the Historical Romance* (regicide [28 n, 32, 33]; "proposal, refusal, and accusation" [156]; and the reemergence of delusion [212]). Regarding the misattribution of the novel to Mary Lyford, see Schwab, "Seduced by Witches," 174. Regarding the novel's comment on Puritan nobility, see Bercovitch, *Office of "The Scarlet Letter,"* 49.

3. Marla Y. Muse, letter to the author.

4. See C. E. Frazer Clark Jr., *Nathaniel Hawthorne,* 63–81, as well as the Hawthorne edition (6:324–25). A catalog of Tappan and Dennet books for mid-1842, listing *Grandfather's Chair*, *Liberty Tree*, and *Famous Old People* (3), but not *Historical Tales for Youth* or *The Salem Belle*, is available at the American Antiquarian Society ("Valuable Books"). The firm is described as "enterprising" in the *Brother Jonathan* (["Messrs. Tappan & Dennet"]). It is briefly mentioned in Tebbel, *History of Book Publishing,* 1:447. For further information on Charles Tappan (brother of the more famous Senator Benjamin Tappan and abolitionist Arthur Tappan, and former apprentice to renowned printer Isaiah Thomas), see his obituaries and the genealogical work by Herbert Tappan, "Tappan (or Toppan) Genealogy," 55, and Daniel Langdon Tappan, *Tappan-Toppan Genealogy,* 37. For further information on Charles F. Dennet (married to the youngest sister of journalists N. P. Willis and Sara Payson Willis Parton ["Fanny Fern"], Ellen H. Willis), see his obituary (["Charles Frederick Dennet"]), as well as Capen, Letter to Horace Mann; and Dennet, "Ramié."

5. For a list of Lucy Cleveland's writings, see Paula Bradstreet Richter, "Lucy Cleveland's 'Figures of Rags,'" 51 n. (For Richter's related essay, which includes color prints, see "Lucy Cleveland, Folk Artist.")

6. The quotations from *The Salem Belle* are drawn from the first edition of that novel. (See [Ebenezer Wheelwright], 1842.)

7. In 1901, Horace E. Scudder stated that Lowell "wrote apparently much of the criticism" of *The Pioneer* (*James Russell Lowell,* 1:105), but Sculley Bradley, in his

introduction to the 1947 facsimile of *The Pioneer*, did not attribute the review of *The Salem Belle* to Lowell (xxvi–xxviii). Bradley did not know, however, a 29 March 1843 letter by Robert Carter, in which Carter identified his contributions to the magazine and did not include the review of *The Salem Belle* (Lease, "Robert Carter"). In light of Carter's not citing the review of *The Salem Belle* as his own, we may ascribe it to the other editor of *The Pioneer*, James Russell Lowell. The full-page ad from Tappan and Dennet appears at the close of the first issue of *The Pioneer*, the inside of the rear wrapper, only five pages from the review. It should be observed, in passing, that Poe, writing in the Philadelphia *Saturday Museum*, termed the reviews in the January 1843 issue of *The Pioneer*, "good and just." (See Mabbott, "Review," 458; and Thomas and Jackson, *Poe Log*, 394.)

8. In 1821, Sophia Peabody was a student at a girl's school in Lancaster, Massachusetts, complementing a boy's school, both of which were overseen by Dorcas Cleveland (whose husband Richard Jeffrey Cleveland was at sea). Dorcas's sister Lucy Cleveland was married to Richard Jeffrey's brother William Cleveland, and they lived together in the Stilwell Mansion. (The brothers were cousins to the sisters. Dorcas was a friend of Sophia's mother Elizabeth Palmer Peabody; Sophia's sister Mary was also a student at the school, and her sister Elizabeth was a teacher.) Sophia later referred to this period at the Clevelands' school as "our Arcadian life in Lancaster" (Letter to Mary Hemenway, 27 Oct. 1869). (The passage is quoted with the permission of the Phillips Library, Peabody Essex Museum, Salem, Massachusetts.) For further information on this interlude, see Marvin, *History of the Town of Lancaster*, 528–30; Tharp, *Peabody Sisters*, 21, 24–28; and Ronda, *Elizabeth Palmer Peabody*, 48–50. (Buford Jones first noted to me Sophia's letters to Hemenway.)

Paula Richter speculates (Conversation with author) that Sophia Peabody and Lucy Cleveland may have exhibited their work at the same April 1833 Salem fair. It is clear, she notes, that Sophia Peabody exhibited paintings there; indeed, the *Catalogue of Articles to be Offered for Sale at the Ladies' Fair* lists "2 splendid Paintings, in Oils, of Scenery near Bristol, in England, by Miss Sophia Peabody," 6. (The Peabody Essex Museum owns one of these paintings.) For Sophia Peabody's account of the fair, see her 11 April 1833 letter to her sister Elizabeth Palmer Peabody. Ms. Richter mentions as catalog items that may have been by vignette-maker Lucy Cleveland, "A very touching representation of a blind girl, with a pathetic appeal in her hand" and a "Very interesting domestic group," 3. The fair is described in the *Essex Register* in "Ladies' Fair," "Salem Fair," and "Report of Ladies"; and a poem by N. P. Knapp is offered in that newspaper, "Ladies' Fair."

During her stay in Cuba (1833–35), arranged with the assistance of Dorcas Cleveland (whose husband was vice-consul), Sophia wrote to her mother, "I wish you would give my love to Mrs. Wm. Cleveland & tell her I shall write to her very soon." (See Sophia Peabody to Mrs. Elizabeth Palmer Peabody, 12 Feb. 1834.) (The passage is quoted with the permission of the Berg Collection of English and American Literature, The New York Public Library, Astor, Lenox and Tilden Foundations.)

Having returned to Salem, Sophia Peabody wrote to Lucy Cleveland, only blocks away from the Peabodys' Charter Street home, on Summer Street, on 11 April 1838. She was inquiring as to whether she could borrow and copy Lucy Cleveland's "magnificent oriental birds" (paintings or figurines, apparently, that Sophia remembered from "days of yore"—their time in Lancaster). Sophia closed her letter affectionately, referring to her visit to Lucy Cleveland at her home: "I hope you are still as well in health as your roundness & bloom testified when I met you in Summer St." She signed the letter, "Truly your friend / S. A. Peabody." (This interesting letter, held by the Phillips Library in Salem, is not listed in Edwin Haviland Miller's "Calendar of the Letters of Sophia Peabody Hawthorne.") Sophia Peabody's friendship with Lucy Cleveland would surely have become known to Sophia's suitor, Nathaniel Hawthorne. (The passages from Sophia Peabody's letter to Lucy Cleveland are quoted with the permission of the Phillips Library, Peabody Essex Museum, Salem, Massachusetts.)

It should be added that the *Salem Directory* of 1842 lists Hawthorne's mother Elizabeth C. Hathorne at 10 Herbert Street, and Lucy Cleveland's husband William Cleveland at 22 Union Street—the street where Hawthorne had been born—only one block from the Hathorne house. Finally, when Hawthorne took the job of surveyor in the Salem Custom House, he would have been sure to hear of the beloved first collector of the port of Salem, Major Joseph Hiller—the father of Lucy Cleveland. Perhaps mention in the second edition of Felt's *Annals of Salem* of Joseph Hiller as a Custom House officer (preceding mention of William R. Lee [father of Hawthorne's inspector; 1:16] and James Miller [Hawthorne's collector; 1:20–24])—on a page facing a page mentioning Surveyor Jonathan Pue (2:380–81)—would have been noted by Hawthorne, who wrote of Pue and Felt's *Annals of Salem* in "The Custom-House" introduction to *The Scarlet Letter* (1:30).

9. Readers may consult Lucy Cleveland, *The Unveiled Heart,* for the passages on Emma Southgate as a "sister of charity" (35, 116), a description of her warning her sister Helen (39), and an account of Edward Harrison's listening to Emma's indistinguishable words (113). Thereafter appears the short story "Retribution," which touches upon "retributive justice" (244).

10. For that derogation, consider his December 1852 comment to publisher James T. Fields, "*All* women, as authors, are feeble and tiresome" (16:124) and his January 1855 remark to publisher William D. Ticknor, "America is now wholly given over to a d____d mob of scribbling women" (17:304). Yet Hawthorne praised Anna Cora Mowatt in January 1854 (17:166; see also 17:261, 277), Fanny Fern in February 1855 (17:307–8), and Elizabeth Barstow Stoddard in January 1863 (18:528; see also 18:524, 531). And clearly, Hawthorne admired Margaret Fuller; see Mitchell, *Hawthorne's Fuller Mystery*. For earlier studies of Hawthorne and women, see Wood, "'Scribbling Women'"; Frederick, "'Scribbling Women'"; and Hull, "'Scribbling' Females." For recent studies, see Idol and Ponder, *Hawthorne and Women*.

11. For this attribution, see the Lilly Library copy of *The Salem Belle*, once owned by J. K. Lilly Jr. Without this attribution, the true authorship of *The Salem Belle* might have been impossible to ascertain. Jane Ann Reed's notations in her copy of the first edition of *The Salem Belle* are quoted courtesy of The Lilly Library, Indiana University, Bloomington, Indiana.

Markings in copies of first editions of *The Salem Belle* may reveal a variety of information. We learn that the book was presented by the author to Clara J. Rider (Phillips Library copy, Peabody Essex Institute) and owned, as well, by Moses Sweetser (Howard B. Lee Library, Brigham Young University), into whose family Clara J. Rider married on 23 September 1849. (For information on Clara J. Rider and her husband Thomas Sweetser, a druggist in South Danvers, Massachusetts, see Nellie Agnes Rider, "Some of the Descendants"; Fremont Rider, *Preliminary Materials*; and

Phillip Starr Sweetser, *Seth Sweetser*. There are several Moses Sweetsers; the likeliest one of them in this context seems to be Moses Foster Sweetser [1848–97], a writer born and raised in Newburyport. See Sweetser, 215–16.)

We also learn that *The Salem Belle* was sometimes given as a gift from a mother to her daughter ("Harriet C. Spooner. / from her mother / 1843" [quoted with the permission of The Huntington Library, San Marino, California]; "Abby Sanford / from / her Mother / Jan. 1845" [quoted with the permission of Special Collections & Archives, Kent State University Libraries]), from a friend to a friend ("Presented To Mariah / By A Friend" [quoted with the permission of the University of South Florida Library]), or from someone with an unidentified relationship to another ("Stephen Henry Osborne / from H. O." [quoted courtesy of the Long Island Studies Institute, Hofstra University, Hempstead, New York]). One inscription states, "One of my Mother's books / when [was?] a child, in / Jany 24th 1843" (quoted with the permission of The Albert and Shirley Small Special Collections Library, University of Virginia Library). Another inscription, presumably for a review copy, reads, "Editor / Congregational Observer / With the Compliments / of Tappan & Dennet" (quoted with the permission of Burton Historical Collection, Detroit Public Library). (The *Congregational Observer* later merged with the *New-York Evangelist*, which published a negative review of *The Salem Belle*, as will be noted.)

12. Jane Ann Reed's brother Edward A. Reed wrote that reading one of her letters "afforded me more pleasure than any other thing than the reception of the other which preceded it" (Letter to Isaac Gardner Reed). (This passage, from a letter in the Reed Family Papers, is quoted with the permission of the Rare Book and Manuscript Library, Columbia University.) And her brother Gardner K. Reed wrote of her "good long old-fashioned letters" (Letter to Jane Ann Reed). (This letter is a part of The Gardner K. Reed Letters and Journals, Yale Collection of Western Americana, Beinecke Rare Book and Manuscript Library, Yale University.) Jane Ann Reed is quoted in Stahl, *History of Old Broad Bay*. For information on the Reed siblings' father Isaac Gardner Reed, see the obituary in the *Boston Recorder*, Dodge, "Hon. Isaac G. Reed" (courtesy of the Harvard University Archives). (The passage from the 26 January 1843 letter of Isaac Gardner Reed, part of the Reed Family Papers, is quoted with the permission of the Rare Book & Manuscript Library, Columbia University.) For dates of birth and death, see also Lilly, *Waldoboro, Maine Cemetery Inscriptions,* 120, 126. Perhaps Isaac Gardner Reed's mention of anachronisms in *The Salem Belle* was prompted by the review of that work in *The Pioneer*, to be discussed shortly. The link between the Reed family and Ebenezer Wheelwright seemed to involve business friends. The Reeds were close to Joseph Ballister, a Boston merchant who, according to the Boston directory for 1836, had been a partner in the firm of McLellan and Ballister. (See also "Joseph Ballister.") Isaac McLellan was a West Indies merchant, as was Wheelwright. Furthermore, as the 1836 Boston directory also reveals, Isaac Jr. and Edward McLellan were in business with Ebenezer Wheelwright in the firm Wheelwright, McLellan and Company.

13. This passage, from a letter in the Reed Family Papers, is quoted with the permission of the Rare Book and Manuscript Library, Columbia University.

14. This biographical sketch is drawn from many sources. For Ebenezer Wheelwright's birthdate, see his letter to John A Vinton, 10 Oct. 1867, 4. For a scholarly treatment of brother William Wheelwright, see Duncan, "New England Heritage." For

the Wheelwright children's strict upbringing and Ebenezer Wheelwright's great trust in others, see ["Mr. Ebenezer Wheelwright, Aged 77"]. For Ebenezer Wheelwright's membership in the First Presbyterian Church, see Cook, *Genealogical Address*, 19. The beginning of Wheelwright's business career is mentioned in Currier, *History of Newburyport*, 2:550, "Death of Eben Wheelwright," and ["Mr. Ebenezer Wheelwright"]. His marriage to Sarah Boddily, daughter of Reverend John Boddily, is listed in *Vital Records*, 505. Wheelwright mentions his three grown children in his letter to Vinton of 10 Oct. 1867. The move to Boston and the shift from flour merchant are evident in the Boston directories, 1835 and later. For his having become a West Indies merchant, see "Death of Eben Wheelwright" and ["Ebenezer Wheelwright"]. Regarding the Bankruptcy Act of 1841, see Balleisen, *Navigating Failure*. Regarding Wheelwright's petition for bankruptcy and declaration of bankruptcy, see National Archives Branch Depository (RG 21, File 730, "Petition by Debtor for Benefit of the Act of Congress" and "Petition by Bankrupt for His Discharge"). The copyright information for *The Salem Belle* was provided by Marla Y. Muse in a letter to the author. The reviews of *The Salem Belle* will be discussed later in this chapter. It is not known for certain how Ebenezer Wheelwright first came in contact with Tappan and Dennet. We may note, in passing, possible connections of Wheelwright with the Tappan family. A friend of the Reed family, Henry Wainwright, was a partner with Sewell Tappan. (See the Boston directory for 1839 and the following years. For the Reed-Wheelwright link, consult note 12 in this chapter.) Daniel Dana Tappan, a cousin of Charles Tappan, was born in Newburyport in 1798, and, like Ebenezer Wheelwright, was married in Portsmouth, New Hampshire, in 1823. (See *Sketch of the Life of Rev. Daniel Dana Tappan.*) Joseph Tappan was a parish clerk at Old South Church in Newburyport. (See Hovey, *Origins and Annals*, 182.) And the Wheelwrights lived in houses on High Street in Newburyport, the street where the Toppan House was located. ("Toppan" was the original spelling of "Tappan." Charles Dennet's great-grandfather Samuel Toppan had lived in this house—see Daniel Langdon Tappan, *Tappan-Toppan*, 7, 22, 125–28.)

15. Ebenezer Wheelwright "espoused early the anti-slavery cause and wrote frequently on its behalf," according to the entry for him in Genealogical Notes, 35–36. (This passage is quoted by permission of the Massachusetts Historical Society.) Ebenezer Wheelwright's sister Elizabeth was antislavery, as well. (See L. M. Robbins to A. W. Weston.) According to Benjamin C. Clark (to whom *Traditions of Palestine* is dedicated), "In July last, a memorial signed by some of the most eminent merchants of Boston, was presented to Congress, soliciting the recognition of Hayti as an Independant State, and praying that she might be placed upon the same footing as other nations," *A Plea for Hayti*, 3. For Wheelwright's move to Newburyport, see the Boston directory entries. His association with Nehemiah P. Mann and his two failures are noted in "Ebenezer Wheelwright" (a credit rating). (Quotation from this credit rating is by permission of Dun and Bradstreet and of the Baker Library, Historical Collections, Harvard Business School. The credit rating may be found in Volume 2, page 665, of the Nineteenth-Century Credit Ledgers, R. G. Dun and Co. Collection, Baker Library, Harvard Business School.) The attribution of *A Review of Dr. Dana's Remonstrance* is provided in the *National Union Catalog*. For sketches of Edwards Amasa Park, see Allibone, *Critical Dictionary*, and Adams, *Dictionary of American Authors*. For the Civil War detail, see Creasey, *City of Newburyport*, 45–46, 195.

Wheelwright's remaining a member of the Old South Church is mentioned in Cook, *Genealogical Address*, 19.

16. The copyright information was provided by Deborah Lloyd, Senior Copyright Research Specialist of the Reference and Bibliography Section in the Copyright Office of the Library of Congress. The copyright entry states "by A. Wayfarer"; the title page of the book states "By a Wayfarer." The book is occasionally listed under "M. H. Sargent," but he was its publisher, not its author. Quotation from the 10 October 1867 letter of Ebenezer Wheelwright is by permission of the New England Historic Genealogical Society. *Traditions of Palestine* went into a fourth edition, published in 1869. For mention of Wheelwright as the author of children's books, see Genealogical Notes, 35–36. Quotation from the relevant passage of this work is by permission of the Massachusetts Historical Society. For two copies of *The Salem Belle* that were gifts from a mother to a daughter; see note 11 this chapter. Quotations from *Traditions of Palestine* are from the third edition. There are only a few copies of this novel extant; the copy I consulted for quotation was that held by the Reconstructionist Rabbinical College Library. There is another work with the same title, published in 1830 and edited by Harriet Martineau; this work also concerns the coming of Jesus. Wheelwright is described as "well known in Massachusetts in the religious world" in an obituary, ["Mr. Eben Wheelwright"]. The inscribed copy of *Traditions of Palestine* is the Harvard copy: the inscription reads "Rev. Dr. Peabody / with the kind remembrances / of the author— / Newburyport March 7 1867." (This inscription is quoted with the permission of the Harvard College Library.) Comparing the handwriting of this inscription with that of Ebenezer Wheelwright's 10 October 1867 letter to John A. Vinton, William Joyce, the Head of Special Collections in Penn State's Pattee/Paterno Library, said, "By all outward appearances, it would appear to be the same handwriting." Andrew Preston Peabody had been Unitarian pastor in Portsmouth, New Hampshire (1833–60)—Wheelwright might have met him there before he moved to Boston—and Peabody later served as editor of the *North American Review* (1852–60). (See *Encyclopaedia Britannica*, 11th ed.) For Wheelwright's editing *The Panoplist* (with "my associate in the Editorial work," "C. D. Pigeon"), see his letter of 21 March 1868. Attempting to initiate an exchange with a southern periodical, Wheelright notes, "Our great object is to support the truth of God, which has been well nigh dissipated in New England, by the Philosophy of the Schools [the Old School and the New School]." (This item is quoted by permission of The Huntington Library, San Marino, California.)

17. For the credit rating in 1867 and 1874, see "Ebenezer Wheelwright." Quotation from the credit rating is by permission of Dun and Bradstreet and of the Baker Library, Historical Collections, Harvard Business School. The credit rating may be found in Volume 2, page 665, of the Nineteenth-Century Credit Ledgers, R. G. Dun and Co. Collection, Baker Library, Harvard Business School. For Wheelwright's own comments on his financial difficulties, see his letter to John A. Vinton of 27 November 1873. Quotation from this letter is by permission of the New England Historic Genealogical Society. For the date and cause of his death, see Pramberg, *Etched in Stone*, 210. The date is alternately given in the *Newburyport Herald* as Sunday, 10 June 1877 (["Mr. Ebenezer Wheelwright, Aged 77"]) and Monday, 11 June 1877 (["Mr. Eben Wheelwright"]).

18. The memorial piece asserts that Ebenezer Wheelwright possessed "sterling integrity" and the "enterprise, energy and indomitable will of a long ancestral line." See

["Mr. Ebenezer Wheelwright, Aged 77"]. He is said to have been "an accomplished writer and essayist" in ["Mr. Ebenezer Wheelwright"] and "a caustic and correct writer" in ["Mr. Eben Wheelwright"].

19. For the comments on the author of "Traditions of Palestine" and the work itself, see the two brief pieces titled "Traditions of Palestine," appearing in the issues of the *Newburyport Herald* in which the first two chapters were published. The clippings are pasted into a book of letters, with the notation, "Brig Monkey" and "John Harrod—1815." (The notation is quoted by permission of the First Presbyterian Church of Newburyport, Massachusetts.) Also in the library of the First Presbyterian Church is Ebenezer Wheelwright's copy of James M. Crowell's *Discourse upon the Life and Death of William W. Caldwell.* For the information on M. H. Sargent, see Hovey, *Origins and Annals*, 201. Benjamin C. Clark was the author of *A Plea for Hayti* (1853), *Remarks upon United States Intervention in Hayti* (1853), and *The Past, Present, and Future* (1867). It is interesting to note that the name B. C. Clark occurs in Wheelwright's bankruptcy papers: "The amount of B. C. Clark & Co. claim is unknown & cannot be ascertained till the unsettled amounts abroad are made up & the property received & sold." (See National Archives Branch Depository ["Amended Schedule B"].) (Quotation is by permission of the National Archives and Records Administration, Northeast Region.) According to the 1842 Boston directory, there was a Benjamin C. Clark and Company. Perhaps this is the company to which Wheelwright owed money, and perhaps the person after whom it was named was the author to whom Wheelwright dedicated *Traditions of Palestine.*

20. "[Advertisement for *Traditions of Palestine*]" states of the novel, "It has received high commendation from the press and from the laity in all directions." The introduction to "A Sabbath in Boston in 1692" states, in part, "The following sketch is founded on the events of those times [the times of the Salem witchcraft trials] and will, we hope, be interesting to our readers." The Sabbath described involves the account of the Willard and Mather sermons that Isaac Gardner Reed so admired in 1843. A run of the *Panoplist* is available at the Andover–Harvard Theological Library.

21. For Lowell's authorship of the review of *The Salem Belle*, see note 7 this chapter. For the review itself, see James Russell Lowell, *Pioneer,* 44. Lowell's paternal genealogy is discussed by Scudder, *James Russell Lowell*, 2:409–17. John Lowell's serving as pastor of Old South Church is noted by Hovey, *Origins and Annals,* 25–26. Abijah White's work as a West Indies merchant is mentioned in Duberman, *James Russell Lowell*, 36. For the advertisement for Jared Sparks's book, *The Life of George Washington*, see the inside of the rear wrapper of the first issue of Lowell's *Pioneer.*

22. Laura Laffrado concurs with Roy Harvey Pearce, in his "Historical Introduction" to volume 6 of the Hawthorne edition, that Elizabeth Peabody negotiated with Tappan and Dennet for Hawthorne (Laffrado, 133–34). For Elizabeth Palmer Peabody's 109 Washington Street address, see Ronda, *Elizabeth Palmer Peabody*, 205. For the 114 Washington Street address of Tappan and Dennet, see the Boston directory for 1842. For information on Elizabeth Palmer Peabody's bookshop, see Ronda, 182–94. For the one block of Tremont Street that separated West Street from Temple Place, see the map in the Boston directory for 1841 or 1842. Elizabeth Palmer Peabody's comment regarding Hawthorne's early reading is offered in Conway, *Life of Nathaniel Hawthorne*, 31.

23. Bruce Ronda asserts Hawthorne's direct relationship with Tappan and Dennet in *Elizabeth Palmer Peabody,* 206. The addresses cited are given in the Boston directory of 1842. (See also the "Directory Advertiser" in the Boston directory of 1842 for publishers' advertisements.) Quotation from Sophia Peabody's 23 March 1843 letter to her mother is by permission of the Berg Collection of English and American Literature, The New York Public Library, Astor, Lenox and Tilden Foundations. For the comment on Theodore Parker's lecture, see *Concord Lyceum Records.* Quotation from these records is by permission of the Concord Free Public Library.

24. Julian Hawthorne, *Nathaniel Hawthorne and His Wife*, 1:125.

25. Sophia Hawthorne to Maria Louisa Hawthorne, 15 Sept. 1843 and 26 Oct. 1843.

26. For Hawthorne's visiting the Concord Athenaeum at this time, see Sophia Hawthorne to Maria Louisa Hawthorne, 4 January 1843, 15:667, and Sophia Hawthorne to Mrs. Elizabeth Palmer Peabody, 28 February 1843.

27. The review of *The Salem Belle* in the *Daily Evening Transcript* of 2 December 1842 was reprinted in the *Newburyport Herald* of 5 and 6 December 1842.

28. I have not mentioned two all-too-brief Boston newspaper notices of *The Salem Belle*—those of the *Boston Daily Courier* and the *Boston Evening Gazette.*

29. The review copy of *The Salem Belle* inscribed to the editor of the *Congregational Observer* is mentioned in note 11 this chapter. A less notable review of *The Salem Belle* than that appearing in the *New York Tribune* or the *New-York Evangelist* is one in the *Albany Evening Journal*, which is reliant on the novel's introduction.

30. Lowell's comment on the need for Hawthorne to return to writing for adults recalls Margaret Fuller's similar comment in her January 1841 review of *Grandfather's Chair*: "Yet we must demand from [Hawthorne] to write again to the older and sadder, and steep them in the deep well of his sweet, humorsome musings."

31. Several days after Hawthorne lost his position at the Salem Custom House, Epes Sargent offered a very positive judgment of Hawthorne's writing ("some of the most exquisite prose in the language"). See Scharnhorst, *Critical Response*, 1.

32. Hawthorne later had his publishers send Tuckerman a copy of *Mosses from an Old Manse*; in an 18 June 1846 letter to Tuckerman, Hawthorne referred to "the pleasure and more than pleasure which I have received from many of your writings" (16:170). Tuckerman published a piece titled "Leaves from the Diary of a Dreamer, No. IX" in the December 1846 issue of the *Columbian Lady's and Gentleman's Magazine*, recalling his first seeing Hawthorne at the Boston Athenaeum in the period 1839–40 and acknowledging his friendship with him. In 1847, Tuckerman helped Rufus W. Griswold with *Prose Writers of America* (23:659 n), an anthology that included Hawthorne. Tuckerman evidently solicited material from Hawthorne for a projected biographical work; Hawthorne responded in a letter of 30 December 1850, "I will see what I can do towards your purpose" (16:381). There is no evidence, however, that Hawthorne sent Tuckerman any biographical material or that Tuckerman subsequently wrote the biographical study. Tuckerman did write a highly favorable essay on Hawthorne in the June 1851 issue of the *Southern Literary Messenger* (Idol and Jones, *Nathaniel Hawthorne*, 419–27), and Hawthorne thanked him for the piece in a letter of 20 June 1851 (16:452). Tuckerman later wrote an appreciation of Hawthorne in *Lippincott's Monthly Magazine* ("Nathaniel Hawthorne"). It is interesting to contrast Tuckerman's appreciation of the kindly Hawthorne with his distaste for the

seemingly severe Poe—we should recall that it was Tuckerman who had rejected "The Tell-Tale Heart" for the *Boston Miscellany*, thus making it available to Lowell and *The Pioneer*. For Tuckerman's expression of love for Hawthorne, see "Leaves," 250. For a brief overview of Tuckerman's critical work, see Lombard, "Neglected Critic."

33. For further discussion of Hawthorne and Upham, see Swartzlander, "'Amid Sunshine and Shadow.'" Consult also Moore, *Salem World of Nathaniel Hawthorne,* 192–98.

34. Julian Hawthorne, *Hawthorne Reading,* 103.

35. For Hawthorne's receiving books from his publishers, see Julian Hawthorne, *Hawthorne Reading,* 117. For the Hawthornes' taking their books from Concord to Salem, see Sophia Peabody to Maria Louisa Hawthorne, 22 September 1845.

36. For Hawthorne's addresses in Salem once he became Surveyor—18 Chestnut Street and 14 Mall Street—see Edwin Haviland Miller, *Salem is My Dwelling Place,* 259. The dates are correct in Mellow, *Nathaniel Hawthorne,* 274, 282–83. The brief announcement in the *Salem Register* of the 1847 reissue is Notice of *The Salem Belle.* John Mark Whittemore was a publisher who was associated with the firms Tappan and Whittemore; Tappan, Whittemore, and Mason; and Whittemore, Niles, and Hall. He later became a prominent Boston stationer. For further information, see his obituary, "John M. Whittemore, Stationer," as well as Whittemore, *Genealogy,* 66; Cutter, *Genealogical and Personal Memoires,* 1703; and Tebbel, *History of Book Publishing,* 430. The squibs for the reissue of *The Salem Belle* are listed here under "Advertisements" for the three newspapers. Henry Whipple both managed his bookstore and published the Salem directory. William and Stephen Bradshaw Ives managed their bookstore; published the *Salem Observer,* Felt's *Annals of Salem,* and other works; and made the first board game in America, *Mansion of Happiness.* For further information on these distinguished Salem booksellers, see Phelps, "Printing, Publishing, and Bookselling," esp. 240, 245, 248, 254, 255, 260, 262; and "Directory of the Salem Book Trade," esp. 278–79 and 294. Notably, Hawthorne suggested in his American notebooks that he write "[a]n article on newspaper advertisements" (8:251). Sophia Hawthorne mentions in her June 1847 journal her borrowing books from Mary Foote for her husband.

37. For Hawthorne's fictional treatment of General Goffe, see "The Gray Champion" (9:9–18). Lea Bertani Vozar Newman suggests that it was in Sir Walter Scott's 1822 novel, *Peveril of the Peak* (*Readers Guide,* 138–39), that Hawthorne first encountered the legend of Goffe's exceptional leadership of the townspeople of Hadley, Massachusetts, during an Indian attack. See also Orians, "Angel of Hadley in Fiction," 262–63. Arlin Turner states that in 1832 Hawthorne visited the Judge's Cave (in New Haven), where "the regicides William Goffe and Edward Whalley supposedly lived in hiding," *Nathaniel Hawthorne,* 70. A "Mr. Lyford" is mentioned at the beginning of the first edition of Felt's *Annals,* 6. He was the Episcopal pastor, John Lyford.

38. For an objection to Hawthorne's blending of historial periods, see Edward H. Davidson, "Question of History in *The Scarlet Letter,*" 3. For Hawthorne's treatment of the persecution of the Quakers, see his short story, "The Gentle Boy" (9:68–105).

39. Hawthorne's time in the Boston Custom House is discussed by George Jepson in "Hawthorne in the Boston Custom House." For discussion of Hawthorne's rela-

tionship with William B. Pike, whom he met at the Boston Custom House, see Holden, "Hawthorne Among His Friends," and Randall Stewart, "Hawthorne and Politics." For Jane Appleton Pierce's residence with the Wheelwrights, see the biographical sketch of Ebenezer's brother, "Isaac Watts Wheelwright." For more on the Wheelwright genealogy, see Bruce, *Ancestry of Mary Wheelwright Codman*.

40. Winthrop, *History of New England*, 1:201, 201 n. And John Wheelwright's daughter-in-law (the wife of his son Samuel) was named Hester. (See Bruce, *Ancestry*.) For a recent thorough study of the Antinomian Controversy, see Michael Winship, *Making Heretics*. For an assessment of the relationship of that controversy to our times, see George McKenna, "'An Holy and Blessed People.'"

41. See Colacurcio, "Footsteps of Ann Hutchinson," especially 464–66. For related studies, see Colacurcio, "'Woman's Own Choice'"; Sarah I. Davis, "Another View of Hester and the Antinomians"; Lang, "American Jezebel"; Franklin, "Hawthorne's Mrs. Hutchinson"; Weinauer, "Considering Possession in *The Scarlet Letter*"; and Scholl, "Winthrop's Anne Hutchinson in *The Scarlet Letter*." It is interesting to note, in passing, that Lowell had once planned to write a work on Anne Hutchinson (Duberman, 40).

42. For Hawthorne's borrowing Winthrop's *History of New England* (1825–26) from the Salem Athenaeum, see Kesselring, "Hawthorne's Reading," 71, 194. The 1825–26 edition of the work is the one cited here. Hawthorne mentions Winthrop's work in the essay "Ann Hutchinson" (23:73), and Arlin Turner comments in "Hawthorne's Literary Borrowings," 551. Winthrop is noted, too, in Ryskamp.

43. Winthrop, *History of New England*, 1:200–202, 214–17, 219–22, 236, 239, 244–47, 259, 280. That Cotton rejected Wheelwright as a pastor in the Boston church to protect Wilson is suggested by Richard S. Dunn in Dunn, Savage, and Yeandle, *Journal of John Winthrop*, 196 n. John Wheelwright's Fast-Day Sermon is included in John Wheelwright, *Writings*, 153–79, and in Hall's *Antinomian Controversy*, 152–72. Hawthorne apparently borrowed Fast Sermons from the Salem Athenaeum (Kesselring, "Hawthorne's Reading,"191). Thomas Hutchinson wrote of John Wheelwright, "Mr. Wheelwright, a zealous minister, of character for learning and piety, was [Anne Hutchinson's] brother in law, and firmly attached to her, and finally suffered with her," *History of Massachusetts*, 1:57.

44. Winthrop, *History of New England*, 1:323; 2:135–36, 162–64. We do not know for certain if Hawthorne read John Winthrop's *A Short Story of the Rise, Reign, and Ruine of the Antinomians, Familists & Libertines* (1644). See Hall, *Antinomian Controversy*, 199–310. We also do not know if he read *Mercurius Americanus* (1645), long attributed to John Wheelwright, but more recently ascribed to Wheelwright's son John Wheelwright Jr. (Bush, "John Wheelwright's Forgotten *Apology*," 42–44). (For the text, see John Wheelwright, *Writings*, 181–228.) It seems unlikely that Hawthorne would have encountered the long-neglected *A Brief, and Plain Apology by John Wheelwright* (1658). For discussion of John Cotton's epistolary effort to persuade the banished John Wheelwright to confess and seek forgiveness, see Bush, "'Revising What We Have Done Amisse.'" Bush notes Cotton's own sense of guilt for not having discerned the Antinomian problem more quickly. The exchange between Cotton and Wheelwright is included in Bush, *Correspondence of John Cotton*, 300–319.

45. Colacurcio, "Footsteps of Ann Hutchinson," 466.

46. Winthrop, *History of New England*, 1:213.

47. For analysis of Hawthorne's dismissal from the Salem Custom-House, see Nissenbaum, "Firing of Nathaniel Hawthorne."

48. R. W. B. Lewis famously investigates Adam in American literature in *American Adam.* Amy Schrager Lang comments on the Puritan comparison of Anne Hutchinson to Eve in *Prophetic Woman,* 55, 57, 58–59, 65, 67. For Thomas Welde's comparison of Hutchinson to Eve, made in his introduction to Winthrop's *Short Story,* see John Wheelwright, *His Writings,* 205–6.

49. Marvell, "On Mr Milton's 'Paradise Lost,'" 119.

50. The passages from the 10 October 1867 and 23 October 1872 letters of Ebenezer Wheelwright to John A. Vinton are quoted with the permission of the New England Historic Genealogical Society. Vinton's manuscript on the Antinomian Controversy is titled "The Antinomian Controversy of 1637. A Memoir of the Life and Times of Rev. John Wheelwright. with a Genealogy of his Descendants." The work was published in the *Congregational Quarterly* in 1873. Vinton's essay defends the Puritans' treatment of John Wheelwright and Anne Hutchinson.

51. The earlier piece titled "The Antinomian Controversy of 1636," complementing the Fast-Day Sermon, states, "The article we have prepared must be deferred to our next number." The subsequent longer piece with the same title is the article promised. For the linking of the Antinomian Controversy to the Salem witchcraft trials, in this latter piece, see 268. Ebenezer Wheelwright's authorship of the two pieces (rather than that of associate C. D. Pigeon) is inferred because of Wheelwright's descent from John Wheelwright and his keen interest in the Antinomian Controversy. Also, Ebenezer Wheelwright mentioned the Fast-Day Sermon and the latter piece on the Antinomian Controversy in his 10 October 1867 letter to John A. Vinton. An earlier piece, "Legality and Antinomianism," concerns only general matters and is signed "W. G."

52. For Burroughs's working for Wheelwright, see Charles H. Bell, "Memoir," 75. It should be noted that there is an affinity between Wheelwright's language on Burroughs in *The Salem Belle* and Hawthorne's own in "Main Street." Wheelwright writes of Burroughs's "administering consolation" to the others condemned to death, and states that "The white robes of innocence and virtue now adorn [Burroughs and the others] in the eye of every beholder" (195). Hawthorne writes that Burroughs "seems to administer counsel" to the condemned Martha Carrier, and asserts that Burroughs is "a Christian saint" (11:76–77). We may wonder whether Hawthorne would have recognized a link between William Goffe, so honored in *The Salem Belle,* and John Wheelwright—both men were, at one time or another, associates of Oliver Cromwell. See Ezra Stiles, 15–21, and Charles H. Bell, 2, 60–63.

CHAPTER 4. THE MATTER OF FORM

1. Edward Dawson divided *The Scarlet Letter* into four acts based on the chronology of events, "Hawthorne's Knowledge," 74. Act 1 included chapters one through four (May 1642); Act 2 comprised chapters 7 and 8 (June 1645); Act 3 featured chapters 12, 14, and 16 through 19 (May 1649); and Act 4 offered chapters 21, 22, and 23 (Election Day, May 1649). (Nondramatic chapters were excluded.) Charles

Ryskamp recapitulated this formulation ("New England Sources," 261). Focusing on the influential characters, John C. Gerber identified four parts to the novel: the first part, chapters 1 through 8, in which the community shapes the action; the second, chapters 9 through 12, in which Chillingworth shapes the action; the third, chapters 13 through 20, in which Hester determines the action; and the fourth, chapters 21 through 24, in which Dimmesdale precipitates the action ("Form and Content," 25). Gordon Roper restated this configuration (Introduction, xxxviii–xlii). Darrel Abel modified Gerber's view: the first part, the community's, includes chapters 1 through 3; the second part, Chillingworth's, includes chapters 4 through 12; the third part, Hester Prynne's, comprises chapters 13 through 19; and the fourth part—God's, not Dimmesdale's—comprises chapters 20 through 23 ("Hawthorne's Dimmesdale," 84–99). G. Thomas Tanselle also modified the Gerber configuration, giving chapter 20 to the fourth part of the novel, and Michael Clark restated Tanselle's view (Clark, "Another Look," 135). Alternatively, Malcolm Cowley ("Five Acts") considered *The Scarlet Letter* to be analogous to a Greek tragedy, with five acts: act 1 is made up of chapters 1 through 4; act 2 is made up of chapters 7, 8, and 10; act 3 is constituted by chapter 12 alone; act 4 includes chapters 14 through 19; and act 5 comprises chapters 21 through 23. Cowley's view may be considered a revision of Dawson's original four-act arrangement. Robert Stanton argued, in "*The Scarlet Letter* as Dialectic of Temperament and Idea," that *The Scarlet Letter* comprised six segments—two halves, each of which included three four-chapter sections, distinguished by philosophical stance. Finally, Leland Schubert, who considered the novel "not really suited to play form," saw seven components: *A*, chapters 1 through 3, "Hester on the scaffold"; *B*, chapters 4 through 8, "Hester and Pearl struggling"; *C*, chapters 9 through 11, "Chillingworth's progress"; *D*, chapter 12, "Dimmesdale on the scaffold"; *E*, chapters 13 through 15, "Hester and Pearl rising"; *F*, chapters 16 through 20, "Hester and Dimmesdale rise as Chillingworth falls"; *G*, chapters 21 through 23, "Hester, Pearl and Dimmesdale on the scaffold" (*Hawthorne, the Artist,* 140). (The introduction and the final chapter constitute the framework.)

2. Matthiessen, *American Renaissance,* 275.

3. See ["Very Brilliant Meteor"]. For an earlier account of a meteor turning night to day, see "Meteor," an article appearing in the Salem children's magazine, *The Hive.*

4. Perry, "Centenary of Hawthorne," 102.

5. The first corresponding phrases have been noted by Edward Stone in "The 'Many Morals' of *The Scarlet Letter,*" 233–34. "Gules," of course, means "red"—the rose is matched by the red letter. For consideration of symmetry involving detail in the introduction and conclusion, including Surveyor Pue and the scarlet letter, see Alfred Weber, "Framing Functions." Additional verbal parallels include the "heraldic honor" and "the best and fittest of all mottoes for the General's shield of arms" (1:23–24), on one hand, and "armorial bearings" and "a herald's wording of which might serve for a motto" (1:264), on the other; and "Aged persons . . . from whose oral testimony he had made up his narrative, remembered her" (1:32) and "the verbal testimony of individuals, some of whom had known Hester Prynne" (1:259–60).

6. It is intriguing to note the resemblance between the structure of *The Scarlet Letter* and the "long-disused writing-desk" (1:43) on which the novel was written: "This writing surface consisted of two lids, hinged at their junction in the centre" (Julian Hawthorne, *Hawthorne and His Circle,* 10).

7. Although Dimmesdale is seen as Christ-like in the second and third scaffold scenes (see chapter 2, note 61), he is finally a man, not a divinity. The judgmental sun—or sunlike meteor—represents Christ.

8. Panofsky, *Meaning in the Visual Arts*, 261–65; see also *Dürer,* 78–79.

9. Kantorowicz, "Dante's 'Two Suns,'" 329–30, 334–35; Fowler, *Triumphal Forms,* 73, and "To Shepherd's Ear," 177; Carey and Fowler, *Poems of John Milton,* 104, 442; and Brooks, *Number and Pattern,* 13.

10. For Hawthorne's early fondness for *Robinson Crusoe*, see Pearson, "Elizabeth Peabody on Hawthorne," 259–60. For Julian Hawthorne's characterization of *Robinson Crusoe* as "our autobiography," see *Hawthorne and His Circle*, 7.

11. Hawthorne's "artistic study" of novels is mentioned by Elizabeth Hawthorne (as noted in chapter 3) in Julian Hawthorne's *Nathaniel Hawthorne and His Wife*, 1:125. Hawthorne's borrowing *Captain Singleton* and *Roxana* is noted in Kesselring, "Hawthorne's Reading," 137–38, 178.

12. Brooks, *Number and Pattern*, 20–21, 38 n.

13. Defoe, *Robinson Crusoe,* 141, 5. For further discussion of Providence in *Robinson Crusoe*, see Hunter, *Reluctant Pilgrim,* 51–75; McFarlane, "Reading Crusoe"; and Zeitz, "Checker-Work of Providence."

14. Brooks, *Number and Pattern,* 20–21, 13.

15. Defoe, *Robinson Crusoe,* 68; Brooks, *Number and Pattern,* 25.

16. The providential form may also be evident in Samuel Taylor Coleridge's seminal romantic poem, "The Rime of the Ancient Mariner"—of which Hawthorne was "very fond" (Julian Hawthorne, *Hawthorne and His Circle*, 127). In the second part, occurring immediately after the mariner has shot the albatross, the seventh of fourteen stanzas reads:

> All in a hot and copper sky,
> The bloody Sun, at noon,
> Right up above the mast did stand,
> No bigger than the Moon. (50)

Perhaps, thus, Christ offers his intense judgment of the guilty mariner. Seven stanzas later, the albatross hangs on the mariner's neck.

Hawthorne was, of course, keenly sensitive to the influence of British literature on American literature, and he appreciated it. At a literary occasion in 1857 in England, he commented on American writers: "it gives me heartfelt happiness to think that we have returned something back of the great debt which we owe to England" ("Hawthorne's Speech," 209). Like Lowell, Longfellow, and Poe, Hawthorne was not especially sympathetic to the resistance to British models that was characteristic of the nationalistic literary group, Young America.

17. For Poe and *Robinson Crusoe*, see Poe's review in *Collected Writings,* 5:98–99, as well as Pollin, "Poe and Daniel Defoe."

18. The argument regarding *Pym* is developed in a series of articles by the author: Kopley, "Secret of *Arthur Gordon Pym*," "Hidden Journey of *Arthur Gordon Pym*," "'*Very* Profound Under-current' of *Arthur Gordon Pym*," as well as "Poe's *Pym*-esque." The argument is elaborated again in the new Penguin edition of *Pym*. Regarding the role of Providence in Poe's novel, see Fukuchi, "Poe's Providential *Narrative*."

19. The providential image of the Sun of Righteousness may be traced in early American literature, too. For example, it is mentioned by Anne Bradstreet in her "Meditations" (*Complete Works,* 50, 200, 202, 206, 207–8) and by Edward Taylor in *Preparatory Meditations* (see especially second series 21 [116–19]; 67A, 67B, 68A, 68B, 69 [200–209]; and 114 [290–91]). Taylor's work, of course, was not published in Hawthorne's lifetime. For a study of Providence in early American literature, see Hartman, *Providence Tales.*

For an instance of the appearance of the Sun of Righteousness in a Boston news-paper of Hawthorne's time, see Beveridge, "Sun of Righteousness." The passage orig-inally appeared in "Thoughts upon the Appearance of Christ the Sun of Righteous-ness, or the Beatific Vision." It is interesting to see how Beveridge characterizes a man without faith in the Sun of Righteousness: "As if a man be born stark blind, though the sun shine never so clear about him, he sees no more than he did before, but lives in dark at noon-day as much as at midnight." In contrast, the Sun of Righteous-ness in *The Scarlet Letter* provides noon at night.

Ralph Waldo Emerson wrote a poem significantly related to the providential form—an 1816 elegy, long unpublished, on the occasion of the death of his cousin Mary Bliss Farnham (von Frank, "Emerson's Boyhood," 32). The seven-stanza poem, titled "Lines on the Death of Miss M. B. Farnham," offers a symmetrical frame com-prising the first words of the first three and final three stanzas: "Come," "Here," "Lowly," and "Long" "Her," "Farewell." And at the center of the poem is the follow-ing revealing quatrain:

> Her's was the brightness of the noonday Sun
> Her fancy brilliant as his golden rays,
> Judgement & Reason, mounted on the throne,
> And pure Religion shone in all her ways. (*Collected Poems,* 286)

With this stanza, which offers such critical markers as "the noonday Sun," "Judge-ment," and "the throne," young Waldo extols his cousin, comparing her to the Sun of Righteousness. Experimenting with a literary convention, he offered his deceased cousin high praise indeed.

Herman Melville seems to have resisted the providential form. It is certainly not ap-parent in his greatest work, *Moby-Dick.* Furthermore, when Starbuck, the most devout character in *Moby-Dick,* confronts the doubloon with the "keystone sun," he says:

> A dark valley between three mighty, heaven-abiding peaks, that almost seem the Trinity, in some faint earthly symbol. So in this vale of Death, God girds us round; and over all our gloom, the sun of Righteousness still shines a beacon and a hope. If we bend down our eyes, the dark vale shows her mouldy soil; but if we lift them, the bright sun meets our glance half way, to cheer. Yet, oh, the great sun is no fixture; and if, at midnight, we would fain snatch some sweet solace from him, we gaze for him in vain! This coin speaks wisely, mildly, truly, but still sadly to me." (*Writings,* 6:432)

Melville seems almost in dialogue with Hawthorne, who had rendered a nighttime Sun of Righteousness in *The Scarlet Letter.* Perhaps the doubting, defiant Melville forbore use of the familiar convention because it implied a faith he did not have. Although Melville did offer a fiction with a Christocentric form in "Bartleby the Scrivener," that work reveals Melville's characteristically dark vision: the returning Christ (Bartleby, "one of the least of these my brethren" [Matthew 25:40])—who appears at the story's midpoint, framed by symmetrical language—goes unrecognized and eventually dies (Kopley, "Circle and Its Center").

20. The scholarly treatment of chiasmus is substantial; a brief selection will be mentioned here. For consideration of chiasmus in classical literature, see Welch, *Chiasmus in Antiquity*. For the assessment of the figure in the Old Testament, see Lund, "Chiasmus in The Psalms" and "The Presence of Chiasmus," and Levenson, *Esther,* 5–12; and in the New Testament, see Lund, *Chiasmus in the New Testament,* and Thomson, *Chiasmus*. For the examination of chiasmus in British literature, see Sanford Budick, "Chiasmus"; Macandrew, "Life in the Maze"; Ralf Norrman, *Samuel Butler and the Meaning of Chiasmus*; and Olson, "'Soul's Imaginary Sight.'" Chiasmus in American literature is investigated by Djelal, "All in All"; Norrman, *Insecure World of Henry James's Fiction,* and *Wholeness Restored*; and Nänny, "Chiasmus in Literature," "Chiastic Structures," "Formal Allusions," "Hemingway's Architecture," "Hemingway's Use," and "The Reinforcement of Meaning."

21. Benoit, "A Letter," 94; Jon B. Reed, "'A Letter,'" 79–80; Gartner, "The Scarlet Letter," 140. Chiasmus in the Book of Esther is explored by Levenson (5–12). Although he does not discuss chiasmus, Robert S. Friedman does discuss the symmetry of the letter *A* (63–67). And Christine Brooke–Rose sees the letter as reflective of Hawthorne's antithetical style.

22. The crossing of Hester and Chillingworth and that of Hester and Dimmesdale anticipate the crossing of Lambert Strether and Chad Newsome in Henry James's *The Ambassadors* (Norrman, *The Insecure World,* 138). However, James himself does not seem to have recognized the chiasmus at the center of *The Scarlet Letter* (*Hawthorne,* 118–19).

23. David Ketterer, "'Shudder': A Signature *Crypt*-ogram in 'The Fall of the House of Usher'" (197). Double *ds* figure at the center of other Poe works, as well: consider "The Man of the Crowd" ("As the night *deepened,* so *deepened* to me . . ." [*Collected Works* 2:510; emphasis added]) and "A Tale of the Ragged Mountains" ("'You arose and *descended* into the city.' 'I arose . . . as you say, and *descended* into the city'" [*Collected Works* 3:946; emphasis added]).

24. For Thoreau on his soundings, see *Walden,* 289. For Charles R. Anderson on the center of *Walden,* see *Magic Circle of Walden,* 222–23. See also Hocks, "Thoreau, Coleridge, and Barfield," 192. For the central passage itself, see *Walden,* 187–88. Richard Tuerk has suggested that Thoreau's reference to a "jarred" "vase of water" owes something to the first verse of the fourteenth canto of Dante's *Paradise,* which concerns the rippling water in a vase. Tuerk notes that Dante's relating his mind to the water tends to reinforce the association of Thoreau's mind with Walden Pond (*Central Still,* 59–60). For circles in *Walden,* see also Charles R. Anderson. For several literary instances of circles of rippling water, see Georges Poulet, *Metamorphoses of the Circle,* 7–8, 174–75, 236–37. For a fuller treatment of Thoreau's use of chiasmus in his greatest work, see Kopley, "Chiasmus in *Walden*."

25. Stowe, *Uncle Tom's Cabin* 190. Notably, the number of the chapter that begins volume two of *Uncle Tom's Cabin,* "XIX," is symmetrical (as my daughter Emily observed).

26. For a consideration of chiasmus as suggestive of the Christian cross, see Tate, "Chiasmus as Metaphor." For a thoughtful contrasting of Hawthorne and Stowe, see Buell, "Hawthorne and Stowe" in his *New England Literary Culture.* For discussion of the scarlet letter as a cross, see Betty Kushen, "Love's Martyrs."

CONCLUSION

1. Irving, *Complete Works*, 8:41. For a comparison of "Rip Van Winkle" and "Peter Klaus the Goatherd," see Pochmann, "Irving's German Sources."

2. For Poe's reliance on "Humorous Adventure—Picking up a Madman" in "The Murders in the Rue Morgue,"see Kopley, *Edgar Allan Poe,* 14–15.

3. Eliade, *Sacred and the Profane*, 81.

4. Fitzgerald, *Great Gatsby*, 140.

5. Irving, *Complete Works*, 8:29.

APPENDIX

1. For the initial assertion, in the *Salem Register*, of an actual Hester Prynne, see M's letter of 21 March 1850. For the newspaper's acknowledgment that the name was "Perrine," not "Prynne," see "Correction." For M's defense of his initial assertion, see his letter of 1 April 1850. M finally admitted his mistake in his letter of 9 May 1850.

2. Lathrop, *Study of Hawthorne*, 70–73; James, *Nathaniel Hawthorne*, 114–17; Julian Hawthorne, "Scenes of Hawthorne's Romances," 387–92; More, "Origins of Hawthorne and Poe," 69–70. For the early reviews of *The Scarlet Letter* that mentioned *Adam Blair*, see Gary Scharnhorst, *Critical Response,* 33, 52.

3. Elizabeth Lathrop Chandler, "Study of the Sources of the Tales and Romances," 42–44; Julian Hawthorne, "Making of 'The Scarlet Letter,'" 410; Randall Stewart, "Hawthorne and *The Faerie Queen*," 203–4.

4. Orians, "Angel of Hadley in Fiction," 63–66; Turner, "Study of Hawthorne's Origins," 310–12 (characters in "The Custom-House"), 389–90 (Hawthorne's method of developing a series of scenes), and "Hawthorne's Literary Borrowings" (558) and "Hawthorne's Method of Using His Source Materials" (307). Regarding characters in "The Custom-House," see also the Leisy edition of *The Scarlet Letter* (286).

5. Edward Dawson, "Hawthorne's Knowledge," 82–83 (Winthrop's *Journal*), 84–94 (Felt's *Annals*), 163–64, 166 (Cotton Mather's *Wonders* and *Magnalia*). For the passages regarding the letter A, see 84, 87.

6. Matthews, "Hawthorne's Knowledge of Dante," 160; Lundblad, *Nathaniel Hawthorne and the Tradition of Gothic Romance*, 55–61; Matthiessen, *American Renaissance*, 305–8; W. Stacy Johnson, "Hawthorne and *The Pilgrim's Progress*," 162–63; Loggins, *Hawthornes*, 278–83; Fiedler, *Love and Death in the American Novel*, 228–30; Lynch, "Devil in the Writings of Irving, Hawthorne, and Poe," 117; Stein, *Hawthorne's Faust*, 104–22; Pearce, Review of *Hawthorne's Faust*, 62; Reid, *Yellow Ruff and "The Scarlet Letter,"* 112 ("principal sources").

7. Laser, "'Head,' 'Heart,' and 'Will' in Hawthorne's Psychology," 135–36; Blair, "Hawthorne" (1956), 125–33; Ryan, "Young Hawthorne at the Salem Theatre," 246; Ryskamp, "New England Sources," 272 (Hawthorne's review of Simms).

8. Warren, *"Scarlet Letter,"* 31.

9. Michael Davitt Bell, *Hawthorne and the Historical Romance of New England*, 134–46; Fogle, "Byron and Nathaniel Hawthorne," 189–90.

10. Waggoner, *Presence of Hawthorne*, 71–72.

11. Turner, *Nathaniel Hawthorne*, 181 (Hawthorne as decapitated Surveyor), 194–202 (Pue and the officials of the Custom House); Ferguson, "Nathaniel Hawthorne and Charles Wentworth Upham," 205–30 (witchcraft in *The Scarlet Letter*); Wright, "Meeting at the Brook-Side," 112; Baym, "Nathaniel Hawthorne and His Mother," 20.

12. Baym, "George Sand in American Reviews," 14.

13. Smolinski, "Covenant Theology and Arthur Dimmesdale's Pelagianism," 224.

14. David S. Reynolds, *Beneath the American Renaissance*, 118–32, 362–63 (reform movements); 211–24, 259–68 (sensational literature); 536–39 (popular humor); 263 ("key stereotypes"); 250–52 (the Salem murder case).

15. Luedtke, *Nathaniel Hawthorne and the Romance of the Orient*, 181–87; Jean Fagan Yellin, "Nathaniel Hawthorne's *The Scarlet Letter*" and "Hawthorne and the American National Sin"; Wagenknecht, *Nathaniel Hawthorne*, 83–85.

16. Benstock, *"The Scarlet Letter,"* 299–300; Dreyer, "'Confession' in *The Scarlet Letter*," 80; Budick, "Hester's Skepticism, Hawthorne's Faith," 210; Sacvan Bercovitch, *The Office of "The Scarlet Letter,"* 70–73 (Choate), and 127–28 (Emerson).

17. O'Keefe, "Echo of Emerson," 10 ("probable supposition"). For Emerson's praise of "The Custom-House" introduction, see Sophia Hawthorne, Letter to Maria Louisa Hawthorne, 28 April 1850. The passage is quoted by permission of the Berg Collection of English and American Literature, The New York Public Library, Astor, Lenox and Tilden Foundations. See also chapter 2, note 53.

18. Claudia Durst Johnson, "Impotence and Omnipotence," 599; Carol M. Bensick, "Dimmesdale and His Bachelorhood," 104, and "Hawthorne and His Bunyan," 5–6; Stephenson and Stephenson, *"Adam Blair* and *The Scarlet Letter,"* 1; Caroline M. Woidat, "Talking Back to Schoolteacher," 535–36.

19. Franchot, *Roads to Rome*, 260–69; Tew, "Hawthorne's P.P.," 20; Dukats, "Hybrid Terrain of Literary Imagination," 57.

20. For quotations from Gussman, see 75–76. For mention of antinomianism in Child's *Hobomok,* see 26, 28; the unpardonable sin, 39; free will and determinism, 127; witchcraft, 13–14; Isaac Johnson's burial ground, 112; and the "electric chain," 117.

21. Gatta, *American Madonna*, 16, 19; Coale, *Mesmerism and Hawthorne*, 69–90; Mitchell, *Hawthorne's Fuller Mystery*, 133; McCall, *Citizens of Somewhere Else*, 18–20 (*Adam Blair*), 74–75 (Emerson's *Nature*); Kennedy-Andrews, *Nathaniel Hawthorne*, 64–93; Crain, *Story of A*, 201–2, 208.

22. Sophia Hawthorne, Letter to Maria Louisa Hawthorne, 31 December 1843 and 1 January 1844. This passage is quoted by permission of the Berg Collection of English and American Literature, The New York Public Library, Astor, Lenox and Tilden Foundations.

Bibliography

Abel, Darrell. "The Devil in Boston." *Philological Quarterly* 32 (1953): 366–81.

———. "Hawthorne's Dimmesdale: Fugitive from Wrath." *Nineteenth-Century Fiction* 11 (1956): 81–105.

———. "Immortality vs. Mortality in *Septimius Felton*: Some Possible Sources." *American Literature* 27 (1956): 566–70.

Abrahamsson, Hans. "The Main Characters of Hawthorne's *The Scarlet Letter* and Their Interrelationships." *Moderna Språk* 68 (1974): 337–48.

Adams, Oscar Fay. *A Dictionary of American Authors*. Boston: Houghton Mifflin, 1897.

Adkins, Nelson F. "The Early Projected Works of Nathaniel Hawthorne." *Papers of the Bibliographical Society of America* 39 (1945): 119–55.

[Advertisement for Bowles & Dearborn]. *The Boston Annual Advertiser, Annexed to the Boston Directory*. Boston: Hunt & Stimpson and J. H. A. Frost, 1827.

[Advertisements for *The Salem Belle*]. *Salem Gazette* 20 July 1847, 3; 23 July 1847, 3; 27 July 1847, 3; 31 July 1847, 4; 3 August 1847, 4; 7 August 1847, 4.

[Advertisements for *The Salem Belle*]. *Salem Observer* 24 July 1847, 3, and 31 July 1847, 1.

[Advertisements for *The Salem Belle*]. *Salem Register* 19 July 1847, 3, and 22 July 1847, 4.

[Advertisements for *Traditions of Palestine*]. *Panoplist,* February–October 1868, inside front wrapper.

Allibone, S. Austin. *A Critical Dictionary of English Literature and British and American Authors*. 2 vols. Philadelphia: J. B. Lippincott & Co., 1858–70.

Anderson, Charles R. *The Magic Circle of Walden*. New York: Holt, Rinehart, and Winston, 1968.

Anderson, Douglas. "Hawthorne's Marriages." In *A House Undivided: Domesticity and Community in American Literature*, 97–120. Cambridge: Cambridge University Press, 1990.

Appendix to the Report of the Trial of John Francis Knapp, on an Indictment for Murder, Containing the New Evidence, the Arguments of Counsel, and the Charge of His Honor Judge Putnam, to the Jury, on the Second Trial. Salem, Mass., 1830.

Arac, Jonathan. "The Politics of *The Scarlet Letter*." In *Ideology and Classic American Literature*, edited by Sacvan Bercovitch and Myra Jehlen, 247–66. Cambridge: Cambridge University Press, 1986.

Austin, William. "Martha Gardner; Or, Moral Re-action." *American Monthly Magazine,* December 1837, 565–74.

Autrey, Max L. "A Source for Roger Chillingworth." *ATQ* 26 Supp. (1975): 24–26.

Balleisen, Edward J. *Navigating Failure: Bankruptcy and Commercial Society in Antebellum America*. Chapel Hill: University of North Carolina Press, 2001.

Barrett, Elizabeth B. Letter to James Russell Lowell. 31 March 1842. *bMS Am 1659 (27)*, Burnett Collection. Houghton Library, Harvard University. Cambridge, Mass.

———. Letter to James Russell Lowell. 1844. In Robert Browning and Elizabeth Barrett Browning, *Browning to His American Friends: Letters between the Brownings, the Storys and James Russell Lowell, 1841–1890*, edited by Gertrude Reese Hudson, 353–54. London: Bowes and Bowes, 1965.

Baughman, Ernest W. "Public Confession and *The Scarlet Letter*." *New England Quarterly* 40 (1967): 532–50.

Bayer, John G. "Narrative Techniques and the Oral Tradition in *The Scarlet Letter*." *American Literature* 52 (1980): 250–63.

Baym, Nina. "George Sand in American Reviews: A Context for Hester." *Hawthorne Society Newsletter* 10 (1984): 12–15.

———. "Nathaniel Hawthorne and His Mother: A Biographical Speculation." *American Literature* 54 (1982): 1–27.

Beebe, Maurice. "The Fall of the House of Pyncheon." *Nineteenth-Century Fiction* 11 (1956): 1–17.

Bell, Charles H. "Memoir of the Reverend John Wheelwright." In John Wheelwright, *John Wheelwright: His Writings,* 1–78.

Bell, Michael Davitt. "Arts of Deception: Hawthorne, 'Romance,' and *The Scarlet Letter*." In *New Essays on "The Scarlet Letter,"* edited by Michael J. Colacurcio, 29–56. Cambridge: Cambridge University Press, 1985.

———. *Hawthorne and the Historical Romance of New England*. Princeton: Princeton University Press, 1971.

Bell, Millicent. *Hawthorne's View of the Artist*. Albany: State University of New York Press, 1962.

Benjamin, Park. Review of *Terrible Tractoration*, by Thomas Green Fessenden. *American Monthly Magazine,* April 1837, 392–95.

———. Review of *The Token, and Atlantic Souvenir [for 1837]*, edited by S. G. Goodrich. *American Monthly Magazine,* October 1836, 405–7.

———. Review of *The Token, and Atlantic Souvenir [for 1838]*, edited by S. G. Goodrich. *American Monthly Magazine,* November 1837, 486–88.

———. "Thomas Green Fessenden." *American Monthly Magazine,* December 1837, 599.

Benoit, Raymond. "A Letter,—the Letter A: Nathaniel Hawthorne." In *Single Nature's Double Name: The Collectedness of the Conflicting in British and American Romanticism*, 83–94. The Hague: Mouton, 1973.

Bensick, Carol M. "Dimmesdale and His Bachelorhood: 'Priestly Celibacy' in *The Scarlet Letter.*" *Studies in American Fiction* 21 (1993): 103–10.

———. "Hawthorne and His Bunyan." *Nathaniel Hawthorne Review* 19 (1993): 1–10.

Benstock, Shari. "*The Scarlet Letter* (a)dorée, or the Female Body Embroidered." In *Nathaniel Hawthorne: "The Scarlet Letter,"* edited by Ross C. Murfin, 288–303. Boston: Bedford Books, 1991.

Bercovitch, Sacvan. *The Office of "The Scarlet Letter."* Baltimore: Johns Hopkins University Press, 1991.

Beveridge, William. "Sun of Righteousness." *Boston Recorder,* 19 January 1843, 9.

———. "Thoughts upon the Appearance of Christ the Sun of Righteousness, or the Beatific Vision." In *The Theological Works of William Beveridge,* 8:460–74. Oxford: John Henry Parker, 1846.

Billington, Ray Allen. "The Burning of the Charlestown Convent." *New England Quarterly* 10 (1937): 4–24.

Blair, Walter. "Hawthorne." In *Eight American Authors: A Review of Research and Criticism,* edited by Floyd Stovall, 100–52. New York: MLA, 1956.

———. "Hawthorne." In *Eight American Authors: A Review of Research and Criticism,* edited by James Woodress, 85–128. Rev. ed. New York: W. W. Norton, 1971.

Blanck, Jacob, and Michael Winship. *Bibliography of American Literature.* 9 vols. New Haven: Yale University Press, 1955–91.

Boewe, Charles, and Murray G. Murphey. "Hester Prynne in History." *American Literature* 32 (1960): 202–4.

"Books Read by Nathaniel Hawthorne, 1828–1850: From the 'Charge-Books' of the Salem Athenaeum." *Essex Institute Historical Collections* 38 (1932): 65–87.

Boston Directories. 1827, 1835–78.

[Boston Map]. *The Boston Annual Advertiser, Annexed to the Boston Directory.* Boston: Hunt & Stimpson and J. H. A. Frost, 1827.

Bouve, Pauline Carrington. "Is Hester Prynne Buried in Boston?" *Boston Evening Transcript,* 11 August 1920, sec. 2, p. 5.

Brack, O. M., Jr. "Hawthorne and Johnson at Uttoxeter." In *American Bypaths: Essays in Honor of E. Hudson Long,* edited by Robert G. Collmer and Jack W. Herring, 1–18. Waco, Tex.: Baylor University Press, 1980.

Bradley, Sculley. Introduction to *The Pioneer: A Literary Magazine,* edited by James Russell Lowell. New York: Scholars' Facsimiles & Reprints, 1947.

———. "Lowell, Emerson, and The *Pioneer.*" *American Literature* 19 (1947): 231–44.

Bradstreet, Anne. *The Complete Works of Anne Bradstreet.* Edited by Joseph R. McElrath Jr. and Allan P. Robb. Boston: Twayne, 1981.

Branch, Watson. "From Allegory to Romance: Hawthorne's Transformation of *The Scarlet Letter.*" *Modern Philology* 80 (1982): 145–60.

Brant, Robert L. "Hawthorne and Marvell." *American Literature* 30 (1958): 366.

Briggs, Charles F. Letter to James Russell Lowell. 22 January 1845. William Page and Page Family Papers. Archives of American Art. Smithsonian Institution. Washington, D.C.

Brooke-Rose, Christine. "A for But: 'The Custom House' in Hawthorne's *The Scarlet Letter.*" *Word and Image* 3 (1987): 143–55.

Brooks, Douglas. *Number and Pattern in the Eighteenth-Century Novel: Defoe, Fielding, Smollett and Sterne.* London: Routledge & Kegan Paul, 1973.

Brown, E. E. *Life of James Russell Lowell.* New York: Werner, 1895.

Brown, Gillian. "Hawthorne, Inheritance, and Women's Property." *Studies in the Novel* 23 (1991): 107–18.

Browning, Robert. Letter to Leigh Hunt. 6 October 1857. In *The Correspondence of Leigh Hunt*, 2 vols., edited by Thornton Leigh Hunt, 264–67. London: Smith, Elder and Co., 1862.

Browning, Robert, and Elizabeth Barrett Browning. *Browning to His American Friends: Letters between the Brownings, the Storys and James Russell Lowell 1841–1890.* Edited by Gertrude Reese Hudson. London: Bowes and Bowes, 1965.

Bruce, Stella P., comp. and ed. *The Ancestry of Mary Wheelwright Codman of Newburyport and Dorchester, Massachusetts, 1792–1857.* Leucadia, Calif.: n.p., 1991.

Budick, Emily Miller. "Hester's Skepticism, Hawthorne's Faith; or, What Does a Woman Doubt? Instituting the American Romance Tradition." *New Literary History* 22 (1991): 199–211.

Budick, Sanford. "Chiasmus and the Making of Literary Tradition: The Case of Wordsworth and 'The Days of Dryden and Pope.'" *ELH* 60 (1993): 961–87.

Buell, Lawrence. "Hawthorne and Stowe as Rival Interpreters of New England Puritanism." In *New England Literary Culture: From Revolution through Renaissance*, 261–80, 469–75. New York: Cambridge University Press, 1986.

Bush, Sargent, Jr. "Hawthorne's Prison Rose: An English Antecedent in the Salem *Gazette.*" *New England Quarterly* 57 (1984): 255–63.

———. "John Wheelwright's Forgotten *Apology*: The Last Word in the Antinomian Controversy." *New England Quarterly* 64 (1991): 22–45.

———. "'Revising what we have done amisse': John Cotton and John Wheelwright, 1640." *William and Mary Quarterly*, 3d ser., 45 (1988): 733–50.

———, ed. *The Correspondence of John Cotton.* Chapel Hill: University of North Carolina Press, 2001.

Cameron, Kenneth Walter. "Literary News in American Renaissance Newspapers (5)." *ATQ* 20 Supp. (1973): 13–36.

———. "New Light on Hawthorne's Removal from the Custom House." *ESQ* 25 (1961): 2–5.

Canaday, Nicholas, Jr. "'Some Sweet Moral Blossom': A Note on Hawthorne's Rose." *Papers on Language and Literature* 3 (1967): 186–87.

Capen, Nahum. Letter to Horace Mann. 4 March 1850. Horace Mann Papers. Massachusetts Historical Society. Boston, Mass.

Carey, John, and Alastair Fowler, eds. *The Poems of John Milton.* London: Longmans, Green, 1968.

Carton, Evan. "'A Daughter of the Puritans' and Her Old Master: Hawthorne, Una, and the Sexuality of Romance." In *Daughters and Fathers*, edited by Lynda E. Boose and Betty S. Flowers, 208–32. Baltimore: Johns Hopkins University Press, 1989.

Catalogue of Articles to be Offered for Sale at the Ladies' Fair, at Hamilton Hall, in Chestnut Street, Salem, on Wednesday, April 10, 1833, for the Benefit of the New-England Asylum for the Blind. Phillips Library. Peabody Essex Museum. Salem, Mass.

Chandler, Elizabeth Lathrop. "A Study of the Sources of the Tales and Romances Written by Nathaniel Hawthorne before 1853." *Smith College Studies in Modern Languages* 7 (1926): 1–64.

Chandler, Eva M. E-mail correspondence to the author. 11 January 1999.

Channing, William Henry. Letter to James Russell Lowell. 27 February 1844. *bMS Am 765 (217)*, Norton Collection. Houghton Library. Harvard University. Cambridge, Mass.

["Charles Frederick Dennet"]. *Boston Evening Transcript,* 4 January 1896, 9.

"Charles Tappan." *Boston Daily Advertiser,* 10 April 1875, 4.

"Charles Tappan." Unidentified newspaper clipping from the Growell Scrapbooks, 12:8. Cahners Publishing Company Library, New York.

Chielens, Edward E., ed. *American Literary Magazines: The Eighteenth and Nineteenth Centuries.* Westport, Conn.: Greenwood Press, 1986.

Child, Lydia Maria. *Hobomok and Other Writings on Indians.* Edited by Carolyn L. Karcher. New Brunswick, N.J.: Rutgers University Press, 1986.

———. Letter to Maria Lowell. 25 December 1844. *bMS Am 765 (226)*, James Russell Lowell Collection. Houghton Library. Harvard University. Cambridge, Mass.

Clark, B[enjamin] C[utler]. *The Past, Present, and Future. In Prose and Poetry.* Toronto: Adams, Stevenson, & Co., 1867.

———. *A Plea for Hayti, with a Glance at Her Relations with France, England and the United States, for the Last Sixty Years.* 2nd ed. Boston: Eastburn's Press, 1853.

———. *Remarks upon United States Intervention in Hayti, with Comments upon the Correspondence Connected with It.* Boston: Eastburn's Press, 1853.

Clark, C. E. Frazer, Jr. *Nathaniel Hawthorne: A Descriptive Bibliography.* Pittsburgh: University of Pittsburgh Press, 1978.

Clark, Michael. "Another Look at the Scaffold Scenes in Hawthorne's *The Scarlet Letter.*" *ATQ* n.s. 1 (1987): 135–44.

Cleveland, Henry Russell. *A Selection from the Writings of Henry R. Cleveland with a Memoir by George S. Hillard.* Boston: Freeman and Bolles, 1844.

Cleveland, Horace William Shaler. *Social Life and Literature Fifty Years Ago.* Boston: Cupples and Hurd, 1888.

Cleveland, Lucy H. "Retribution." In *The Unveiled Heart; A Simple Story*, 243–62. Boston: John Allen, 1835.

———. *The Unveiled Heart; A Simple Story.* Boston: John Allen, 1835.

Coale, Samuel Chase. *Mesmerism and Hawthorne: Mediums of American Romance.* Tuscaloosa: University of Alabama Press, 1998.

———. "The Romance of Mesmerism: Hawthorne's Medium of Romance." In *Studies in the American Renaissance 1994*, edited by Joel Myerson, 271–88. Charlottesville: University Press of Virginia, 1994.

Cody, David C. "'The Dead Live Again': Hawthorne's Palingenic Art." *ESQ* 35 (1989): 23–41.

Cohen, B. Bernard. "Hawthorne's Library: An Approach to the Man and His Mind." In *The Nathaniel Hawthorne Journal 1971*, edited by C. E. Frazer Clark Jr., 125–39. Washington, D.C.: Microcard Editions, 1971.

Cohen, Daniel A. "Alvah Kelley's Cow: Household Feuds, Proprietary Rights, and the Charlestown Convent Riot." *New England Quarterly* 74 (2001): 531–79.

Colacurcio, Michael J. "Footsteps of Ann Hutchinson: The Context of *The Scarlet Letter*." *ELH* 39 (1972): 459–94.

———. "The Sense of an Author: The Familiar Life and Strange Imaginings of Nathaniel Hawthorne." *ESQ* 27 (1981): 108–33.

———. "'The Woman's Own Choice': Sex, Metaphor, and the Puritan 'Sources' of *The Scarlet Letter*." In Colacurcio, *New Essays,* 101–35.

———. ed. *New Essays on "The Scarlet Letter."* Cambridge: Cambridge University Press, 1985.

Coleridge, Samuel Taylor. "The Rime of the Ancient Mariner." In *Samuel Taylor Coleridge*, 46–65. Oxford: Oxford University Press, 1985.

Concord Lyceum Records 1828–1922. Concord Free Public Library. Concord, Mass.

Conway, Moncure D. *Life of Nathaniel Hawthorne*. New York: Scribner & Welford, 1890.

Cook, Moody D. *A Genealogical Address, Giving a Brief History of the Parishioners and Founders of the Federal Street Church, from 1745–6 to 1862. . . .* Newburyport, Mass.: William H. Huse & Co., 1862.

Cooke, George Willis. *A Bibliography of James Russell Lowell.* Boston: Houghton Mifflin, 1906.

"Correction." *Salem Register,* 28 March 1850, 2.

Cox, Clara B. "'Who Killed Judge Pyncheon?': The Scene of the Crime Revisited." *Studies in American Fiction* 16 (1988): 99–103.

Cowley, Malcolm. "Five Acts of *The Scarlet Letter*." *College English* 19 (1957): 11–16.

Crain, Patricia. *The Story of A: The Alphabetization of America from "The New England Primer" to "The Scarlet Letter."* Stanford, Calif.: Stanford University Press, 2000.

Creasey, George W. *The City of Newburyport in the Civil War from 1861 to 1865.* Boston: Griffith-Stillings Press, 1903.

Crews, Frederick. *The Sins of the Fathers: Hawthorne's Psychological Themes.* New York: Oxford University Press, 1966. Reprint, with a new afterword, Berkeley: University of California Press, 1989.

Crowell, James M. *Discourse upon the Life and Death of William W. Caldwell.* Philadelphia: Alfred Martin, 1868. Library, First Congregational Church. Newburyport, Mass.

Currier, John J. *History of Newburyport, Mass, 1764–1909.* 2 vols. Newburyport, Mass.: n.p., 1909.

Cutter, William Richard. *Genealogical and Personal Memoirs Relating to the Families of Boston and Eastern Massachusetts.* Vol. 4. New York: Lewis Historical Publishing Co., 1908.

Dameron, J. Lasley. "*Bold Hawthorne* and Rufus W. Griswold." *University of Mississippi Studies in English,* n.s. 1 (1980): 50–57.

Dana, Daniel. *A Remonstrance Addressed to the Trustees of Phillips Academy, on the State of the Theological Seminary Under Their Care; September 1849.* Boston: Crocker and Brewster, 1853.

Darnell, Donald. "*The Scarlet Letter:* Hawthorne's Emblem Book." *Studies in American Fiction* 7 (1979): 153–62.

Davidson, Edward H. "The Question of History in *The Scarlet Letter.*" *ESQ* 25 (1961): 2–3.

Davidson, Frank. "'Young Goodman Brown'—Hawthorne's Intent." *ESQ* 31 (1963): 68–71.

Davis, Sarah I. "Another View of Hester and the Antinomians." *Studies in American Fiction* 12 (1984): 189–98.

Davis, W. A. Review of *Poems*, by James Russell Lowell. *Christian Examiner,* March 1844, 173–81.

Dawson, Edward. "Hawthorne's Knowledge and Use of New England History: A Study of Sources." Ph.D. diss., Vanderbilt University, 1937.

Dawson, Hugh J. "*The Scarlet Letter*'s Angry Eagle and the Salem Custom House." *Essex Institute Historical Collections* 122 (1986): 30–34.

———. "The Triptych Design of *The Scarlet Letter.*" *Nathaniel Hawthorne Review* 13 (1987): 12–14.

"Death of Eben Wheelwright." *Boston Daily Globe*, 12 June 1877.

Defoe, Daniel. *Robinson Crusoe.* 2nd ed. Edited by Michael Shinagel. New York: W. W. Norton, 1994.

Delano, Sterling F. *"The Harbinger" and New England Transcendentalism: A Portrait of Associationism in America.* Rutherford, N. J.: Fairleigh Dickinson University Press, 1983.

Dennet, Charles F. "Le Ramié—Nouvelle Fibre Textile." Broadside. Massachusetts Historical Society. Boston, Mass.

Derby, J. C. *Fifty Years among Authors, Books and Publishers.* New York: G. W. Carleton, 1884.

Derby, Sarah R. Letter to Mary Gardner Reed. 13 October 1841. Reed Family Papers. Rare Book & Manuscript Library. Columbia University. New York, N.Y.

Derrick, Scott S. "'A Curious Subject of Observation and Inquiry': Homoeroticism, the Body, and Authorship in Hawthorne's *The Scarlet Letter.*" *Novel* 28 (1995): 308–26.

Djelal, Juana Celia. "All in All: Melville's Poetics of Unity." *ESQ* 41 (1995): 219–37.

D[odge], J[ohn]. "Hon. Isaac G. Reed." *Boston Recorder,* 1 April 1847: 1. HUG 300. Harvard University Archives. Pusey Library. Cambridge, Mass.

Douglass, Frederick. *Narrative of the Life of Frederick Douglass, An American Slave. The Frederick Douglass Papers.* Series Two: *Autobiographical Writings.* Vol. 1. Edited by John W. Blassingame, John R. McKivigan, and Peter P. Hinks. New Haven: Yale University Press, 1999.

Downing, David B. "The Swelling Waves: Visuality, Metaphor, and Bodily Reality in *The Scarlet Letter.*" *Studies in American Fiction* 12 (1984): 13–28.

Dreyer, Eileen. "'Confession' in *The Scarlet Letter.*" *Journal of American Studies* 25 (1991): 78–81.

Duberman, Martin. *James Russell Lowell*. Boston: Houghton Mifflin, 1966.

Dukats, Mara L. "The Hybrid Terrain of Literary Imagination: Maryse Condé's Black Witch of Salem, Nathaniel Hawthorne's Hester Prynne, and Aimé Césaire's Heroic Poetic Voice." *College Literature* 22 (1995): 51–61.

Duncan, Roland E. "The New England Heritage of William Wheelwright of Newburyport, Massachusetts." *Essex Institute Historical Collections* 98 (1962): 239–48.

Dunn, Richard S., James Savage, and Laetitia Yeandle, eds. *The Journal of John Winthrop, 1630–1649*. Cambridge: Harvard University Press, 1996.

Duyckinck, Evert A. Letter to James Russell Lowell. 17 January 1850. *bMS Am 765* (299–301), Norton Collection. Houghton Library. Harvard University. Cambridge, Mass.

"Ebenezer Wheelwright." Vol. 2, p. 665. R. G. Dun & Co. Collection. Nineteenth-Century Credit Ledgers. Baker Library. Harvard Business School. Boston, Mass.

["Ebenezer Wheelwright"]. *Boston Morning Journal,* 12 June 1877, 2.

Ehrlich, Gloria C. *Family Themes and Hawthorne's Fiction: The Tenacious Web*. New Brunswick, N.J.: Rutgers University Press, 1984.

———. "Hawthorne and the Mannings." In *Studies in the American Renaissance 1980*, edited by Joel Myerson, 97–117. Boston: G. K. Hall, 1980.

Elbert, Monika. "Hester on the Scaffold, Dimmesdale in the Closet: Hawthorne's Seven-Year Itch." *Essays in Literature* 16 (1989): 234–55.

Eliade, Mircea. *The Sacred and the Profane: The Nature of Religion*. Translated by Willard R. Trask. New York: Harcourt, Brace & World, 1959.

Emerson, Ralph Waldo. *Ralph Waldo Emerson: Collected Poems and Translations*. Edited by Harold Bloom and Paul Kane. New York: Library of America, 1984.

Eveleth, George W. *The Letters from George W. Eveleth to Edgar Allan Poe*. Edited by Thomas Ollive Mabbott. New York: New York Public Library, 1922.

"Facts and Opinions." *Literary World,* 27 April 1850, 425–56.

Felker, Christopher D. *Reinventing Cotton Mather in the American Renaissance: "Magnalia Christi Americana" in Hawthorne, Stowe, and Stoddard*. Boston: Northeastern University Press, 1993.

Felt, Joseph B. *Annals of Salem*. 2nd ed. 2 vols. Salem: W. & S. B. Ives, 1845 and 1849.

[———]. *The Annals of Salem, from Its First Settlement*. Salem: W. & S. B. Ives, 1827.

Felton, C. C. Review of *Poems*, by James Russell Lowell. *North American Review,* April 1844, 283–99.

Ferguson, Helen Myatt. "Nathaniel Hawthorne and Charles Wentworth Upham: The Witchcraft Connection." Ph.D. diss., University of Maryland, 1980.

Fessenden, Thomas Green. *"New England Farmer's Almanack, for 1828." New England Farmer,* 31 August 1827, 74.

Fiedler, Leslie. *Love and Death in the American Novel*. 1960. New York: Anchor, 1992.

Fitzgerald, F. Scott. *The Great Gatsby*. 1925. In *Cambridge Edition of the Works of F. Scott Fitzgerald*, edited by Matthew J. Bruccoli. Cambridge: Cambridge University Press, 1991.

Fleischner, Jennifer. "Hawthorne and the Politics of Slavery." *Studies in the Novel* 23 (1991): 96–106.

Fogle, Richard Harter. "Byron and Nathaniel Hawthorne." In *Romantic and Victorian Studies in Memory of William H. Marshall*, edited by W. Paul Elledge and Richard L. Hoffman, 181–97. Rutherford, N.J.: Fairleigh Dickinson University Press, 1971.

———. "The Great English Romantics in Hawthorne's Major Romances." In *The Nathaniel Hawthorne Journal 1976*, edited by C. E. Frazer Clark Jr., 62–68. Englewood, Colo.: Information Handling Services, 1978.

Fowler, Alastair. "'To Shepherd's Ear': The Form of Milton's 'Lycidas.'" In *Silent Poetry: Essays in Numerological Analysis*, 170–84. London: Routledge & Kegan Paul, 1970.

———. *Triumphal Forms: Structural Patterns in Elizabethan Poetry*. Cambridge: Cambridge University Press, 1970.

Franchot, Jenny. *Roads to Rome: The Antebellum Protestant Encounter with Catholicism*. Berkeley: University of California Press, 1994.

Franklin, Benjamin, V. "Hawthorne's Mrs. Hutchinson." *B. A. S.: British and American Studies/Revista de Studii Britanice si Americane* 1 (1996): 93–98.

Frederick, John T. "Hawthorne's 'Scribbling Women.'" *New England Quarterly* 48 (1975): 231–40.

Friedman, Robert S. *Hawthorne's Romances: Social Drama and the Metaphor of Geometry*. Amsterdam: Harwood Academic Publishers, 2000.

Fukuchi, Curtis. "Poe's Providential *Narrative of Arthur Gordon Pym*." *ESQ* 27 (1981): 147–56.

Fuller, Margaret. Review of *Grandfather's Chair*, by Nathaniel Hawthorne. In *Essays on American Life and Letters*, edited by Joel Myerson, 58. Albany, N.Y.: NCUP, 1978.

Gabler-Hover, Janet. "'I Take the Shame Upon Myself': Ethical Veracity in *The Scarlet Letter*." In *Truth in American Fiction: The Legacy of Rhetorical Idealism*, 85–120. Athens: University of Georgia Press, 1990.

Gartner, Matthew. "*The Scarlet Letter* and the Book of Esther: Scriptural Letter and Narrative Life." *Studies in American Fiction* 23 (1995): 131–51.

Gatta, John, Jr. *American Madonna: Images of the Divine Woman in Literary Culture*. New York: Oxford University Press, 1997.

———. "The Apocalyptic End of *The Scarlet Letter*." *Texas Studies in Literature and Language* 32 (1990): 506–21.

Genealogical Notes. Box 4. Wheelwright Family Papers. Massachusetts Historical Society. Boston, Mass.

Geraldi, Robert. "Biblical and Religious Sources and Parallels in *The Scarlet Letter*." *The USF Language Quarterly* 15 (1976): 31–34.

Gerber, John C. "Form and Content in *The Scarlet Letter*." *New England Quarterly* 17 (1944): 25–55.

Gervais, Ronald J. "'A Papist among the Puritans': Icon and Logos in *The Scarlet Letter*." *ESQ* 25 (1979): 11–16.

Gilkes, Lillian B. "Hawthorne, Park Benjamin, and S. G. Goodrich: A Three-Cornered Imbroglio." In *The Nathaniel Hawthorne Journal 1971,* edited by C. E. Frazier Clark Jr., 83–112. Englewood, Colo.: Microcard Editions Books, 1971.

Gollin, Rita K. "Hawthorne." *American Literary Scholarship: An Annual / 1982,* edited by J. Albert Robbins, 25–42. Durham, N. C.: Duke University Press, 1984.

———. *Portraits of Nathaniel Hawthorne: An Iconography.* DeKalb: Northern Illinois University Press, 1983.

Green, Carlanda. "The Custom-House: Hawthorne's Dark Wood of Error." *New England Quarterly* 53 (1980): 184–95.

Griffin, Gerald R. "Hawthorne and 'The New England Village': Internal Evidence and a New Genesis of *The Scarlet Letter.*" *Essex Institute Historical Collections* 107 (1971): 268–79.

Griswold, Rufus W., ed. *The Poets and Poetry of America.* 8th ed. Philadelphia: Carey and Hart, 1847.

———. *The Poets and Poetry of America.* 10th ed. Philadelphia: Carey and Hart, 1850.

Gross, Seymour. "Poe's Revision of 'The Oval Portrait.'" *Modern Language Notes* 74 (1959): 16–20.

Gussman, Deborah. "Inalienable Rights: Fictions of Political Identity in *Hobomok* and *The Scarlet Letter.*" *College Literature* 22 (1995): 58–80.

Hale, Edward Everett. *James Russell Lowell and His Friends.* Boston: Houghton Mifflin, 1901.

Hall, David D., ed. *The Antinomian Controversy, 1636–1638: A Documentary History.* 2d ed. Durham, N. C.: Duke University Press, 1990.

Hallowell, Anna D. "An Episode in the Life of James Russell Lowell." *Harper's Weekly,* 23 April 1892, 393–95.

Hartman, James D. *Providence Tales and the Birth of American Literature.* Baltimore: Johns Hopkins University Press, 1999.

Hawthorne, Julian. *Hawthorne and His Circle.* New York: Harper & Brothers, 1903.

———. *Hawthorne Reading: An Essay.* Cleveland: The Rowfant Club, 1902.

———. "The Making of 'The Scarlet Letter.'" *The Bookman* 74 (1931): 401–11.

———. *Nathaniel Hawthorne and His Wife: A Biography.* 2 vols. Boston: James R. Osgood, 1885.

———. "Scenes of Hawthorne's Romances." *Century* 28 (1884): 380–97.

Hawthorne, Nathaniel. *Centenary Edition of the Works of Nathaniel Hawthorne.* Edited by William Charvat, et al. 23 vols. Columbus: Ohio State University Press, 1962–97.

———. "Fessenden's *Poems.*" *American Magazine of Useful and Entertaining Knowledge,* June 1836, 403–4.

———. "Fragments from the Journal of a Solitary Man." *American Monthly Magazine,* July 1837, 45–56.

———. *Hawthorne's Lost Notebook, 1835–1841.* Transcript and preface by Barbara S. Mouffe, introduction by Hyatt H. Waggoner. University Park: Pennsylvania State University Press, 1978.

———. "Hawthorne's Speech to the Friends of the William Brown Library, 15 April 1857." In *The Nathaniel Hawthorne Journal 1972,* edited by C. E. Frazer Clark Jr., 208–10. Washington, D.C.: Microcard Editions, 1973.

————. "Thomas Green Fessenden." *American Monthly Magazine,* January 1838, 30–41.

Hawthorne, Sophia Peabody. Journal. 10–18 June 1847. Berg Collection. New York Public Library. New York, N.Y.

————. Letter to Mrs. Lucy Cleveland. 11 April 1838. Nathaniel Hawthorne Collection. Mss. #68. Phillips Library. Peabody Essex Museum. Salem, Mass.

————. Letter to Maria Louisa Hawthorne. 17 April 1843. Berg Collection. New York Public Library. New York, N.Y.

————. Letter to Maria Louisa Hawthorne. 15 September 1843. Berg Collection. New York Public Library. New York, N.Y.

————. Letter to Maria Louisa Hawthorne. 26 October 1843. Berg Collection. New York Public Library. New York, N.Y.

————. Letter to Maria Louisa Hawthorne. 31 December 1843 and 1 January 1844. Berg Collection. New York Public Library. New York, N.Y.

————. Letter to Maria Louisa Hawthorne. 22 September 1845. Berg Collection. New York Public Library. New York, N.Y.

————. Letter to Maria Louisa Hawthorne. 3 May 1846. Berg Collection. New York Public Library. New York, N.Y.

————. Letter to Maria Louisa Hawthorne. 28 April 1850. Berg Collection. New York Public Library. New York, N.Y.

————. Letter to Mrs. Mary Hemenway. 28 February1869. Hawthorne-Manning Collection. Mss. #69. Phillips Library. Peabody Essex Museum. Salem, Mass.

————. Letter to Mrs. Mary Hemenway. 27 October 1869. Hawthorne-Manning Collection. Mss. #69. Phillips Library. Peabody Essex Museum. Salem, Mass.

————. Letter to Elizabeth Palmer Peabody. 2 November 1822. Berg Collection. New York Public Library. New York, N.Y.

————. Letter to Elizabeth Palmer Peabody. 11 April 1833. Berg Collection. New York Public Library. New York, N.Y.

————. Letter to Elizabeth Palmer Peabody. 2 December 1849. Berg Collection. New York Public Library. New York, N.Y.

————. Letter to Mrs. Elizabeth Palmer Peabody. 12 February1834. ("Cuba Journal" 1: 28–31). Berg Collection. New York Public Library. New York, N.Y.

————. Letter to Mrs. Elizabeth Palmer Peabody. 28 February1843. Berg Collection. New York Public Library. New York, N.Y.

————. Letter to Mrs. Elizabeth Palmer Peabody. 23 March 1843. Berg Collection. New York Public Library. New York, N.Y.

————. Letter to Mrs. Elizabeth Palmer Peabody. 20 April 1843. Berg Collection. New York Public Library. New York, N.Y.

————. Letter to Mrs. Elizabeth Palmer Peabody. 19 August 1849. Berg Collection. New York Public Library. New York, N.Y.

Herbert, T. Walter. *Dearest Beloved: The Hawthornes and the Making of the Middle-Class Family.* Berkeley: University of California Press, 1993.

————. "Nathaniel Hawthorne, Una Hawthorne, and *The Scarlet Letter:* Interactive Selfhoods and the Cultural Construction of Gender." *PMLA* 103 (1988): 285–97.

Higginson, Thomas Wentworth. "A Precursor of Hawthorne." *Independent* 40 (1888): 385–86.

Hocks, Richard A. "Thoreau, Coleridge, and Barfield: Reflections on the Imagination and the Law of Polarity." *The Centennial Review* 17 (1973): 175–98.

Hoeltje, Hubert H. "Captain Nathaniel Hathorne, Father of the Famous Salem Novelist." *Essex Institute Historical Collections* 89 (1953): 329–56.

———. "The Writing of *The Scarlet Letter.*" *New England Quarterly* 27 (1954): 326–46.

Hoffman, Elizabeth Aycock. "Political Power in *The Scarlet Letter.*" *ATQ,* n.s. 4 (1990): 13–29.

[Holden, George Henry]. "Hawthorne among His Friends." *Harper's Monthly* 63 (1881): 260–67.

Hoover, Merle M. *Park Benjamin: Poet and Editor.* New York: Columbia University Press, 1948.

Hovey, Horace C., ed. *Origins and Annals of "The Old South" First Presbyterian Church and Parish, in Newburyport, Mass., 1746–1896.* Boston: Damrell & Upham, 1896.

Howard, Leon. *Victorian Knight-Errant: A Study of the Early Literary Career of James Russell Lowell.* Berkeley: University of California Press, 1952.

Hull, Raymona E. "'Scribbling' Females and Serious Males: Hawthorne's Comments from Abroad on Some American Authors." In *The Nathaniel Hawthorne Journal 1975,* edited by C. E. Frazer Clark Jr., 35–58. Englewood, Colo.: Microcard Editions, 1975.

Hunter, J. Paul. *The Reluctant Pilgrim: Defoe's Emblematic Method and Quest for Form in "Robinson Crusoe."* Baltimore: Johns Hopkins University Press, 1966.

Hutchinson, Thomas. *The History of Massachusetts: From the First Settlement Thereof in 1628, until the Year 1750.* 2 vols. 3rd ed. Boston: Thomas and Andrews, 1795.

Hutchison, Earl R., Sr. "Antiquity and Mythology in *The Scarlet Letter*: The Primary Sources." *Arizona Quarterly* 36 (1980): 197–210.

Idol, John L., Jr., and Buford Jones, eds. *Nathaniel Hawthorne: The Contemporary Reviews.* Cambridge: Cambridge University Press, 1994.

Idol, John L., Jr., and Melinda M. Ponder, eds. *Hawthorne and Women: Engendering and Expanding the Hawthorne Tradition.* Amherst: University of Masschusetts Press, 1999.

"Intelligence Office." *Salem Tri-Weekly Gazette,* 6 November 1847, 1.

Irving, Washington. *Complete Works.* Edited by Richard Dilworth Rust, et al. 30 vols. Boston: Twayne, 1969–88.

"Isaac Watts Wheelwright." In *History of Essex County, Massachusetts, with Biographical Sketches of Many of Its Pioneers and Prominent Men,* compiled by D. Hamilton Hurd, 2:1827–29. Philadelphia: J. W. Lewis & Co., 1888.

Isani, Mukhtar Ali. "Hawthorne and the Branding of William Prynne." *New England Quarterly* 45 (1972): 182–95.

James, Henry. *Hawthorne.* New York: Harper, 1879.

Jepson, George. "Hawthorne in the Boston Custom House." *The Bookman* 19 (1904): 573–80.

"John M. Whittemore, Stationer." *Boston Evening Transcript,* 20 November 1901, 2.

Johnson, Claudia Durst. "Impotence and Omnipotence in *The Scarlet Letter*." *New England Quarterly* 66 (1993): 594–612.

———. *Understanding "The Scarlet Letter": A Student Casebook to Issues, Sources, and Historical Documents*. Westport, Conn.: Greenwood Press, 1995.

Johnson, W. Stacy. "Hawthorne and *The Pilgrim's Progress*." *JEGP* 50 (1951): 156–66.

Jones, Buford. "'The Hall of Fantasy' and the Early Hawthorne-Thoreau Relationship." *PMLA* 83 (1968): 1429–38.

["Joseph Ballister"]. *Boston Daily Advertiser*, 14 November 1876.

Joyce, William. Interview by author. University Park, Pa., 2 February 2001.

Kantorowicz, Ernst H. "Dante's 'Two Suns.'" In *Selected Studies*, 325–38. Locust Valley, N.Y.: J. J. Augustin, 1965.

Kearns, Francis E. "Margaret Fuller as a Model for Hester Prynne." *Jahrbuch für Amerikastudien* 10 (1965): 191–97.

Kehler, Dorothea. "Hawthorne and Shakespeare." *ATQ* 22 (1974): 104–5.

Keil, James C. "Reading, Writing, and Recycling: Literary Archaeology and the Shape of Hawthorne's Career." *New England Quarterly* 65 (1992): 238–64.

Kennedy, J. Gerald. "'Trust No Man': Poe, Douglass, and the Culture of Slavery." In *Romancing the Shadow: Poe and Race*, edited by J. Gerald Kennedy and Liliane Weissberg, 225–57. New York: Oxford University Press, 2001.

Kennedy-Andrews, Elmer, ed. *Nathaniel Hawthorne: "The Scarlet Letter."* New York: Columbia University Press, 1999.

Kesselring, Marion L. "Hawthorne's Reading, 1828–1850." *Bulletin of The New York Public Library* 53 (1949): 55–71, 121–38, 173–94.

Ketterer, David. "'Shudder': A Signature *Crypt*-ogram in 'The Fall of the House of Usher.'" *Resources for American Literary Study* 25 (1999): 192–205.

Kilcup, Karen L. "'Ourselves Behind Ourself, Concealed—': The Homoerotics of Reading in *The Scarlet Letter*." *ESQ* 42 (1996): 1–28.

King, Caroline Howard. *When I Lived in Salem, 1822–1866*. Brattleboro, Vt.: Stephen Daye Press, 1937.

Knapp, N. P. "Ladies' Fair." *Essex Register*, 15 April 1833, 1.

Kopley, Richard. "Chiasmus in *Walden*." *New England Quarterly*, forthcoming.

———. "The Circle and Its Center in 'Bartleby the Scrivener.'" *ATQ*, n.s. 2 (1988): 191–206.

———. *Edgar Allan Poe and "The Philadelphia Saturday News."* Baltimore: Enoch Pratt Free Library and Edgar Allan Poe Society of Baltimore, 1991.

———. "Hawthorne's Transplanting and Transforming 'The Tell-Tale Heart.'" *Studies in American Fiction* 23 (1995): 231–41.

———. "The Hidden Journey of *Arthur Gordon Pym*." In *Studies in the American Renaissance 1982*, edited by Joel Myerson, 29–51. Boston: G. K. Hall, 1982.

———. "Poe's *Pym*-esque 'A Tale of the Ragged Mountains.'" In *Poe and His Times: The Artist and His Milieu*, 167–77. Baltimore: Edgar Allan Poe Society, 1990.

———. "The Secret of *Arthur Gordon Pym*: The Text and the Source." *Studies in American Fiction* 8 (1980): 203–18.

————. "The 'Very Profound Under-current' of *Arthur Gordon Pym*." In *Studies in the American Renaissance 1987*, edited by Joel Myerson, 143–75. Charlottesville: University Press of Virginia, 1987.

————, ed. *The Narrative of Arthur Gordon Pym of Nantucket*, by Edgar Allan Poe. New York: Penguin Books, 1999.

Korobkin, Laura Hanft. "The Scarlet Letter of the Law: Hawthorne and Criminal Justice." *Novel* 30 (1997): 193–217.

Krappe, Edith Smith. "A Possible Source for Poe's 'The Tell-Tale Heart' and 'The Black Cat.'" *American Literature* 12 (1940): 84–88.

Kushen, Betty. "Love's Martyrs: The Scarlet Letter as Secular Cross." *Literature and Psychology* 22 (1972): 109–20.

"The Ladies' Fair." *Essex Register,* 15 April 1833, 2.

Laffrado, Laura. *Hawthorne's Literature for Children*. Athens: University of Georgia Press, 1992.

Lang, Amy Schrager. *Prophetic Woman: Anne Hutchinson and the Problem of Dissent in the Literature of New England*. Berkeley: University of California Press, 1987.

Laser, Marvin. "'Head,' 'Heart,' and 'Will' in Hawthorne's Psychology." *Nineteenth-Century Fiction* 10 (1955): 130–40.

Lathrop, George Parsons, ed. *Complete Works of Nathaniel Hawthorne*. 12 vols. Boston: Houghton Mifflin, 1883.

————. *A Study of Hawthorne*. Boston: James R. Osgood, 1876.

Lathrop, Rose Hawthorne. *Memories of Hawthorne*. Boston: Houghton Mifflin, 1897.

Lease, Benjamin. "Robert Carter, James Russell Lowell, and John Neal: A Document." *Jahrbuch für Americastudien* 13 (1968): 246–48.

Leisy, Ernest E., ed. *The Scarlet Letter: A Romance*, by Nathaniel Hawthorne. New York: Thomas Nelson, 1929.

Levenson, Jon D. *Esther: A Commentary*. Louisville, Ky: Westminster John Knox Press, 1997.

Leverenz, David. *Manhood and the American Renaissance*. Ithaca, N.Y.: Cornell University Press, 1989.

Lewis, R. W. B. *The American Adam: Innocence, Tragedy, and Tradition in the Nineteenth Century*. Chicago: University of Chicago Press, 1955; reprint, Chicago: University of Chicago Press, 1971.

Li, Haipeng. "Hester Prynne and the Folk Art of Embroidery." *University of Mississippi Studies in English,* n.s. 10 (1992): 80–85.

Lilly, Georgiana, copier. *Waldoboro, Maine Cemetery Inscriptions*. N.p., n.d. Recopied by Virginia T. Merrill, Solon, Maine.

Littlefield, Walter. "James Russell Lowell in 1842." In *Early Prose Writings of James Russell Lowell,* xvi–xxxviii.

Ljungquist, Kent P. "The 'Little War' and Longfellow's Dilemma: New Documents in the Plagiarism Controversy of 1845." *Resources for American Literary Study* 23 (1997): 28–59.

Lloyd, Deborah. Letter to the author from the senior copyright research specialist of the Reference & Bibliography Section, Copyright Office, Library of Congress. Washington, D.C. 20 July 2001.

Loewentheil, Stephan, and Tom Edsall, comps. *The Poe Catalogue: A Descriptive Catalogue of the Stephan Loewentheil Collection of Edgar Allan Poe Material.* Baltimore: The 19th Century Shop, 1992.

Loggins, Vernon. *The Hawthornes: The Story of Seven Generations of an American Family.* New York: Columbia University Press, 1951.

Lombard, C. M. "A Neglected Critic—Henry T. Tuckerman." *Etudes Anglaises* 22 (1969): 362– 69.

Longfellow, Henry Wadsworth. *Kavanagh: A Tale.* Boston: Ticknor, Reed, and Fields, 1849.

———. *The Letters of Henry Wadsworth Longfellow.* Edited by Andrew Hilen. 6 vols. Cambridge: Harvard University Press, 1967–82.

Loring, George Bailey. "Loring on Hawthorne." *Salem Register,* 8 May 1882, 2. See *Biographical Clippings* at the Phillips Library of the Peabody Essex Museum Library, 26: 364.

Lowell, James Russell. "The Ballad of the Stranger." In *The Token and Atlantic Souvenir, an Offering for Christmas and the New Year*, 133–37. Boston: Daniel H. Williams, 1842. Reprinted in *Uncollected Poems of James Russell Lowell.*

———. *Conversations on Some of the Old Poets.* Cambridge, Mass.: John Owen, 1845.

———. *Early Prose Writings of James Russell Lowell.* Prefatory note by Edward Everett Hale and Introduction by Walter Littlefield. New York: John Lane, 1902.

———. "The First Client, with Incidental Good Precepts for Incipient Attorneys." *Boston Miscellany,* May 1842, 228–30. Reprinted in *Early Prose Writings of James Russell Lowell,* 2–15.

———. Letter to Edward M. Davis. 13 January 1850. *bMS Am 1054 (110–123)*, Davis Letters. Houghton Library. Harvard University. Cambridge, Mass.

———. Letter to Nathaniel Hawthorne. 24 April 1851. Berg Collection. New York Public Library. New York, N.Y.

———. *Letters of James Russell Lowell.* 2 vols. Edited by Charles Eliot Norton. New York: Harper & Brothers, 1894.

———. *New Letters of James Russell Lowell.* Edited by M. A. DeWolfe Howe. New York: Harper and Brothers, 1932.

———. "The Old English Dramatists." *Boston Miscellany,* April 1842, 45–54; May 1842: 201–8; August 1842, 49–54.

———. "The Plays of Thomas Middleton." In *Pioneer,* 32–39.

———. *Poems.* Cambridge, Mass.: John Owen, 1844.

———. *Poems.* 2 vols. Boston: Ticknor, Reed, and Fields, 1849. Inscribed to Hawthorne. Berg Collection. New York Public Library. New York, N.Y.

———. Review of *Historical Tales for Youth,* by Nathaniel Hawthorne. In *Pioneer,* 42–43.

———. Review of *The Salem Belle.* In *Pioneer,* 44.

———. *Uncollected Poems of James Russell Lowell.* Edited by Thelma M. Smith. Philadelphia: University of Pennsylvania Press, 1950.

———. *The Writings of James Russell Lowell.* 10 vols. Cambridge, Mass.: Houghton Mifflin, 1890.

———. *A Year's Life*. Boston: C. C. Little and J. Brown, 1841.

———, ed. *The Pioneer: A Literary Magazine*. Introduction by Sculley Bradley. New York: Scholars' Facsimiles and Reprints, 1947.

Lowell, James Russell, and John Owen. [Contract for "Poems by James Russell Lowell"]. Morgan Library. New York, N.Y. MA 648

Lowell, Maria White. *Letter of Maria White [Mrs. James Russell] Lowell to Sophia [Mrs. Nathaniel] Hawthorne*. N.p, n.d. Ca. 1910. Reprinted ("Letter of Maria White Lowell") in *Yearbook* (of the Bibliophile Society) 11 (1912): 107–14.

———. Letter to Caroline King. 4 October 1842. Typescript transcription. Loring Family Papers. Schlesinger Library. Radcliffe Institute. Harvard University. Cambridge, Mass.

———. Letter to Sarah Blake Sturgis Shaw. 4 November 1842. James Russell Lowell Papers. Massachusetts Historical Society. Boston, Mass.

———. *The Poems of Maria Lowell with Unpublished Letters and a Biography*. Edited by Hope Jillson Vernon. Providence, R.I.: Brown University Press, 1936.

Lowes, John Livingston. *The Road to Xanadu: A Study in the Ways of the Imagination*. Boston: Houghton Mifflin, 1927.

Lucke, Jessie Ryon. "Hawthorne's Madonna Image in *The Scarlet Letter*." *New England Quarterly* 38 (1965): 391–92.

Luedtke, Luther S. *Nathaniel Hawthorne and the Romance of the Orient*. Bloomington: Indiana University Press, 1989.

Lund, Nils W. *Chiasmus in the New Testament: A Study in Formgeschichte*. Chapel Hill: University of North Carolina Press, 1942.

———. "Chiasmus in the Psalms." *American Journal of Semitic Languages and Literatures* 49 (1933): 281–312.

———. "The Presence of Chiasmus in the Old Testament." *American Journal of Semitic Languages and Literatures* 46 (1930): 104–26.

Lundblad, Jane. *Nathaniel Hawthorne and the Tradition of Gothic Romance*. Uppsala, Sweden: A.-B. Lundequistska Bokhandeln, 1946.

Lynch, James J. "The Devil in the Writings of Irving, Hawthorne, and Poe." *New York Folklore Quarterly* 8 (1952): 111–31.

M. Letter. *Salem Register* (21 March 1850): 2.

———. Letter. *Salem Register* (1 April 1850): 2.

———. Letter. *Salem Register* (9 May 1850): 2.

Mabbott, T. O. "A Review of Lowell's Magazine." *Notes and Queries* 178 (1940): 457–58.

Macandrew, Elizabeth. "Life in the Maze—Johnson's Use of Chiasmus in *The Vanity of Human Wishes*." In *Studies in Eighteenth-Century Culture*, edited by Roseann Runte, 9:517–27. Madison: University of Wisconsin Press, 1979.

Maes-Jelinek, Hena. "Roger Chillingworth: An Example of the Creative Process in 'The Scarlet Letter.'" *English Studies* 49 (1968): 341–48.

Male, Roy R. *Hawthorne's Tragic Vision*. 1957. Reprint, New York: Norton, 1973.

Marks, Alfred H. "*The Scarlet Letter* and Tieck's 'The Elves.'" *Nathaniel Hawthorne Review* 17 (1991): 1, 3–5.

———. "Two Rodericks and Two Worms: 'Egotism; or, the Bosom Serpent' as Personal Satire." *PMLA* 74 (1959): 607–12.

Martineau, Harriet, ed. *Traditions of Palestine.* London: Longman, Rees, Orme, Brown, and Green, 1830.

Marvell, Andrew. "On Mr Milton's 'Paradise Lost.'" In Marvell, *The Oxford Authors: Andrew Marvell*, 119–20.

———. *The Oxford Authors: Andrew Marvell*, edited by Frank Kermode and Keith Walker. Oxford: Oxford University Press, 1990.

———. "The Unfortunate Lover." In Marvell, *The Oxford Authors: Andrew Marvell*, 25–27.

Marvin, Abijah P. *History of the Town of Lancaster, Massachusetts.* Lancaster, Mass.: n.p., 1879.

Masheck, J. D. C. "Samuel Johnson's Uttoxeter Penance in the Writings of Hawthorne." *Hermathena* 111 (1971): 51–54.

Mathews, J. Chesley. "Hawthorne." "Bibliographical Supplement: A Selective Check List, 1955–1962." In *Eight American Authors: A Review of Research and Criticism*, edited by Floyd Stovall, 428–34. New York: MLA, 1963.

———. "Hawthorne's Knowledge of Dante." *University of Texas Studies in English* 20 (1940): 157–65.

Matthiessen, F. O. *American Renaissance: Art and Expression in the Age of Emerson and Whitman.* New York: Oxford University Press, 1941.

Mayhook, J. Jeffrey. "'Bearings Unknown to English Heraldry' in *The Scarlet Letter*." In *The Nathaniel Hawthorne Journal 1977*, edited by C. E. Frazer Clark Jr., 173–214. Detroit: Gale Research, 1980.

McCall, Dan. *Citizens of Somewhere Else: Nathaniel Hawthorne and Henry James.* Ithaca, N.Y.: Cornell University Press, 1999.

McCorison, Marcus. "Thomas Green Fessenden, 1771–1837: Not in *BAL*." *Papers of the Bibliographical Society of America* 89 (1995): 5–59.

McDonald, John J. "A Guide to Primary Source Materials for the Study of Hawthorne's Old Manse Period." In *Studies in the American Renaissance 1977*, edited by Joel Myerson, 261–312. Boston: G. K. Hall, 1978.

———. "The Old Manse Period Canon." In *The Nathaniel Hawthorne Journal 1972*, edited by C. E. Frazer Clark Jr., 13–39. Washington, D.C.: Microcard Editions, 1973.

McFadyen, Alvan R. "The Contemporaneous Reputation of James Russell Lowell." Ph.D. diss., University of Florida, 1955.

McFarlane, Cameron. "Reading Crusoe Reading Providence." *English Studies in Canada* 21 (1995): 257–67.

McKeithan, D. M. "Poe and the Second Edition of Hawthorne's *Twice-Told Tales*." In *The Nathaniel Hawthorne Journal 1974*, edited by C. E. Frazer Clark Jr., 257–69. Englewood, Colo.: Microcard Editions Books, 1975.

McKenna, George, "'An Holy and Blessed People': The Puritan Origins of American Patriotism." *The Yale Review* 90 (2002): 81–98.

Mellow, James R. *Nathaniel Hawthorne and His Times.* Boston: Houghton Mifflin, 1980.

Melville, Herman. *The Writings of Herman Melville*. Edited by Harrison Hayford, et al. 13 vols. to date. Evanston, Ill.: Northwestern University Press and The Newberry Library, 1968–.

["Messrs. Tappan and Dennet"]. *Brother Jonathan,* 18 February 1843, 195.

"The Meteor." *The Hive* (of Salem, Mass.), 28 June 1830, 160.

Miller, Edwin Haviland. "A Calendar of the Letters of Sophia Peabody Hawthorne." In *Studies in the American Renaissance 1986*, edited by Joel Myerson, 199–281. Charlottesville: University Press of Virginia, 1986.

———. *Salem is My Dwelling Place: A Life of Nathaniel Hawthorne*. Iowa City: University of Iowa Press, 1991.

Miller, Harold P. "Hawthorne Surveys His Contemporaries." *American Literature* 12 (1940): 228–35.

Milne, Gordon. *George William Curtis and the Genteel Tradition*. Bloomington: Indiana University Press, 1956.

Mitchell, Thomas R. *Hawthorne's Fuller Mystery*. Amherst: University of Massachusetts Press, 1998.

Moore, Margaret B. *The Salem World of Nathaniel Hawthorne*. Columbia: University of Missouri Press, 1998.

More, Paul Elmer. "The Origins of Poe and Hawthorne." In *Shelburne Essays*, first series, 51–70. New York: G. P. Putnam's Sons, 1904.

Morrison, Toni. *Playing in the Dark: Whiteness and the Literary Imagination*. Cambridge: Harvard University Press, 1992.

Mott, Frank Luther. *A History of American Magazines, 1741–1850*. Vol. 1. Cambridge: Harvard University Press, 1938.

["Mr. Eben Wheelwright"]. *Newburyport Herald,* 19 June 1877, 3.

["Mr. Ebenezer Wheelwright"]. *Boston Daily Advertiser*, 12 June 1877, 1.

["Mr. Ebenezer Wheelwright, Aged 77"]. *Newburyport Daily Herald*, 13 June 1877, 3.

Muse, Marla Y. Letter to the author from the senior copyright research specialist, Reference and Bibliography Section, Copyright Office, Library of Congress. 23 October 1998.

Nänny, Max. "Chiasmus in Literature: Ornament or Function?" *Word and Image* 4 (1988): 51–59.

———. "Chiastic Structures in Literature: Some Forms and Functions." In *The Structure of Texts*, edited by Udo Fries, 75–87. Tubingen: Gunter Narr, 1987.

———. "Formal Allusions to Visual Ideas and Visual Art in Hemingway's Work." *European Journal of English Studies* 4 (2000): 66–82.

———. "Hemingway's Architecture of Prose: Chiastic Patterns and Their Narrative Functions." *North Dakota Quarterly* 64 (1997): 157–76.

———. "Hemingway's Use of Chiastic Centering as an Interpretive Clue." *North Dakota Quarterly* 65 (1998): 174–85.

———. "The Reinforcement of Meaning by Subliminal Patterns of Repetition." In *Anglistentag 1990 Marburg: Proceedings*, edited by Claus Uhlig and Rüdifer Zimmermann, 109–16. Tübingen: Max Niemeyer Verlag, 1991.

National Archives Branch Depository, Waltham, Mass. ["Amended Schedule B"]. Records of the Bankruptcy of Ebenezer Wheelwright. File 730. RG 21.

National Union Catalog: Pre–1956 Imprints. Chicago: Mansell, 1968–80.

Newberry, Frederick. *Hawthorne's Divided Loyalties: England and America in His Works.* Rutherford, N.J.: Fairleigh Dickinson University Press, 1987.

———. "A Red-Hot A and a Lusting Divine: Sources for *The Scarlet Letter.*" *New England Quarterly* 60 (1987): 256–64.

———. "Tradition and Disinheritance in *The Scarlet Letter.*" *ESQ* 23 (1977): 1–26.

Newman, Lea Bertani Vozar. *A Reader's Guide to the Short Stories of Nathaniel Hawthorne.* Boston: G. K. Hall, 1979.

"The New-York Booksellers' Dinner." *American Monthly Magazine,* May 1837, 521–24.

Nissenbaum, Stephen. "The Firing of Nathaniel Hawthorne." *Essex Institute Historical Collections* 114 (1978): 37–86.

Normann, Ralf. *The Insecure World of Henry James's Fiction: Intensity and Ambiguity.* New York: St. Martin's Press, 1982.

———. *Samuel Butler and the Meaning of Chiasmus.* New York: St. Martin's Press, 1986.

———. *Wholeness Restored: Love of Symmetry as a Shaping Force in the Writings of Henry James, Kurt Vonnegut, Samuel Butler, and Raymond Chandler.* Frankfurt am Main: Peter Lang, 1998.

Notice of *The Salem Belle. Boston Daily Courier,* 30 November 1842, 2.

Notice of *The Salem Belle. Boston Evening Gazette,* 3 December 1842, 3.

Notice of *The Salem Belle. Salem Register,* 22 July 1847, 2.

O'Keefe, Richard R. "An Echo of Emerson in Hawthorne's 'The Custom-House'?" *Nathaniel Hawthorne Review* 18 (1992): 9–11.

Olson, Kristen. "The 'Soul's Imaginary Sight': Visuality and Mimesis in Early Modern Poetics." Ph.D. diss., Case Western Reserve University, 2001.

"The Organ." *The Columbian* (Hartford, Conn.), 2 March 1844, 1.

Orians, G. Harrison. "The Angel of Hadley in Fiction: A Study of the Sources of Hawthorne's 'The Grey Champion.'" *American Literature* 4 (1932): 257–69.

———. "New England Witchcraft in Fiction." *American Literature* 2 (1930): 54–71.

Osborn, Robert, and Marijane Osborn. "Another Look at an Old Tombstone." *New England Quarterly* 46 (1973): 278–79.

Owens, Louis. "Paulding's 'The Dumb Girl,' A Source of *The Scarlet Letter.*" In *The Nathaniel Hawthorne Journal 1974*, edited by C. E. Frazer Clark Jr., 240–49. Englewood, Colo.: Microcard Editions, 1975.

Panofsky, Erwin. *The Life and Art of Albrecht Dürer.* 4th ed. 1955. Reprint, Princeton: Princeton University Press, 1971.

———. *Meaning in the Visual Arts: Papers in and on Art History.* Garden City, N.Y.: Doubleday Anchor, 1955.

Peabody, Mary. Letter to Sophia Hawthorne. 5 October 1842[?] Berg Collection. New York Public Library. New York, N.Y.

Pearce, Roy Harvey. Review of *Hawthorne's Faust. Modern Language Notes* 71 (1956): 61–63.

Pearson, Norman Holmes. "Elizabeth Peabody on Hawthorne." *Essex Institute Historical Collections* 94 (1958): 256–76.

Perry, Bliss. "The Centenary of Hawthorne." In *Park-Street Papers*, 63–103. Boston: Houghton Mifflin, 1908.

Person, Leland S., Jr. *Aesthetic Headaches: Women and a Masculine Poetics in Poe, Melville, and Hawthorne*. Athens: University of Georgia Press, 1988.

———. "Hawthorne's Love Letters: Writing and Relationship." *American Literature* 59 (1987): 211–27.

"Peter Klaus: The Legend of the Goatherd—Rip Van Winkle." *London Magazine* 5 (1822): 229–30.

Peterson, Charles J. Letter to James Russell Lowell. 10 January 1844. *bMS Am 1355 (31)*, Norton Collection. Houghton Library. Harvard University. Cambridge, Mass.

———. "Lowell's Poems. A New School of Poetry at Hand" (Review of *A Year's Life*). *Graham's Magazine,* April 1842, 195–99.

———. Review of *Poems*, by James Russell Lowell. *Ladies' National Magazine,* February 1844, 71–72.

———. Review of *Poems*, by James Russell Lowell. *Ladies' National Magazine,* March 1844, 95–99.

Pfister, Joel. *The Production of Personal Life: Class, Gender, and the Psychological in Hawthorne's Fiction*. Stanford, Calif.: Stanford University Press, 1991.

Phelps, C. Deirdre. "Directory of the Salem Book Trade." *Essex Institute Historical Collections* 124 (1988): 264–95.

———. "Printing, Publishing, and Bookselling in Salem, Massachusetts, 1825–1900." *Essex Institute Historical Collections* 124 (1988): 227–64.

Phillips, Mary E. *Edgar Allan Poe—The Man*. 2 vols. Chicago: John C. Winston, 1926.

Pochmann, Henry A. "Irving's German Sources in *The Sketch Book*." *Studies in Philology* 27 (1930): 477–507.

Poe, Edgar Allan. *Collected Works of Edgar Allan Poe*. Edited by Thomas Ollive Mabbott. 3 vols. Cambridge: Harvard University Press, 1969–78.

———. *Collected Writings of Edgar Allan Poe*. Edited by Burton R. Pollin. 5 vols. to date. Boston: Twayne, 1981; New York: Gordian Press, 1985–.

———. *The Complete Works of Edgar Allan Poe*. Edited by James A. Harrison. 17 vols. New York: T. Y. Crowell, 1902. Reprint, New York: AMS Press, 1979.

———. *The Letters of Edgar Allan Poe*. Edited by John Ward Ostrom. 2 vols. New York: Harvard University Press, 1948. Reprint, with a supplement, New York: Gordian, 1966.

———. Review of *Conversations on Some of the Old Poets*, by James Russell Lowell. In *Bibliography of the Writings of Edgar A. Poe*, by John W. Robertson 1:214. San Francisco: Russian Hill Private Press, 1934.

———. "Von Jung, the Mystific." *American Monthly Magazine,* June 1837, 562–71.

Pollin, Burton R. "Poe and Daniel Defoe: A Significant Relationship." *Topic* 16 (1976): 3–22.

———. "Poe's Authorship of Three Long Critical and Autobiographical Articles of 1843 Now Authenticated." *American Renaissance Literary Report: An Annual* 7 (1993): 139–71.

———. "A Posthumous Assessment: The 1849–1850 Periodical Press Response to Edgar Allan Poe." *American Periodicals* 2 (1992): 6–50.

Poulet, Georges. *The Metamorphoses of the Circle.* Translated by Carley Dawson and Elliott Coleman. Baltimore: Johns Hopkins University Press, 1966.

Pound, Louise. "Lowell's 'Breton Legend.'" *American Literature* 12 (1940): 348–50.

Pramberg, Noreen C., comp. *Etched in Stone: Newburyport, Mass., Cemeteries.* Vol. 1. N.p., 1991.

Prestwich, Ann. "Charles Jacobs Peterson, Editor, and Friend of Lowell and Poe." M.A. diss., Columbia University, 1938.

Pribek, Thomas. "Hawthorne's Blackstone." *American Notes & Queries* 24 (1986): 142–44.

Reed, Edward A. Letter to Isaac Gardner Reed. 29 December 1833. Reed Family Papers. Rare Book and Manuscript Library. Columbia University. New York, N.Y.

Reed, Gardner K. Letter to Jane Ann Reed. 27 October 1867. The Gardner K. Reed Letters and Journals, Yale Collection of Western Americana. Beinecke Rare Book and Manuscript Library. Yale University. New Haven, Conn.

Reed, Isaac Gardner. Letter to Mary Gardner Reed. 26 January 1843. Reed Family Papers. Rare Book & Manuscript Library. Columbia University. New York, N.Y.

Reed, Jon B. "'A Letter,—the Letter A': A Portrait of the Artist as Hester Prynne." *ESQ* 36 (1990): 79–107.

Regan, Robert. "Hawthorne's 'Plagiary'; Poe's Duplicity." *Nineteenth-Century Fiction* 25 (1970): 281–98.

Reid, Alfred S. *The Yellow Ruff and "The Scarlet Letter": A Source of Hawthorne's Novel.* Gainesville: University of Florida Press, 1955.

"Remarks on the Scarabæus Roseus, or Rose-Bug." *New England Farmer,* 31 August 1827, 41–42; 7 September 1827, 49–50.

["The Report of Ladies"]. *Essex Register,* 15 April 1833, 2.

Review of *Poems,* by James Russell Lowell. *Boston Recorder,* 25 January 1844, 14.

Review of *Poems,* by James Russell Lowell. *The Critic,* 15 April 1844, 152–54.

Review of *Poems,* by James Russell Lowell. *Knickerbocker,* February 1844, 171.

Review of *Poems,* by James Russell Lowell. *Littell's Living Age,* November 1844, 161–65.

Review of *Poems,* by James Russell Lowell. *New Jerusalem Magazine,* March 1844, 249–54.

Review of *Poems,* by James Russell Lowell. Portland *Transcript,* 20 January 1844, 327.

Review of *Poems,* by James Russell Lowell. *New York Tribune,* 30 January 1844, 1.

Review of *Robinson Crusoe. Boston Miscellany,* February 1843, 94.

Review of *Robinson Crusoe. Boston Evening Gazette,* 3 December 1842, 3.

Review of *The Salem Belle. Albany Evening Journal,* 16 December 1842, 2.

Review of *The Salem Belle. American Traveller,* 9 December 1842, 2.

Review of *The Salem Belle. Bay State Democrat,* 1 December 1842, 2.

Review of *The Salem Belle. Boston Miscellany,* February 1843, 94.

Review of *The Salem Belle. Boston Post,* 5 December 1842, 1. Reprint, *Boston States-man,* 10 December 1842, 4.

Review of *The Salem Belle. Boston Recorder,* 30 December 1842, 206.

Review of *The Salem Belle. Boston Daily Atlas,* 1 December 1842, 2.

Review of *The Salem Belle. Boston Daily Evening Transcript,* 2 December 1842, 2. Reprint, *Newburyport Herald,* 5 December 1842, 2.

Review of *The Salem Belle. Evening Mercantile Journal,* 1 December 1842, 2.

Review of *The Salem Belle. Knickerbocker,* January 1843, 102.

Review of *The Salem Belle. New England Puritan,* 9 December 1842, 2.

Review of *The Salem Belle. New-York Evangelist,* 8 December 1842, 192.

Review of *The Salem Belle. New York Tribune,* 6 December 1842, 1.

Review of *The Salem Belle. Newburyport Herald,* 5 December 1842, 2; 6 December 1842: 2.

Review of *The Salem Belle. Salem Gazette,* 2 December 1842, 2.

Review of *The Salem Belle. Salem Observer,* 3 December 1842, 2.

Review of *The Salem Belle. Salem Register,* 5 December 1842, 2.

Review of *The Salem Belle. Sargent's New Monthly Magazine,* February 1843, 95–96.

Reynolds, David S. *Beneath the American Renaissance: The Subversive Imagination in the Age of Emerson and Melville.* New York: Knopf, 1988.

Reynolds, Larry J. "*The Scarlet Letter* and Revolutions Abroad." *American Literature* 57 (1985): 44–67.

Richter, Paula Bradstreet. Conversation with author, Salem, Mass., 26 April 1999.

———. "Lucy Cleveland, Folk Artist." *The Magazine Antiques,* August 2000, 204–13.

———. "Lucy Cleveland's 'Figures of Rags': Textile Arts and Social Commentary in Early-Nineteenth-Century New England." In *Textiles in Early New England: Design, Production, and Consumption,* edited by Peter Benes. The Dublin Seminar for New England Folklife Annual Proceedings 1997. Boston: Boston University Scholarly Publications, 1999.

Rider, Fremont, comp. *Preliminary Materials for a Genealogy of the Rider (Ryder) Families in the United States.* Middletown, Conn.: Godfrey Memorial Library, 1959.

Rider, Nellie Agnes. "Some of the Descendants of Samuel[2] Rider son of Samuel Rider of Yarmouth, Mass." Portion of third volume of a three-volume manuscript at the New England Historic Genealogical Society, Boston, Mass.

Ripley, George. ["The Gothic, the Supernatural, the Imagination"]. In *Critical Essays on Hawthorne's "The Scarlet Letter,"* edited by David B. Kesterson, 25–27. Boston: G. K. Hall, 1988.

———. Review of *The Scarlet Letter,* by Nathaniel Hawthorne. In *Hawthorne: The Critical Heritage,* edited by J. Donald Crowley, 158–59. New York: Barnes & Noble, 1970.

———. Review of *The Works of the Late Edgar Allan Poe,* edited by Rufus Wilmot Griswold. In *Edgar Allan Poe: The Critical Heritage,* edited by I. M. Walker, 333–36. London: Routledge & Kegan Paul, 1986.

Robbins, Chandler. Letter to James Russell Lowell. 23 November 1844. *bMS Am 765 (682)*, Norton Collection. Houghton Library. Harvard University. Cambridge, Mass.

Robbins, L. M. Letter to A. W. Weston. 16 March 1844. Department of Rare Books and Manuscripts. Boston Public Library. Boston, Mass.

Robinson, Danny. "Rufus Wilmot Griswold and Hawthorne's 'Early Unavowed Romance.'" *Resources for American Literary Study* 12 (1982): 43–48.

Ronda, Bruce A. *Elizabeth Palmer Peabody: A Reformer on Her Own Terms*. Cambridge, Mass.: Harvard University Press, 1999.

Roper, Gordon. Introduction to *The Scarlet Letter and Selected Prose Works*, by Nathaniel Hawthorne. New York: Hendricks House, 1949.

Rozakis, Laurie. "Another Possible Source of Hawthorne's Hester Prynne." *ATQ* 59 (1986): 63–71.

Ryan, Pat M., Jr. "Young Hawthorne at the Salem Theatre." *Essex Institute Historical Collections* 94 (1958): 243–55.

Ryskamp, Charles. "The New England Sources of *The Scarlet Letter*." *American Literature* 31 (1959): 257–72.

Salem Directory. 1842.

"The Salem Fair." *Essex Register,* 15 April 1833, 2. Reprinted from the Boston *Evening Gazette,* 13 April 1833.

Sanborn, F. B. *Hawthorne and His Friends*. Cedar Rapids, Iowa: Torch Press, 1908.

Sandeen, Ernest. "*The Scarlet Letter* as a Love Story." *PMLA* 77 (1962): 425–35.

Schamberger, J. Edward. "The Failure of 'A City upon a Hill': Architectural Images in *The Scarlet Letter*." *Essex Institute Historical Collections* 125 (1989): 9–24.

Scharnhorst, Gary, ed. *The Critical Response to Nathaniel Hawthorne's "The Scarlet Letter."* New York: Greenwood Press, 1992.

Scheuermann, Mona. "The American Novel of Seduction: An Exploration of the Omission of the Sex Act in *The Scarlet Letter*." In *The Nathaniel Hawthorne Journal 1978*, edited by C. E. Frazer Clark Jr., 105–18. Detroit: Gale Research, 1984.

———. "Outside the Human Circle: Views from Hawthorne and Godwin." In *The Nathaniel Hawthorne Journal 1975*, edited by C. E. Frazer Clark Jr., 182–91. Englewood, Colo.: Microcard Editions, 1975.

Scholl, Diane G. "Winthrop's Anne Hutchinson in *The Scarlet Letter*: Hester as Hagar." *Nathaniel Hawthorne Review* 28 (2002): 29–51.

Schubert, Leland. *Hawthorne, the Artist: Fine-Art Devices in Fiction*. 1944. New York: Russell & Russell, 1963.

Schultz, Nancy Lusignan. *Fire and Roses: The Burning of the Charlestown Convent, 1834*. New York: Free Press, 2000.

Schwab, Gabriele. "Seduced by Witches: Nathaniel Hawthorne's *The Scarlet Letter* in the Context of New England Witchcraft Fictions." In *Seduction and Theory: Readings of Gender, Representation, and Rhetoric*, edited by Dianne Hunter, 170–91. Urbana: University of Illinois Press, 1989.

Schwarz, Peter. "Zwei Mögliche 'Faust'—Quellen für Hawthorne's Roman *The Scarlet Letter*." *Jahrbuch für Amerikastudien* 10 (1965): 198–205.

Scudder, Horace Elisha. *James Russell Lowell: A Biography*. 2 vols. Boston: Houghton Mifflin, 1901.

Shelley, Percy Bysshe. "The Indian Serenade." In *The Complete Poetical Works of Percy Bysshe Shelley*, edited by Thomas Hutchinson, 575. London: Oxford University Press, 1912.

———. "Lines to an Indian Air." In *Posthumous Poems*. London: John and Henry L. Hunt, 1824.

Shurr, William H. "Eve's Bower: Hawthorne's Transition from Public Doctrines to Private Truths." In *Ruined Eden of the Present: Hawthorne, Melville, and Poe*, edited by G. R. Thompson and Virgil L. Locke, 143–69. West Lafayette, In.: Purdue University Press, 1981.

Sir Nathaniel [pseud.]. Review of *The Scarlet Letter*, by Nathaniel Hawthorne. In *The Critical Response to Nathaniel Hawthorne's "The Scarlet Letter,"* edited by Gary Scharnhorst, 51–55. New York: Greenwood Press, 1992.

A Sketch of the Life of Rev. Daniel Dana Tappan with an Account of the Tappan Family. "Prepared by His Children." Boston: Samuel Usher, 1890.

Smith, David E. *John Bunyan in America*. Bloomington: Indiana University Press, 1966.

Smith, Evans Lansing. "Re-Figuring Revelations: Nathaniel Hawthorne's *The Scarlet Letter*." *ATQ*, n.s. 4 (1990): 91–104.

Smith, Julian. "Hawthorne and a Salem Enemy." *Essex Institute Historical Collections* 102 (1966): 299–302.

Smith, Nolan E. "Author-Identification for Six Wright I Titles: Cleveland and Doughty." *Papers of the Bibliographical Society of America* 65 (1971): 173–74.

Smolinski, Reiner. "Covenant Theology and Arthur Dimmesdale's Pelagianism." *ATQ*, n.s. 1 (1987): 211–31.

Stahl, Jasper Jacob. *History of Old Broad Bay and Waldoboro*. Vol. 1. Portland, Maine: Bond Wheelwright, 1956.

Stanton, Robert. "Hawthorne, Bunyan, and the American Romances." *PMLA* 71 (1956): 155–65.

———. "*The Scarlet Letter* as Dialectic of Temperament and Idea." *Studies in the Novel* 2 (1970): 474–86.

Stein, William Bysshe. *Hawthorne's Faust: A Study of the Devil Archetype*. Gainesville: University of Florida Press, 1953.

The Stephen H. Wakeman Collection of Books of Nineteenth Century American Writers. New York: American Art Association, 1924.

Stephen, Leslie. *Hours in a Library*. New ed., with additions. 3 vols. London: Smith, Elder, 1892.

Stephenson, Will, and Mimosa Stephenson. "*Adam Blair* and *The Scarlet Letter*." *Nathaniel Hawthorne Review* 19 (1993): 1–10.

Stewart, Charles Oran. *Lowell and France: A Study of the French Element in the Collected Writings of James Russell Lowell*. Nashville, Tenn: Vanderbilt University Press, 1951.

Stewart, Randall. "Hawthorne and Politics: Unpublished Letters to William Pike." *New England Quarterly* 5 (1932): 237–63.

———. "Hawthorne and *The Faerie Queen.*" *Philological Quarterly* 12 (1933): 196–206.

———. Introduction. *The American Notebooks,* by Nathaniel Hawthorne. New Haven, Conn.: Yale University Press, 1932.

Stiles, Ezra. *A History of Three of the Judges of King Charles I.* Hartford, Conn.: Elisha Babcock, 1794.

Stoddard, Roger E. *"Put a Resolute Hart to a Steep Hill": William Gowans, Antiquary and Bookseller.* New York: Book Arts Press of the School of Library Service, Columbia University, 1990.

Stone, Edward. "The 'Many Morals' of *The Scarlet Letter.*" In *The Nathaniel Hawthorne Journal 1977,* edited by C. E. Frazer Clark Jr., 215–38. Detroit: Gale Research, 1980.

———. "More on Hawthorne and Melville." In *The Nathaniel Hawthorne Journal 1975,* edited by C. E. Frazer Clark Jr., 59–70. Englewood, Colo: Microcard Editions, 1975.

Stowe, Harriet Beecher. *Uncle Tom's Cabin.* Edited by Elizabeth Ammons. New York: W. W. Norton, 1994.

Stubbs, John C. "A Note on the Source of Hawthorne's Heraldic Device in 'The Scarlet Letter.'" *Notes and Queries* 15 (1968): 173–74.

Swartzlander, Susan. "'Amid Sunshine and Shadow': Charles Wentworth Upham and Nathaniel Hawthorne." *Studies in American Fiction* 15 (1987): 227–33.

Sweeney, Susan Elizabeth. "The Madonna, the Women's Room, and *The Scarlet Letter.*" *College English* 57 (1995): 410–25.

Sweetser, Philip Starr. *Seth Sweetser and His Descendants.* Philadelphia: Integrity Press, 1938.

Tanselle, G. Thomas. "A Note on the Structure of *The Scarlet Letter.*" *Nineteenth-Century Fiction* 17 (1962): 283–85.

Tappan, Daniel Langdon. *Tappan-Toppan Genealogy: Ancestors and Descendants of Abraham Toppan of Newbury, Massachusetts, 1606–1672.* Arlington, Mass.: n.p., 1915.

Tappan, Herbert, comp. "The Tappan (or Toppan) Genealogy." *The New-England Historical and Genealogical Register* 34 (1880): 48–57.

Tate, George S. "'Chiasmus as Metaphor: The 'Figura Crucis' Tradition and 'The Dream of the Rood.'" *Neuphilologische Mitteilungen* 79, no. 2 (1978): 114–25.

Taylor, Edward. *The Poems of Edward Taylor.* Edited by Donald E. Stanford and Louis L. Martz. New Haven, Conn.: Yale University Press, 1960.

Tebbel, John. *A History of Book Publishing in the United States.* Vol. 1. New York: R. R. Bowker, 1972.

Tew, Arnold G. "Hawthorne's P.P.: Behind the Comic Mask." *Nathaniel Hawthorne Review* 20 (1994): 18–22.

Tharp, Louise Hall. *The Peabody Sisters of Salem.* Boston: Little, Brown, 1950

Thomas, Brook. *Cross-Examinations of Law and Literature: Cooper, Hawthorne, Stowe, and Melville.* Cambridge, England: Cambridge University Press, 1987.

Thomas, Dwight, and David K. Jackson. *The Poe Log: A Documentary Life of Edgar Allan Poe 1809–1849.* Boston: G. K. Hall, 1987.

Thomson, Ian H. *Chiasmus in the Pauline Letters.* In *Journal for the Study of the New Testament,* supplement series 111. Sheffield, England: Sheffield Academic Press, 1995.

Thoreau, Henry David. *Walden.* Edited by J. Lyndon Shanley. Princeton, N.J.: Princeton University Press, 1971.

Thornton, Horace. "Hawthorne, Poe, and a Literary Ghost." *New England Quarterly* 7 (1934): 146–54.

Todd, Robert E. "The Magna Mater Archetype in *The Scarlet Letter.*" *New England Quarterly* 45 (1972): 421–29.

"Traditions of Palestine." *Newburyport Herald,* 27 June 1863, 2.

"Traditions of Palestine." *Newburyport Herald,* 4 July 1863, 2.

"Tragedy in Tale of Love." *Boston Sunday Herald,* 31 August 1902, 40.

Tucker, Edward L. "James Russell Lowell and Robert Carter: The *Pioneer* and Fifty Letters from Lowell to Carter." In *Studies in the American Renaissance 1987,* edited by Joel Myerson, 187–246. Charlottesville: University Press of Virginia, 1987.

Tuckerman, Henry T. "Leaves from the Diary of a Dreamer, No. IX." *Columbian Lady's and Gentleman's Magazine,* December 1846, 249–52.

———. "Nathaniel Hawthorne." *Lippincott's Magazine* 5 (1870): 498–507.

———. "Nathaniel Hawthorne." *Southern Literary Messenger* 17 (1851): 344–49. Reprint in Idol and Jones, *Nathaniel Hawthorne,* 419–27.

Tuerk, Richard. *Central Still: Circle and Sphere in Thoreau's Prose.* The Hague: Mouton, 1975.

Turner, Arlin. "Hawthorne's Literary Borrowings." *PMLA* 51 (1936): 543–62.

———. "Hawthorne's Methods of Using His Source Materials." In *Studies for William A. Read: A Miscellany Presented by Some of His Colleagues and Friends,* edited by Nathaniel M. Caffee and Thomas A. Kirby, 301–12. Baton Rouge: Louisiana State University Press, 1940.

———. *Nathaniel Hawthorne: A Biography.* New York: Oxford University Press, 1980.

———. "Needs in Hawthorne Biography." In *The Nathaniel Hawthorne Journal 1972,* 43–45. Washington, D.C.: Microcard Editions, 1973.

———. "Park Benjamin on the Author and the Illustrator of 'The Gentle Boy.'" In *The Nathaniel Hawthorne Journal 1974,* edited by C. E. Frazier Clark Jr., 85–91. Englewood, Colo.: Microcard Editions Books, 1975.

———. "A Study of Hawthorne's Origins." Ph.D. diss., University of Texas, Austin, 1934.

Underwood, Francis H. *The Poet and the Man: Recollections and Appreciations of James Russell Lowell.* Boston: Lee and Shepard, 1893.

Upham, Charles W. *Lectures on Witchcraft, Comprising a History of the Delusion in Salem, in 1692.* Boston: Hendee and Babcock, 1831.

"Valuable Books, Just Published and for Sale by Tappan & Dennet." Boston, 1842. American Antiquarian Society. Worcester, Mass.

Van Doren, Mark. *Nathaniel Hawthorne.* New York: Viking, 1949.

Van Leer, David. "Hester's Labyrinth: Transcendental Rhetoric in Puritan Boston." In Colacurcio, *New Essays,* 57–100.

Vernon, Hope Jillson. "The Life of Maria (White) Lowell 1821–1853." In *The Poems of Maria Lowell with Unpublished Letters and a Biography*. Providence, R.I.: Brown University Press, 1936.

["A Very Brilliant Meteor"]. *Salem Tri-Weekly Gazette,* 6 November 1847, 1.

Villemarqué, Th. Hersart de la, trans. *Barzas-Breiz Chants Populaires de le Bretagne.* 2 vols. 10th ed. Paris: Delloye, 1840.

Vinton, John A. "The Antinomian Controversy of 1637." *Congregational Quarterly,* April 1873, 263–85; July 1873, 395–426; October 1873, 542–73.

———. "The Antinomian Controversy of 1637. A Memoir of the Life and Times of Rev. John Wheelwright, with a Genealogy of his Descendants." Wheelwright Collection. New England Historic Genealogical Society. Boston, Mass.

Vital Records of Newburyport Massachusetts to the End of the Year 1849. Vol. 2, *Marriages and Deaths.* Salem, Mass.: Essex Institute, 1911.

von Frank, Albert J. "Emerson's Boyhood and Collegiate Verse: Unpublished and New Texts Edited from Manuscript." In *Studies in the American Renaissance 1983,* edited by Joel Myerson, 1–56. Charlottesville: University Press of Virginia, 1983.

Von Mehren, Joan. *Minerva and the Muse: A Life of Margaret Fuller.* Amherst: University of Massachusetts Press, 1994.

Voss, Arthur W. M. "Lowell's 'A Legend of Brittany.'" *Modern Language Notes* 61 (1946): 343–45.

W. G. "Legality and Antinomianism." *Panoplist,* June 1867, 167–68.

Wagenknecht, Edward. *Nathaniel Hawthorne: The Man, His Tales and Romances.* New York: Continuum, 1989.

Waggoner, Hyatt H. *The Presence of Hawthorne.* Baton Rouge: Louisiana State University Press, 1979.

Walsh, Louis S. *Origin of the Catholic Church in Salem, and Its Growth in St. Mary's Parish and the Parish of the Immaculate Conception.* Boston: Cashman, Keating, 1890.

Walsh, Thomas F. "Dimmesdale's Election Sermon." *ESQ* 45 (1966): 64–66.

Walter, James. "The Letter and the Spirit in Hawthorne's Allegory of American Experience." *ESQ* 32 (1986): 36–54.

Warren, Austin. "Hawthorne's Reading." *New England Quarterly* 8 (1935): 480–97.

———. "*The Scarlet Letter*: A Literary Exercise in Moral Theology." *Southern Review,* n.s. 1 (1965): 22–45.

Weber, Alfred. "The Framing Functions of Hawthorne's 'The Custom-House' Sketch." *Nathaniel Hawthorne Review* 18 (1992): 5–8.

Webster, Daniel. *Speeches and Forensic Arguments.* Vol. 1. Boston: Perkins & Marvin, 1830.

Weinauer, Ellen. "Considering Possession in *The Scarlet Letter*." *Studies in American Fiction* 29 (2001): 93–112.

Welch, John W., ed. *Chiasmus in Antiquity: Structures, Analyses, Exegesis.* Hildesheim, Germany: Gerstenberg Verlag, 1981.

Wellborn, Grace Pleasant. "Plant Lore and *The Scarlet Letter*." *Southern Folklore Quarterly* 27 (1963): 160–67.

Wentersdorf, Kent P. "The Element of Witchcraft in *The Scarlet Letter*." *Folklore* 83 (1972): 132–53.

Wheelwright, Ebenezer. Letter to John A. Vinton. 10 October 1867. Wheelwright Collection. New England Historic Genealogical Society. Boston, Mass.

———. Letter to John A. Vinton. 23 October 1872. Wheelwright Collection. New England Historic Genealogical Society. Boston, Mass.

———. Letter to John A. Vinton. 27 November 1873. Wheelwright Collection. New England Historic Genealogical Society. Boston, Mass.

———. Letter to unknown correspondent. 21 March 1868. "Regarding the Panoplist." Brock Collection. BR Box 120 (38). The Huntington Library, San Marino, Calif.

———. "The Antinomian Controversy of 1636." *Panoplist,* July 1867, 222.

———. "The Antinomian Controversy of 1636." *Panoplist,* September 1867, 263–68.

[———]. *A Review of Dr. Dana's Remonstrance Addressed to the Trustees of Phillips Academy, September 1849. On the State of the Theological Seminary Under Their Care.* Boston: Crocker and Brewster, 1853.

[———]. "A Sabbath in Boston in 1692." *Panoplist,* November 1868, 335–44.

[———]. *The Salem Belle: A Tale of 1692.* Boston: Tappan & Dennet, 1842.

[———]. *The Salem Belle: A Tale of 1692.* Boston: Tappan & Dennet, 1842. Special Collections. Howard B. Lee Library. Brigham Young University. Salt Lake City, Utah.

[———]. *The Salem Belle: A Tale of 1692.* Boston: Tappan & Dennet, 1842. Burton Historical Collection. Detroit Public Library. Detroit, Mich.

[———]. *The Salem Belle: A Tale of 1692.* Boston: Tappan & Dennet, 1842. Long Island Studies Institute. Hofstra University. Hempstead, N.Y.

[———]. *The Salem Belle: A Tale of 1692.* Boston: Tappan & Dennet, 1842. The Huntington Library. San Marino, Calif.

[———]. *The Salem Belle: A Tale of 1692.* Boston: Tappan & Dennet, 1842. The Lilly Library. Indiana University. Bloomington, Ind.

[———]. *The Salem Belle: A Tale of 1692.* Boston: Tappan & Dennet, 1842. Special Collections and Archives. Kent State University Libraries. Kent, Ohio.

[———]. *The Salem Belle: A Tale of 1692.* Boston: Tappan & Dennet, 1842. Phillips Library. Peabody Essex Museum. Salem, Mass.

[———]. *The Salem Belle: A Tale of 1692.* Boston: Tappan & Dennet, 1842. Special Collections. University of South Florida Library. Tampa, Fla.

[———]. *The Salem Belle: A Tale of 1692.* Boston: Tappan & Dennet, 1842. Taylor Collection of American Best Sellers. The Albert and Shirley Small Special Collections Library. University of Virginia Library. Charlottesville, Va.

[———]. *The Salem Belle: A Tale of Love and Witchcraft in the Year 1692.* Boston: John M. Whittemore, 1847.

[———]. "Traditions of Palestine." *Newburyport Herald,* 27 June 1863, 1; 4 July 1863, 1; 11 July 1863, 1; 18 July 1863, 1; 25 July 1863, 1; 1 August 1863, 1; 8 August 1863, 1; 15 August 1863, 1; 22 August 1863, 1; 29 August 1863, 1; 5 September 1863, 1; 12 September 1863, 1; 19 September 1863, 1; 26 September 1863, 1; 3 October 1863, 1.

[———]. "Traditions of Palestine." Clippings of the *Newburyport Herald*'s fifteen installments of "Traditions of Palestine," pasted into a book of letters. Library, First Presbyterian Church. Newburyport, Mass.

[————]. "Traditions of Palestine." *Herald of Gospel Liberty*, July–October 1863.

[————]. *Traditions of Palestine; or, Scenes in the Holy Land in the Days of Christ.* 3rd ed. Boston: M. H. Sargent, 1864.

[————]. *Traditions of Palestine; or, Scenes in the Holy Land in the Days of Christ.* 3rd ed. Boston: M. H. Sargent, 1864. Inscribed to Andrew Preston Peabody. Widener Library. Harvard College Library. Cambridge, Mass.

Wheelwright, John. *John Wheelwright, His Writings, Including His Fast-Day Sermon, 1637 and His Mercurius Americanus, 1645; with a Paper upon the Genuineness of the Indian Deed of 1629 and a Memoir by Charles H. Bell, A.M.* 1876. Reprint, New York: Burt Franklin, n.d.

————. "A Sermon Preached at Boston in New England, upon a Fast Day, the 19th of January, 1636." *Panoplist,* July 1867, 202–12; August 1867, 240–46.

White, Paula K. "Puritan Theories of History in Hawthorne's Fiction." *Canadian Review of American Studies* 9 (1978): 135–53.

[Whitney, Louisa Goddard]. *The Burning of the Convent: A Narrative of the Destruction, by a Mob, of the Ursuline School on Mount Benedict, Charlestown, As Remembered by One of the Pupils.* Boston: James R. Osgood, 1877.

Whittemore, B[arnard] B[emis]. *A Genealogy of Several Branches of the Whittemore Family.* Nashua, N.H.: Francis P. Whittemore, 1890.

Wilbur, Richard. "Poe and the Art of Suggestion." *University of Mississippi Studies in English*, n.s. 3 (1982): 1–13.

Winship, Michael. *Making Heretics: Militant Protestantism and Free Grace in Massachusetts, 1636–1641.* Princeton, N.J.: Princeton University Press, 2002.

Winthrop, John. *The History of New England from 1630 to 1849.* 2 vols. Boston: Phelps and Farnham, 1825–26.

Woidat, Caroline M. "Talking Back to Schoolteacher: Morrison's Confrontation with Hawthorne in *Beloved.*" *Modern Fiction Studies* 39 (1993): 527–46.

Wood, Ann D. "The 'Scribbling Women' and Fanny Fern: Why Women Wrote." *American Quarterly* 23 (1971): 3–24.

Woodson, Thomas. "Hawthorne, Upham, and *The Scarlet Letter.*" In *Critical Essays on Hawthorne's "The Scarlet Letter,"* edited by David B. Kesterson, 183–93. Boston: G. K. Hall, 1988.

Wright, Dorena Allen. "The Meeting at the Brook-Side: Beatrice, the Pearl-Maiden, and Pearl Prynne." *ESQ* 28 (1982): 112–20.

X. Letter. *Louisville Daily Journal,* 26 March 1850, 3.

Yellin, Jean Fagan. "Hawthorne and the American National Sin." In *The Green American Tradition: Essays and Poems for Sherman Paul*, edited by H. Daniel Peck, 75–97. Baton Rouge: Louisiana State University Press, 1989.

————. "Nathaniel Hawthorne's *The Scarlet Letter.*" *Women and Sisters: The Antislavery Feminists in American Culture.* 125–50. New Haven, Conn.: Yale University Press, 1989.

Young, Philip. *Hawthorne's Secret: An Un-Told Tale.* Boston: Godine, 1984.

Zeitz, Lisa M. "'A Checker-Work of Providence': The Shaping of *Robinson Crusoe.*" *English Studies in Canada* 9 (1983): 255–71.

Index